Seven Years Behind the Veil

a memoir of my early years in Arabia

Ann Hellewell

"In Love & Light...."
Ann Hellewell

Copyright © 2017 Ann Hellewell

All rights reserved.

ISBN: 1544695128

ISBN 13: 9781544695129

Acknowledgements

My heartfelt "thanks" flows out to all the loving souls who opened their hearts and their homes to a young, naive girl from America. Each one of these foreign and Arabic friends/relatives are alive in my memory banks.

A lasting gratitude extends to Edward Swartz, a NY Agent who believed that the world would be a better place if the West could see the East through "*Arab Eyes*."

Esther Baruch from Finishing Touches Editing did a marvelous job editing the manuscript and became my friend.

My sister Barb Henley and I spent many fun times disecting the pages between full cups of coffee. A talented writer in her own right...she constantly probed me to go deeper and expand the scenes.

I sincerely thank Julie Scherer, who encouraged me to edit and publish the manuscript when I was in the deep valley of doubt.

Finally, none of my written works would be possible without the patience and support of Ben...my loving husband.

for my Arabic Relatives and Mac.....
and for my two sons who are the essance of my life

Author's Note

"After nourishment, shelter, and companionship, stories are the things we need most in all the world."
Philip Pullman

My own story keeps running through my mind, piercing my everyday moments, until I finally put pen to paper. Hence, ***Seven Years Behind the Veil: A True Story*** is born. I write that in the year 1970 I land on Arabian sand with my Saudi husband and son. With a freshly printed university diploma and a suitcase packed with our worldly possessions, we enter the cloaked Kingdom.

Ordinary hours, weeks, months, rainy mornings, and hot blistering days pass by in all their mundane details. Meanwhile, every aspect of my life turns inside out. Such an absolute transformation is almost impossible to imagine. In order to survive, my journal becomes my life companion. This lifeline sustains the real me, the essence of my spirit, the core of myself.

Over time, the experiences recorded in my journal demand to be shared. ***Seven Years Behind the Veil: A True Story*** refuses to stuff itself into a drawer to be lost for all time. Instead, the words jump onto the pages of the following book. Enjoy the journey!!

Chapter 1

The Journey

"The minute he started telling a story, his eyes would light up, as if he had just come back from black and white into full color."

Doris Kearns Goodwin about Abraham Lincoln

My story begins in the spring of 1947. Life is good in our Ohio home, which overlooks the shores of Lake Erie. My two sisters, born right after me, become wonderful playmates. I spend my early years playing foursquare, hopscotch, jump rope, and a million other games on our dead-end street.

Each summer our family drives to our cottage in Canada, where we spend six weeks surrounded by relatives. The lake breezes blow off the Georgian Bay and my sisters and I romp on our beach.

As I grow, I slowly evolve into two beings. My physical appearance blends into my surroundings. Blond hair, blue eyes, and an attractive white face are sure entry cards. Emotionally, however, I paint life with bold strokes and rainbow colors. I am too different to fit easily into my world.

As I enter my teens, my conservative, middle-class surroundings begin to suffocate my free soul, and I turn to a fantasy life for survival. I dream of distant shores and far-off adventures. Little do I realize that I am creating my future reality.

The college years find me at a large Ohio university during the 60s. Coming from a sheltered environment, I find that it's quite an adjustment. One out of every three freshmen flunk out and the competition is fierce. Unfortunately, the students who don't make the grade often land in the rice paddies of Vietnam.

Semesters pass as I submerge myself under mounds of multi-topic books. While I study, I observe the transformation of university life. By my sophomore year, the war in Vietnam is in full swing and so are the anti-war demonstrations. Rebellion against any kind of established authority soon gains my attention. I join in my generation's demands that our elders shatter their outdated institutions, and I watch in fascination as old ways fall apart around me. As I listen and watch, I learn that the youth of a society can indeed change a culture.

During the second half of my junior year, I begin volunteering in a Mexican migrant camp off campus. Determined to make a difference, I join the team that is responsible for the migrant camp's nursery school classes, English classes, and a coffeehouse for high school students.

Every weekend finds our team in the camp, establishing a rapport with the Mexican-Americans. Soon it becomes clear that we need a larger staff. In search of quality help, I decide that sociology students could become the best source of new volunteers. So I ask Dr. Snyder, an upper level Minorities Course professor, if I can speak to his seminar.

The next week I walk into University Hall and make my way to the podium in Dr. Snyder's classroom. As I scan the room, I notice many of my friends. Most of them wear curious expressions, wondering what I am doing there. Slowly, I pull myself together and put my energies into a persuasive speech.

As I continue, I can sense by the feedback that many students are interested. Toward the end of the talk, my eyes are drawn to a student sitting directly in front of me. There is something about his face. His deep-set eyes register on my preoccupied mind.

After the presentation I send a piece of paper around the room, asking anyone who is interested in the migrant camp to write down their name and telephone number. Meanwhile, several students ask questions, including the student in front of me. He says, "My American friends have a hard time understanding my Arabian accent. If I work in the migrant camp, how can the Mexicans understand me?" His comment brings laughter from the class. Watching him, I secretly hope he signs my sheet.

The following Saturday, I meet with the students on the interest list. It is a fun evening and after the session, I find my conversation directed toward the student with the accent. I discover that his name is Osane. I ask him where he is from and he tells me Saudi Arabia. Although our first communication is short, my initial assumption is correct. He promises to be an interesting person.

Throughout the rest of the semester, Osane and I see each other frequently at the migrant camp. Our friendship grows, but only to a point, for we are each dating someone else. Besides, I know that on the college campus of the 60s, anything and everything is permissible; I also realize that off campus, mixed couples are not only unheard of, they are strictly taboo! Even thinking of dating a Saudi is a rebellion I'm not brave enough to consider.

With my hours totally occupied, time passes quickly. A few days before Easter vacation, I walk through the dorm lobby to pick up my mail. I notice Osane sitting on a couch, so I sit down beside him. As we talk about nothing in particular, my eyes are drawn to his foreign-looking watch. The dial is square with a black background, while the watchband is made of large, flexible gold links. Curious, I ask him about it. Instantly his eyes revert inward, as he pictures his uncle giving him this prized graduation gift. He then refocuses into the present and begins his story.

"I finished at the top of my high school class and won a scholarship to America," Osane states. "At that time I was living in Taif, a mountainous town far from Riyadh. The only way to drive through the desert to the capital city to accept my scholarship was on top of huge Mercedes trucks that followed old caravan routes. These convoys traveled through the sands with full loads, so the only place for passengers was on top of the truck cabs. With the sum of my possessions wrapped in one small scarf, I spent several days hanging onto various cabs as they bounced through the desert. Each night at sunset, the trucks circled and made camp. As I crawled under my truck to sleep, I prayed to Allah for protection against the desert bandits, who would most certainly steal my prized watch."

As Osane finishes reminiscing, he looks up and unexpectedly our eyes lock. An instantaneous feeling of familiarity consumes me. Suddenly I feel firmly connected to his essence, as if I have spent several lifetimes by his side. Then, with no warning, a low hum begins to vibrate in my ears, my heart begins to throb, and my body breaks into a sweat. Shocked, I physically shake myself. Sensing by his ashen face that Osane has had a similar experience, I mumble something and excuse myself.

When I reach my dorm room, the world is still spinning. I sit on the bed and bury my head in my hands. "What was that?" I scream to myself. Mentally, I immediately back-peddle, trying to delete the experience from my existence. All I need is a relationship with a foreign student! My parents warned me to never bring home a Catholic. What will they say if I introduce them to a dark-skinned, Muslim Arab from some country called Saudi Arabia? The idea is simply too absurd. It is a loaded bomb with the capability of blowing my present life to shreds. Dismissing the whole incident, I pack for Easter.

My week at home is hardly fun. I break up with a boyfriend I had cared a great deal about. I also can't get Osane out of my thoughts. His face keeps flashing through my mind. No matter how hard I try, it seems that my path is already beginning its curve toward strange new worlds.

I return to campus feeling full of turmoil. On the third day back I receive a call from Osane asking me to dinner. I tighten my grip on the phone. My inner confusion breaks into bedlam, causing a long pause of indecision. Finally, to my surprise, I hear myself say, "Sure."

As I dress for our first date, red flags explode, creating a mental minefield. Several times I sit down and hold my sick stomach. Indecision is making me nauseous and I marvel that my feet keep moving toward the door. "You are certainly mad," I say to myself as I wait for the elevator.

I meet Osane in the dorm lobby and he walks me to his car. As he opens the door for me, I push my apprehensions aside and smile at him. Soon we are driving through campus on our way to the other side of town. It doesn't take long to arrive at the house he rents with his two roommates.

As we pull into his driveway I am much more at ease, for I am finding it difficult to be nervous around Osane. The minute

I see his small house surrounded by empty lots, I like it. Upon entering, I am impressed by how tidy it is. The table in the dining room is already set and when Osane walks into the kitchen to put the finishing touches on his chicken dinner, I have an opportunity to talk with his roommates.

During the conversation, I glance around the living room. The one couch and two armchairs have brightly patterned cushions scattered around. The sun is shining in the front windows, giving the room a bright and airy feel. Thick textbooks are thrown on the coffee table, and backpacks hang on hooks by the door.

Soon the meal is served, and the four of us sit around the table eating a delicious dinner. Somehow, I am totally at home in this little house, as if I belong here.

After dinner, Osane's roommates clean up, allowing us alone time. We sit on the couch and as Osane lights his pipe, our eyes meet once again. Finding it impossible to look away, I feel as though electrical shocks are pulsing through me. I can feel my insides fluttering and a droning interference overwhelms my mind. Just before I slide into a puddle of nothingness, I look deeper into Osane's eyes. I suddenly realize that he is also fighting his emotions.

With my brain in full reverse, I stand up. I attempt to leave the room, but irresistible magnetic forces pull our bodies together. In a daze, I watch Osane tenderly pick up my hand. As our flesh touches, our combined energy sizzles and sparks into a flame. This feverish blaze transforms into a seasoned fire as the weeks pass.

Soon Osane and I can't see enough of each other. The hours between meetings are simply tolerated. We become obsessed with one another. Familiarity begins to dim the voices of prejudice I had ingested as a child. The more we talk, the more real Osane becomes, and I am finally able to truly see him.

What materializes before me is a handsome human being. Osane's thin frame stands just a little shorter than mine. His skin is a beautiful shade of tan, like a deerskin in midsummer. He has inherited the fine features of his desert brethren, and when his full, strong mouth breaks into a smile, his whole face becomes charismatic. The hint of a cleft in Osane's chin provides a balance to his features. Osane's hair is thick, curly, and beautiful, but the focal points of his face are his burnt-amber eyes. From the first moment I saw him, they have mesmerized me. Full of sensitivity, humor, depth, shadows, and dark clouds, his eyes enchant and captivate, pulling me into his personal space.

Being so absorbed in one another makes the weeks pass quickly. Osane and I desert our friends, drop outside activities, and skip classes. As we dig further into each other, what we uncover is that we are kindred spirits. Somehow, brought up in two different worlds, we have developed the same value systems, interests, goals, and a similar way of looking at life. Neither of us wants to be cornered into a suburb, nor do we want any country to consume us. Let the world be our home. Our spiritual beliefs also blend, for in our world God is not dead.

In our isolated college world, our relationship blossoms. After all, we are the New Age children of the 60s. We are embodying the emotions of our era. John Lennon sings, *All You Need is Love*, and we believe him. This mood carries us through the semester and into the summer.

Chapter 2

Crossroads

"Don't worry that you're not strong enough before you begin. It is in the journey that God makes you strong."
Unknown author

The summer means separation. Osane flies overseas to Saudi Arabia and I return to the suburbs.

While waiting for my parents to pick me up, I feel reality strike me like an invisible bullet. What have I been thinking? How can I even mention Osane to my family? Our relationship will mix with their worldview like water with oil. Or maybe like a bomb that will blow our family to bits.

My feet shuffle nervously as I watch my parents drive into the dorm parking lot. As usual, their greeting is warm and loving. They don't seem to notice that I am pre-occupied and distant. Looking out the window, I watch as we pull away from the university and all that is familiar. Farms speed by unnoticed, for I am battling erupting doubts that crash down on me like tidal waves. Slowly we wind around the shores of Lake Erie and onto our little street. Grabbing my sides, I can feel my old way of life engulfing me, suffocating me in its sameness.

For two months I suffer the "now" in silence, my past and future lives noiselessly ripping me apart. I pray that peace will return when we pack our bags and head north to our Canadian cabin. However, even there in the stillness of the summer woods, my inner chaos continues.

I spend days staring at waves of grass blowing in the breeze, and marvel at the widening ripples of water each time a fish jumps. The busy bees hum in my ears, and the birds compose songs to sooth my soul. Still, I can't find a way to blend Osane into my everyday life. While I fish I quietly ponder; when I swim I deliberate; during my solitary hikes I contemplate; and while the house sleeps I secretly re-run memories of Osane. Through all these deliberations, the puzzle remains unsolved and I remain in turmoil.

The night before we're to return home, the whirl of the wind through the pine trees keeps sleep at bay. Surrounded by moonless darkness, I wrap my mind around the stories Osane has told me. Through the breezes, Osane whispers to me.

"My father was tribal chief of an agricultural village in the mountains of southern Arabia. Father had the reputation of being a hard but fair leader, and throughout the whole area he was respected. With his position came many responsibilities. He was required to entertain, mediate disputes, and keep order. Over the course of his life, he married thirty-two wives. He only kept two wives at a time, for many of his marriages were political, and most of his wives died in childbirth.

"My mother was remembered for her beauty and strength of character. When she became ill after my birth, she left her husband's home and returned to her mother's house. When she died a few months later, she left me to be raised by my grandmother, two older aunts, and an uncle.

"My grandmother's family lived on the top two stories of a tower home. The ground floor was reserved for sheep, goats, and donkeys. When I was not tending the animals, I was required to attend school. Classes consisted of rote memorization and whacks with a cane. They were hard on my free young spirit. Many mornings I ran to the mountains, only to be found, tied to one of my father's slaves, and delivered back to school.

"One afternoon, my uncle brought my grandmother a wooden viewfinder and five slides. These pictures portrayed strange foreigners from Europe and America. The family laughed at the different clothes, hairstyles, and backgrounds, and I was excited when my turn came. My relatives watched, anticipating my amusement. Instead, I became silent and distant. Many moments went by as I studied the first picture. When I finally put the viewfinder down, my eyes held a faraway look, and I prophesied to my grandmother, 'Someday I will travel west, and visit the strange foreigners in the picture.'

"As I matured, my life became confused. Periodically I was required to leave my grandmother's house and spend time with my father. This was a difficult transition. In my grandmother's house life was simple and full of love, but at my father's "Big House" I found silence and responsibility. I was required to pour tea and coffee for the male guests, spread their bedding, serve meals, and I was to keep silent until spoken to. These environments were too far apart on the emotional scale. I experienced a lack of balance and the extreme differences complicated me."

"Time passed and I internalized the desert culture and my village's tribal laws. I learned about hospitality, politeness, honor, truth, control, and family loyalty. The center of my life became the Muslim religion and the Koran. Five times a day I faced Mecca and joined the other sons of the village in prayer. I was taught that Allah was compassionate and merciful. The Imam, our spiritual leader, taught the boys in my class that the Koran's underlying message was harmony in everyday life. In the Koran, Allah commanded us to live an ethical life and treat others better than they treat you.

"Just as I was blossoming into my mid-teens, tragedy struck. My sister's husband and oldest son were killed when their car sped off a cliff. As their closest male relative, it became my cultural responsibility to move into my sister's home in Taif, a mountain town outside of Mecca.

"This forced transition from my beloved village to an unknown town was very hard on me. One day I was tucked into my grandmother's mud tower home, surrounded by love. The next day I was thrown into a large, modern villa full of mourning. Although I was given fine robes and there was enough water to bathe regularly, the emotional turmoil of the household began to take root within my young soul. Traditional screams of mourning haunted the long nights. My sister's depression also began to affect me. I escaped into my schoolbooks. To find a way out of the cultural maze I was in, I became determined to earn a scholarship abroad. With this in mind, I lost myself in studies and the semesters passed.

"Finally, my last year of high school drew near and I began preparing for my final. I joined the other high school students as they entered the drama of their senior test. We strolled through parks and gardens, studying for the one exam that decided our whole grade.

"After taking my final, I returned home and turned on the radio for test results. Each student and his class rank were announced for the entire city to hear. In a simple society, these results were headline news. I was overjoyed when my exam result ranked me *first* in my class. This top rank guaranteed a government scholarship. The door to the West was finally open.

"Transition again awaited me as I flew from Saudi Arabia to a small New England town in the middle of winter. While I attended an English Language School, everything in my life turned inside out. Absolutely everything changed. The only things that felt remotely familiar were the Christmas Nativity Scenes. There, the people looked and dressed like Arabs. The animals and the hay were all familiar. I often walked through the deep snow and sat on bales of hay beside sheep, camels, baby Jesus, and the rest of my countrymen.

"After only one semester of language study, I transferred into the university. It wasn't enough. In an era where one out of three Americans flunked out, I had little chance to succeed. With sheer determination, I studied and struggled until I was finally able to pull myself up to the rank of a C student.

"Finally out of academic danger, I was able to stabilize and I slowly gained my Western gait. My sense of humor resurfaced and by the time I was an upperclassman, I had merged with my fellow students. I had not only visited the foreign lands as I had prophesied years before, I had actually become one of the foreign people I had seen so long ago in my uncle's viewfinder."

With Osane's stories still ringing in my ears, and soothed by the scent of White Canadian Pines I finally slip into a deep sleep. For the first time in weeks, my soul is at peace, for I dream that Osane's arms are wrapped around me. Trying to hold onto this dream, I fight the summer sun, which is shining through the bedroom window.

Eventually, I open my eyes and find a new day. With dawn comes the realization that I truly love Osane. In life, when a heart recognizes a heart it is a Godly gift. My choice is to trust, embrace, and acknowledge this love. Osane will be my future.

To this fate I finally surrender. My internal war is over and love has won.

These past tumultuous months, however, have crushed my rose-colored glasses. My sense of denial has shattered and I know that the price of this love will be exorbitant. For an indeterminable amount of time, I will need to part with my family, country, lifestyle, culture, and religion. This will require a blind leap off a monstrous cliff. In this free flight, I must trust God and life to direct my path.

On the other side of the world, while I am waking, Osane is occupied with his own emotional tug-of-war. Surrounded by his large extended family, he, too, is detached and quiet. Instructed by centuries of communal living, his relatives give Osane space and privacy to sort out his inner turmoil. As children swirl in play around him, he contemplates.

Late at night, he also argues with himself. With an angry voice, he inwardly screams that he has *never* considered marrying an American or any foreigner. In fact, he used to criticize the few people he knew who did. Bringing home an American bride would be swimming against a strong cultural current. Osane questions if he is willing to make the sacrifices.

After many days of painful deliberation, he also makes his decision. Even oceans away, distance can't blur my image or his love for me. No matter how he tries, he can't keep me out of his mind. Finally, Osane also surrenders to his feelings and our mutual future.

The passage of time finally puts the summer of turmoil behind me. I wave goodbye to my departing parents with infinite relief. Walking across campus, I can finally breathe. In this space between worlds, my life with Osane can actually become a reality.

That evening, while keeping up a carefree banter with my roommates, I unpack my things. The next morning I walk to the bookstore to buy books for the semester, and I casually wonder when Osane will call me. Three days slip by. When I still haven't heard from Osane, I begin to panic. Did he decide to stay in Saudi Arabia? Is he back in classes, but has decided not to see me?

Each day that passes finds my emotions winding tighter and tighter. Just before I internally explode, a friend tells me that she's seen Osane and gives me his new address.

That evening my feet bring me to Osane's apartment door. Sweating from my hurried walk, I concentrate on my heavy breathing. I raise my arm, but I'm not able to knock on the door. Minutes pass. I hear movement within the apartment and my heart quickens when I hear Osane's voice.

"Why hasn't he called me?" hurt voices from within scream. More minutes pass. I feel dizzy and my queasy stomach is tied in knots. Finally, I grip my fingers into a fist and knock boldly. Slowly the door opens and I find myself staring at Osane's roommate.

"Yes?" he asks.

"Is Osane in?" I whisper.

"Come in," his roommate replies.

As I step into the apartment, I immediately see Osane standing in the middle of the room. When he sees me, all time stops and the world stands still. For at least a lifetime, we remain as still as rocks. In between my thundering heart and the ringing in my ears, I search his eyes, trying to decipher his feelings.

Suddenly, I feel our souls connect. With this validation, I run toward him. We grab onto one another with incredible fierceness, daring the world to separate us again. As our summer's intense struggles whirl in our minds, we both begin sobbing.

"Hard… it's been so hard," I mutter between sobs.

"It's going to be alright now," Osane whispers as he pulls out his handkerchief.

Refusing to release one another, we walk into Osane's bedroom and close the door. My heart is pounding. Osane catches my bottom lip between his teeth. Just as I feel my knees buckle, Osane lifts me into his bed.

When I look up and see his clouded eyes, a spear of lust shoots through me. We desperately cling to each other, and as Osane's hands trace my body, each second seems endless. As we slide toward surrender, we both tremble and ride huge waves that crash onto sandy beaches. And then, slowly and tenderly, Osane claims me as his own.

When we blend into one, elusive peace encompasses us. The world has tried to break us apart but couldn't, for we are meant to be together. Secure in each other's presence, we both sleep deeply. Early the next morning, as the sun rises and a cool breeze blows in the window, we hold one another. United on all levels and looking at the new day, we both commit to the next step. It's now time to plan our wedding day.

Naively we begin the process of uniting our worlds. Barbara Kingsolver states, "Every choice is a world made new for the chosen." Unfortunately, the new reality Osane and I have chosen for ourselves is a life out of the box. The challenges associated with swimming against society's tide become evident immediately.

We drive from one church to another, full of excitement. We meet with the ministers I once thought were my friends. Something in their 1968 white Christian beings rebels at our attempt at a mixed marriage. Skepticism shadows their smiles and their body language is clear: we should both back up and carefully review our union. Every door we knock on closes, or takes us to a new dead-end. We feel suffocating resistance all around us, dragging us down. Our love is the only force propelling us forward.

With no options left, we resign ourselves to the fact that our life together will begin in the bureaucratic Justice of the Peace office. Our wedding will lack color, flowers, bridesmaids, and family members. It will, however, be blessed by three carloads of Arab and American friends, who are determined to make our ceremony lively.

Meanwhile, I attempt to introduce Osane to my family. I'm not surprised when my family slams the door shut. They claim I'm naive, impulsive, and caught up in the rebellious attitude of my generation. That I am young enough to believe I am invincible and that I haven't known this "boy" long enough to even think of marriage. Their trump card is that society as a whole forbids mixed marriages.

I agree with them. Then I try to explain that Osane and I have a connection that's strong and true, and that our love transcends any cultural differences.

After endless calls, face-to-face meetings mediated by our minister, letters, tears, and broken hearts on both sides, we reach an impasse. Eventually, it is a simple choice between Osane and my family. I finally announce that my decision had already been made that summer. With a heavy but hopeful heart, I determinedly veer my life path due east, toward the Arabian sands and the man I love.

With our life spinning in drama, the time flies by. The day before our Justice of the Peace appointment, the phone rings. Suddenly I catch my breath, for I can feel an energy shift. Gingerly, I pick up the receiver and Greg, Osane's former roommate speaks.

As a philosophy graduate student, he shares his office with another graduate student who also happens to be a minister. Over coffee that morning, Greg tells the minister our plight.

His officemate can't believe that none of the town ministers will marry us. He declares that we are a couple ahead of our time, making choices that are counter to the status quo. He tells Greg, "I will be honored to perform their marriage ceremony anytime they wish."

When I hang up the phone, I scream in pure delight. Finally, a campus minister who resides in *our world* has provided the missing piece to our wedding puzzle. Is it possible that my dream of being married in our small college church can become reality?

I close my eyes and picture Prout Chapel, which is quaint enough to grace the cover of a Hallmark card. Its white frame snuggles under ancient oaks and maples in the center of campus. When spring breezes stir the blood of winter-weary students, it's to the chapel grounds that they wander to renew their spirits. Under huge trees they linger, study, and sprawl on the newly sprouting grass.

Inside the chapel, the simplicity of the lined pews demands silence and the space resonates peace. A cross sits on a Quaker table in the middle of the altar, creating reverence. Many times I have taken my troubled soul to the healing solitude of this chapel. Sitting in an empty pew, I ask for and receive guidance and strength. To this space I am no stranger. I therefore feel that it is the perfect place to legally unite Osane's East with my West. It is here that we will profess our love, and it is in this Godly space that we will open the first chapter of our new life.

With my heart full of wonder, I somehow know that the details of the wedding are going to rapidly fall into place. I keep hearing my inner voices repeating the pattern of "struggle / persistence / flow."

Immediately I call my old roommates and we arrange to meet that evening. Miraculously, these friends patch their talents and closets together, and the results are striking. While one plays with my hair, the other dresses me in a long, white, satin skirt and blouse. At the waist, she ties a multicolored Arab turban. Within a few hours, I stand in front of the mirror, an instant bride.

Meanwhile, another friend takes on the wedding cake as her project. She calls her mother who lives in a small farm town not far from the university. Inspired by our story, the mother calls their local baker. With a beaming smile, this dear friend tells us that a beautiful, five-layer wedding cake, with a silver peace symbol sticking out of the top layer, is being donated to our wedding.

Within the next three days, everything else falls into place. We reserve the chapel and Dr. Seller donates the International Center for our wedding reception. Our friends plan the reception as their present to us, buying the decorations and refreshments. At the last minute, two music majors volunteer to be our organist and soloist.

The final job is left to Osane. He is determined to fill the entire chapel, for he doesn't want to walk down the aisle of an empty church. Since there is no time for written invitations, word of mouth will have to do. With a determined stride, Osane pounds on doors and walks into the offices of the many professors he knows. Each time he says, "I would be honored if you would attend my wedding... tomorrow."

The sun shines on our wedding day, bathing the chapel in light. We wait in the side room of the church. Osane keeps peeking through the curtains and bending down to look through the keyhole. He is frightened that no one will come. But they do come. The pews slowly fill with a wonderfully strange, mixed crowd. There is not a child among the guests; none of my family attends; Osane's relatives are oceans away. Our union is, instead, blessed by students and professors of the ivory tower. Our vows are said, we slip twenty-five cent friendship rings on our fingers, the organ music bellows, and we walk down the aisle as man and wife.

Osane and I run through a shower of rice and walk to the International Center for our wedding reception. There is a feeling of unrestrained camaraderie at the party, for everyone knows one another. Hussein, our Persian photographer, keeps the mood swinging with his antics to capture the ultimate wedding picture. Soon, it is time to cut the cake. My hand shakes and Osane steadies the knife, as I glance up and see Hussein trying to take another perfect picture. If only he knew that Osane, in his nervousness, has loaded the camera improperly. Not one picture captures our day of magic.

We leave the reception and drive through town in our decorated car, tin cans rattling. Our wedding car deposits us home to our waiting beds, where we fall into each other's arms. Osane and I make love, for the first time as husband and wife. After he slips into a deep sleep, I review the events of the last three days.

My heart hums with gratitude for each of our friends, who took up our wedding as a cause. They are the ones who planned it, donated it, and made the wedding a reality. They have also poured their positive love over the negative skepticism that was starting to grow inside us, and gave us the strength to unite two worlds into one.

I slowly turn over and hug my sleeping husband. As I contemplate the future, I am not afraid, for my strength lies beside me. Osane has two more years before he graduates. There will be enough time in the future to tackle the Arabian challenge. For now, I am simply content to be his American wife.

Chapter 3

A Time to Gather Information

"My mind is a lock pick always looking for another door to open. I often find those doors by exploring minds of others."
Hewitt E. Moore

During the next two years, we are busy developing a stable foundation for our marriage, taking classes, and preparing for our eventual departure to Saudi Arabia. In between all these activities, my personal assignment is to unlock the mysteries surrounding the concealed Kingdom of Saudi Arabia. In the late '60s, most Americans don't even realize this remote country of sand exists. Its invisibility is so complete that its cloaked reality is almost impenetrable.

My most available resources are our Middle Eastern friends, from all over the Arab world. I spend hours talking to them about their cultures. They know Saudi Arabia is my future and they help as much as they can, but I sense everything they tell me is sugar-coated. They know the truth is too stark to reveal.

I also spend hours in our university's new, multimillion-dollar library. I shuffle through a vast number of card files, but all I find is an informational void. The only materials are outdated encyclopedia articles. Occasionally, I find a romantic novel such as *Love Under the Arabian Sky,* which is fun to read but doesn't contain any relevant information. I can't even find anything in National Geographic. I soon confirm my opinion that as far as America is concerned, Saudi Arabia does not exist.

My only pertinent informational source is an Aramco Oil magazine that is delivered to Osane every month. The articles focus on early oil explorations in the eastern deserts. However, in the back section of one magazine, some wonderful editor has slipped in an historical article on Abdul Aziz Ibn Sa'ud. Most of the information comes from *The Desert King,* by David A. Howarth. With great anticipation, I sit down on our couch and begin reading.

In 1744, Muhammad Ibn Saud combined forces with a religious leader named Ibn Abdul Wahhab. This alliance was powerful as it linked a charismatic leader with a ready-made force of Islamic fundamentalists. This religious group of austere, desert-hardened men stood for the denial of worldly pleasures. Soon, a mighty army was on the march. At their height, this force spread Islam over one million miles and gained the allegiance of many fragmented tribes.

When Saud and his Wahhabi soldiers attacked Mecca, the Sultan of Constantinople sent a Turkish army to roust them out of the Holy Land. In 1813, Saud's army was pushed out of Mecca. A rival Arabian family, the Al Rashids, took advantage of the Sauds' weakened condition. This dynasty pushed them out of Riyadh and into the desert. The Sauds were forced to retreat to Kuwait, where they spent eight destitute years.

Then in 1901, Muhammad's son, Abdul Aziz Ibn Saud, left Kuwait with forty camel-men. He seized his father's former castle and reclaimed the capitol city of Riyadh. Abdul Aziz spent the next several years fighting the Turks, local tribesmen, and his rivals, the Rashid family. He was assisted by Britain, whose support during and after the fall of the Ottoman Empire in World War I made the Saudi state possible. Religious zealots also fired up Abdul Aziz's army. This twentieth century revival of the Wahhabi fringe was called the Ikhwan. They were God's soldiers, heedless of death and thirsty for glory.

This army marched for the next thirty years, until 1932, when the nation of Saudi Arabia was united. During his war years, Ibn Saud personally led the Saudi's baby boom, unifying his realm by fathering children with the daughters of as many tribal leaders as possible. Then, in 1933, a year after Saudi Arabia was founded with Riyadh as its capitol, Ibn Saud granted an exclusive oil exploration concession to the Standard Oil Company of California. The partnership evolved into Saudi Aramco. By 1953, the House of Saud was receiving surpluses of oil money. Ibn Saud died that year.

Throughout the history of the Saud Dynasty, the Wahhabi and the Ikwan were instrumental in helping the family win their wars. What they demanded in return was to spread their fundamentalist Islamic beliefs. They felt it was the duty of good Muslims to put their lives in order and purify those around them. If fellow Muslims would not respond to friendly persuasion, then stronger methods, such as Holy Wars, or Jihads, were called for.

By the time I finish the article it is getting late. Expecting Osane home any minute, I start dinner. As I chop onions for meat loaf, my mind wanders back over the history I have just read. Although I am thankful for any facts, I am still more interested in the *ordinary Arabian*… not the royal family and religious zealots. What are the men, women, and children of mainstream Saudi Arabia like? What events comprise their days? They are the unknown essence and heart of the Kingdom, and they are what intrigue me. These Saudis will be my future neighbors and I will pass my time in their company.

Frustrated by my lack of information and the reality that my well at the library has already run dry, I turn to my last resource—Osane. Every time I attempt to question him, however, he sidesteps my effort. I sense he is convinced that if I hear about the true nature of the Kingdom, he will be returning to Saudi Arabia alone.

Late one rainy evening, I prepare two cups of tea and sit him down. Realizing he is fearful, I softly ask him to describe his homeland. He fidgets, holding back until I gently take his hand and look into his eyes.

"OK, Christie, you win," he says. "But I warn you: The only way to grasp the Arab mentality is to step out of your American mind and begin to see through *Arab eyes*."

With relief, I reply, "I know this is difficult for you Osane, but I'm already committed to changing worlds. Before I leave physically, it will really assist me to take a mental trip…so let's go…"

"Your new country," he reluctantly begins, "is extremely isolated, poor, and tribal. There are 830,000 square miles, most of which is desert. It's the twelfth largest country in the world. Few of the women are educated and the men are taught mainly the Koran or the Sha'ria."

"The best way to truly understands life as a Saudi," he continues, "is to become one. Pretend you are born into an extended Arabian family in the 1960s. As a child, you not only live with your mother, father, brothers, and sisters, but also with stepmothers and stepbrothers. Your sole entertainment is based on visiting cousins, aunts, uncles, and grandparents. There are no museums, libraries, symphonies, art galleries, or any other outlets. Because of primitive medicine, death is a constant visitor. Women dying during childbirth and the death of young children are the most frequent casualties. Pain will become a familiar companion. With the lack of proper medical facilities, most of the cures you will be using are passed down through generations or prescribed by elder villagers with "the gift."

Osane nervously continues. "Family life is the backbone of your whole life. In such a support system, there is no loneliness. Warmth and unconditional love shape your life. Your uncles, aunts, and cousins consider you as important as their own children. When you are in the safety of your home, freedom of behavior is allowed. Outside your own dwelling, tribal customs and culture demand strict behavior patterns for almost *every* occasion.

At an early age you will learn the structure of life. There are levels of authority: God, King, tribe, father, uncle, and brother. There is no separation between Church and State. The word "God" enters into most sentences you will be speaking. Arabian Law is based on the Sha'ria, and most of your education is spent memorizing this religious law and the Koran. The Koran, unlike the Bible, lays down rules for most aspects of your life. The ever-present factor ruling your life will be tribal pride. If the family/tribal laws are broken, resulting in loss of face, the discipline is severe. There is no flexibility in the punishment for thievery, murder, or adultery."

Osane pauses and asks, "Christie, do you really want to hear more?" A quick look into my eyes affirms that I do. A reluctant Osane proceeds. "The five-to-ten-year-olds carry many responsibilities. If you are male, you begin attending school. Before and after school you tend to your family's livestock. You make daily trips to the market for food, material, and any other goods the women of the household need. Many hours are spent caring for the guests of your father. While the men visit you must pour coffee and tea, and lay out their bedding. You must also attend Friday Mosque, and prayers five times a day become an absolute."

"As a female," Osane states, "just as much will be demanded of you. At the age of nine or ten, you will be veiled. Although the Kingdom has just opened elementary schools for girls, most of your learning will be in homemaking. The women of the family will begin your apprenticeship with sewing, for all dresses are hand-sewn. Education in cooking will also occupy many hours, for the families are large and food is prepared from scratch. Not only are the females of the house required to cook for their families, but also for the many male guests. You will also learn how to do the laundry and in between your household chores, you will take a large part in raising the younger children. It is also customary to pray five times a day within the home. Soon, you will become an important part of the female harem (the many women living and caring for the same home). Without modern conveniences, it takes many hands to keep a large residence. With many of the harem dying in childbirth, multiple wives serve a definite need."

Osane concludes his delivery by stating, "With the discovery of oil, the ancient Kingdom is just *beginning* to change. You, however, will be stepping into an Arabia which has stood still through the ages, a land time has forgotten."

Finally finished, Osane stares down at his hands. I gently take his arm and pull him towards me, seeing insecurity and fear of abandonment in his eyes. I kiss those eyes and thank him for taking me on a mental journey, for now I know what to expect.

As he walks out the door in relief, an unwanted wave of doubt comes crashing down on my mind and soul. Knowing what to anticipate is not necessarily a guarantee that my Arab lenses won't shatter, and be rapidly buried under mounds of desert sand.

Chapter 4

Birthing and Departure Preparations

"The two most important days in your life are the day you are born and the day you find out why."
Mark Twain

As the weeks fly by, I begin to realize that the Arabian relatives will meet more than one new member of the family. To say this pregnancy is planned is a misstatement, for we are still coming to terms with early marriage. We are also living on a financial shoestring. My source of income from my parents has been terminated, and after four years of support, the Arabian Educational Mission has cut Osane's salary in half.

As the baby grows, Osane studies and I work one menial job after another. Finally, I am able to pay my way back into school and the spring finds me student teaching in a small farm town outside our university. As I teach, the baby keeps developing. Soon it is kicking, and I can feel a new love begin to grow in my heart.

My student teaching ends, and as blossoms appear across campus, I begin attending my last two courses of summer school before graduation. My first course is especially demanding. Japanese history is mentally complex enough, without fitting it into a short summer semester. An interesting physical complication of late pregnancy becomes the classroom desk. No matter which way I sit, I hardly fit. Often in the middle of some dynasty, the baby will give a good kick. Its foot will hit the edge of the desk, sending my pen flying.

Caught up in the swirls of life, I feel the summer days flying by. My only moments of peace are in the public gardens down the street from our apartment. During these short moments of repose, it's sheer bliss to hear the birds sing and smell the brilliant flowers. Feeling the life move within me, I hug myself. My Madonna eyes stare into the distance and I enter the world where all mothers go who are with child. In this space cushioned with love, time stands still, and I always re-enter the present rejuvenated and optimistic.

During mid-summer, the night before my Japanese History final exam, I receive a phone call from my aunt and two cousins. It seems they have appointed themselves an official peace-making party between my family and myself. While I applaud the sentiment of this impromptu visit, it brings up a problem. None of my relatives know that I'm pregnant.

The next afternoon, Osane drives me to the local Holiday Inn to meet our visitors. Waiting in the lobby in my pregnant splendor, I shuffle my feet as I nervously wait. After the initial surprise, the visit turns into a success. Osane wines, dines, and charms the relatives, and we say goodbye around midnight amid hugs and congratulations.

The following morning, Osane gives me a kiss before driving our only car to the library. I leisurely roll over, for I am looking forward to sleeping in. I am exhausted from the strain of the last five weeks of Japanese history, yesterday's final, and the relatives' visit.

My deep sleep is interrupted mid-morning, when water starts gushing out of me. I lie in bed thinking that bedwetting must be another nuisance of late pregnancy. As the streams turns into a lake, I decide to hurry to the bathroom.

As I sit there alone, stark reality hits. I am having our baby five weeks early! No, I think. I can't let this happen. We aren't prepared. We don't have a crib, diapers, or anything for the baby—and I haven't graduated! I have one more session of summer school and then the baby is due. We planned it this way and this is the way it has to be!

I quickly learn that mind over matter doesn't work in these situations, for water continues to drip. Suddenly a thought shoots through my mind. How can I get to the hospital? Osane has taken our car. As I attempt to push back panic, I hear a light knock at the door. I fling a towel between my legs in an attempt to dam up the flow of water, and grope towards the door.

I open it to find my relatives, armed to the teeth with baby presents. They see me standing there with wide eyes, pale face, and little trickles flowing down my legs, and quickly grasp the situation. Between them they have delivered seven children, so they are more than qualified to take control.

After letting them in, I walk to the table and attempt to dial the phone. Seeing my hands shaking, my aunt takes the receiver and calls the doctor for me. As happens in such dire emergencies, the line is busy.

While waiting for an open line, my relatives sit me down and begin handing me baby presents. Through my numb fingers pass little T-shirts, rattles, receiving blankets and all the things I will need for our baby's early weeks. Emotional tears of thanksgiving drip down my face as I carefully place all the new gifts on a corner of the couch.

Meanwhile, my aunt reaches the doctor, who tells her to drive me straight to the hospital. Seeing the apprehension in my eyes, my aunt gently leads me to her car while my cousins drive to the library to find Osane.

As I lie in the delivery room watching the summer breezes blow the oak limbs outside the window, I shake with fear of the unknown. There is no mistaking the first pains. As they grow in intensity and frequency, I become preoccupied with breathing exercises. Consumed with my visualization of waves crashing onto a beach and then ebbing out to sea, I hardly notice Osane when he slips into the delivery room. His olive skin is the color of ash, and he seems more in shock than I am. I'm much too busy keeping my waves afloat. Although my labor is quite hard, it isn't long. On the afternoon of July 26, 1969, our little Nazar enters the world.

It must be the same experience for every new mother who truly wants her child. I am overwhelmed by this new miracle of life. He is so perfect and just the way I'd pictured him. Each time I look at my newborn infant, I feel centered into the very essence of life. He has already grounded me, and my heart is overflowing with love.

After Nazar's birth, the relatives reappear. They find it hard to believe that they had come to visit, and ended up helping to deliver a baby. After loading me down with compliments about our new son, they hug me. I thank them for their presents, support, and shared wisdom. Assuring them that they had taken the edge of fear out of Nazar's birth, I fondly say good-bye.

Osane pays his first formal visit a few hours afterwards. He arrives dressed in his best suit, carrying the biggest bouquet of flowers the local florist can create. He spreads his visitation time between looking at his new son and hugging me. Next, our friends start arriving. Each one brings their own special gift, and soon Nazar has more supplies than any baby could need.

As dusk falls, visiting hours end, and the nurses bring out the babies for their evening milk. This is my first opportunity to be with my newborn son. The second the nurse tenderly places Nazar in my arms I feel a primordial cord, connecting me to the deepest cycles of life. Running my finger across his infant cheek, I sense a cosmic bonding cementing us together, joining us through this lifetime and those to come. As I stare into his face, I experience a contentment and peace that resonates in every molecule of my being. On the first day of Nazar's life, I am also reborn.

Physically, I conclude, Nazar is simply beautiful. Born with black sideburns and hair right down his neck, his features are strong and wonderfully pronounced. Each time I search his face I find what I had hoped for. Peering up at me are Osane's eyes and chin dimple. My white pigments tone down his skin color one shade, and the straightness of my hair takes out the tight curls. In total, however, this is Osane in miniature and I couldn't love either of them more.

After the feeding period is over, I hand Nazar back to the nurse and settle down for a well-earned rest. Even on this sunny day of perfection, when my heart is overflowing with wonder, gathering rain clouds keep sleep at bay.

The reality is, we can't pay for our son's birth. With a total of $22 in the bank, it is impossible for us to pay the $500 we owe the hospital and doctor. Desperate, Osane has spent days searching for a solution. We discussed several options, but always arrived at a dead end. Osane's Arab pride had kept him from borrowing the money from his friends or taking out a bank loan. Exhaustion finally dims the thoughts of swirling bills, and I fall into a troubled sleep.

The next morning Osane arrives with a twinkle in his eyes. After a large hug, he places a strange-looking envelope in my hand. I touch it gingerly, as one would handle a rare piece of art, for it seems to come from another world. It has Arabic writing in the corner and a colorful, Asian-looking stamp.

The interior holds the *real surprise*. For inside is a bank check made out for $500, the exact amount we need to pay our hospital bills. I am overwhelmed. Tears of disbelief fill my eyes and I lie in my hospital bed completely spellbound. My soul overflows with gratitude. In the end, our families have paved the road for Nazar's birth. One side of the family has comforted and supplied our baby with all the clothes and things he will need, while the other side of the family has paid for his birth.

We have witnessed grace working in our lives twice now. The first time was at our wedding, and again at the birth of our son. Is this a sign that we are walking the right path, or is this the gift of a lazy river, balancing the raging rapids that might be in our near future?

As the days pass, I grow stronger. Soon we are both going back to school, for I have one more course to finish before I graduate. I sign up for a morning class and Osane signs up for afternoon classes. This way someone is always with Nazar.

Time passes, and my university graduation comes and goes. I shed the title of student only to accept the new role of waitress and sole supporter of our family. It's hard to make ends meet, and the contents of our fridge depend on my tips.

For the next several months, life has a rhythm. Nazar grows, Osane studies, and I work evenings. Each day is more or less the same; a time out, to strengthen us for the next gigantic step. Our routine is full of contentment and scattered with lazy times in which we simply enjoy being together. A part of me wishes to freeze these days and to continue in this pattern forever. Too soon however, it's time to break this cycle. Our new lives in Saudi Arabia are tapping at our door. It's time to refocus our energies and prepare for our next chapter.

My first purchases on our departure list are two metal trunks. As I study my piles of property, I know that most things must be discarded. The hardest things to give up are my clothes, my outer identity. Knowing none of my mini-skirts, sweaters, nylons, tights, knee socks or coats will be culturally acceptable in Arabia, I still feel compelled to include some of them. Over my clothes, Nazar's clothes are packed. On top of these I pile birth control pills, Raggedy Andy fabric, pictures, a two-year supply of makeup and anything else I think will be relevant. The crowning glory is Jell-O. Osane feels that this exotic substance might dazzle the relatives, and buy enough time for me to develop my Arabian cooking skills. So into the tight corners of the trunk go boxes of cherry, grape, lemon, and pineapple Jell-O.

The next step on our departure to-do list is quite a big step. Knowing that a Christian marriage is not accepted in Saudi Arabia, Osane makes all the arrangements for our Muslim wedding. Within a week, we are seated in the office of the local mosque. Osane sits in one office chair, while Nazar and I sit in another. As the Imam reads our vows, the silence is only broken by Nazar. Our young son is determined to pull the telephone off the Imam's desk.

After our Muslim vows are read, two Arab male witnesses and the Imam sign the papers. As congratulations are handed out, the Imam picks up Nazar. While I stand there hoping our energetic son will behave, Nazar decides he wants to investigate the Imam's glasses. After he tries to grab them, Nazar is handed back to me, and the men go into the mosque to pray.

I sit in a chair outside the mosque, listening to Osane's voice singing out the long ritual of the Islamic prayer. Even though I am still in my country, I am now in his world. He is uttering strange new words I didn't even know he knew. Meanwhile I'm in the lobby, sitting outside the male world, an excluded woman.

Chapter 5

Resistance

"Resistance is common to the unusual."
Toba Beta

While I'm packing, a quote from an unknown author keeps whispering in my ear. "Don't think you're on the right road just because it's a well-beaten path."

As the days proceed, I begin to realize that being nonconformists and swimming upstream creates ripples. The first roadblock in our departure becomes my entry visa into Saudi Arabia. Osane had warned me about this possibility before we were married.

"Christie," he shared one evening. "About ten years ago, the Saudi government began sending the first and second waves of

Saudi sons abroad on government scholarships. Some of these sons brought back foreign wives, but their numbers were too limited to cause currents. However, as time passed, it became evident that these mixed marriages led to divorce and foreign mothers taking Saudi children out of the country. I am on the cusp of the third wave of scholarships. I know there is turmoil in the Ministry of Education and that the government is positioning for a decisive move."

Months pass. Our wedding comes and goes and neither Osane nor I mention my entry visa until late one night, when Osane pulls me aside. "There's something I need to tell you, Christie. Right after we were married, the Government issued a Royal Decree, banning all marriages to foreign spouses. I kept this official proclamation quiet from you because of everything else going on in our lives."

Spinning from this news, I sit down on the bed.

Osane continues by saying, "Well, Christie, it's finally time to face this demon. I have my degree in hand and I have proof that we were married *before* the Royal Decree. Our ace in the hole is our Saudi son. With a 10-hour difference, the appropriate time to call is *now*." He walks towards the phone but instead of picking it up, he begins pacing back and forth.

"Christie," he worries aloud. "If the government doesn't allow our marriage, we both know they won't approve an entry visa for you and Nazar. What will we do then?"

Suddenly engulfed in fear, I reply, "I don't know, Osane. I truly don't know, but we have to try."

Looking into my eyes for support, Osane picks up the receiver and dials the Educational Mission in Saudi Arabia. I can see moist sweat on his palms as he holds the phone. Meanwhile, I sit helplessly beside him, with my heart sinking into my stomach.

Osane begins the phone call in English and quickly slips into Arabic. With frustration, I listen to this heated Arabic discussion, which seems to continue forever. I watch Osane's face to decipher the course of the conversation, but his expression remains a neutral mask. Just when I am about to explode, Osane hangs up the phone.

"Tell me, tell me," I plead.

Osane gives me a big smile and says, "In the end, mainly because of our Saudi son, the Educational Mission has agreed to issue not one but three tickets... *and* they're also sending your entry visa!"

Ecstatic to have all the tension and apprehension of the dreaded issue behind us, the three of us go out to dinner the next evening to celebrate. On the way to the restaurant, the moon seems to shine with brilliance and the leaves in the trees rustle a victory song in our ears. With such a positive decision from the Educational Mission, it seems to us that our trip into the Kingdom will be an effortless flow.

We should have known better than to prematurely celebrate.

Weeks pass and every day Osane checks the mailbox for my entry visa. He has already written the Ministry several times, but one delay leads to the next and still... no visa.

Late one afternoon, Osane slowly walks into our living room and finds me playing with Nazar. "Christie," he says as I look up into his frustrated face. "I simply don't know what else we can do about your visa. There's only one other thing I can think of. If you become a Muslim, this could grease the wheels. You might think about studying the Koran and the Five Pillars of Wisdom of the Muslim faith. If you don't object morally and philosophically, we can return to the mosque and have the papers signed."

Caught off guard by such a blunt request, my heart skips a beat. I am, however, determined to keep an open mind. "OK," I say. "I'll begin my studies tomorrow and let you know how I feel."

So once again, I enter the library stacks. This time I am successful, finding a wonderful collection of books on Islam. I open my first source to read a quote from Don Belt of *National Geographic*. He claims that, "A fifth of humankind follows Islam, the fastest-growing and perhaps most misunderstood religion on earth. For these people, Islam is a personal connection to the same God worshiped by Jews and Christians."

I find another quote from Prince Talal of Jordan. He says, "Peace is the essence of Islam."

While Nazar sleeps, I study. Soon baby bottles, diapers, and a mass of wonderful books intermingle. I become fascinated with Islamic history. I find that Judaism, Christianity, and Islam trace their lineage to Abraham. Muslims believe in the Hebrew prophets, including Moses, and the Old Testament. They also believe that Jesus cannot be the son of God for there are no Gods on earth, only prophets. The ultimate messenger for Muslims is the last Prophet from God. His name is Muhammad. As Tad Szulc states, "Muhammad is recognized as the last in a series of prophets, including Adam, Abraham, Moses and Jesus, all of whom appear, redefined, in the Holy Book of Islam."

Another article by Don Belt states that, "Muhammad is born in Mecca about 570 A.D. He is an orphan and is raised by his grandfather and uncle. As he grows, he rejects the popular polytheism of his day. He instead begins to worship the one God of the Jewish communities. When he is forty, Muhammad retreats to a cave outside Mecca. While deep in meditation, he is visited by the archangel Gabriel, who recites to him the Word of God. Until his death, he spreads these teachings to his followers. When he dies, in 632 A.D., these words are written down in the Koran. Muslims consider the Koran to be the literal Word of God and a refinement to the Jewish and Christian scriptures.

Inspired by Muhammad, Islam spreads like wildfire. Its momentum is multi-tiered. On one level, the golden words of the spirit spread truth while on the human level, Islamic warlords and men thirst for conquest and women. When Islam has taken over much of Europe and Northern Africa, it offers a blossoming of science, arts, philosophy, and medicine. After the Crusades, Islam withdraws into itself, leaving in its wake the path of enlightenment."

I am lucky enough to find an English language Koran among my collection of textbooks. As I glance through its ornate pages, I notice that the Koran consists of 114 suras, or chapters. These suras cover everything from the nature of God to the laws governing the affairs of men.

One of Osane's requests is that I learn the Five Pillars of Wisdom, which stand at the heart of the Muslim religion. Opening the description pages in my English Koran, I read that the first Pillar is the call to prayer five times a day. Over the entire Muslim world, the same call has been sung for nearly 1,400 years. "Allah...u akbar," the faithful sing out. "Allahhhh...u akbar! – God is great!"

The second Pillar of Wisdom is the pilgrimage to Mecca. The Koran states that Abraham and his son Isma'il travel to Mecca. Here they raise "The House" as a celebration to God. The only thing remaining of Abraham's and Isma'il's "House" is a corner of its foundation called the Kaaba, or Great Stone. This Kaaba is shrouded in black cloth and has become Islam's holiest shrine. It is required of Muslims who can manage it, to make a Pilgrimage to Mecca at least once in their lifetime. Muhammad was the first Hajji, or Pilgrim. He returned to Mecca from Medina. Once in Mecca, he destroyed the fake idols of the Kaaba, and re-dedicated it to the God of Abraham. Each year, as many as 2.5 million Muslims circle the Kaaba in the footsteps of Abraham, Isma'il and Muhammad.

The third Pillar of Islam is fasting during the holy month of Ramadan. The fourth Pillar is charity. An Arabic proverb states that the right hand should give, while the left hand does not see what's being given. An illustration of this was Osane's uncle's late-night rides. This Uncle would drop food at the doors of the hungry and would tell no one. The only reason Osane knew was that, at times, he also would make these rides.

The fifth and final Pillar of Islam was: "La ilaha illa Allah, Muhammad rasul Allah – There is no god but God, and Muhammad is his Messenger."

While I am reading, Osane walks into the room. He looks at my book and sits down beside me. "There are a few concepts you may not infer from your readings, Christie," he states. "To become a practicing Muslim demands dedication and discipline. There are two pillars that are particularly rigorous.

"The third pillar orders that a Muslim fast during the month of Ramadan. This requires a great deal of sacrifice, especially when fit into the daily routines of work, study, and family care. It is not easy to fast, and it's not meant to be. While *hungry,* the worshiper is instructed to empathize with the poor and their continually growling, empty stomachs.

"The first pillar is particularly demanding. It orders the practicing Muslim to pray five times a day. It requires that life stops, and that the timely washing ritual be observed. The praying requires kneeling and rising and kneeling and prostrations. This exercise routine is insisted of the very young and the very old… five times a day."

I stare at Osane, trying to digest the exacting nature of this desert religion.

"Don't worry, Christie," Osane smiles. "An orthodox following might not be for you. However, an acknowledgment of the way God fills the everyday life of practicing Muslims should be kept in your mind. Their dedication should be honored and respected."

I take Osane's hand and thank him for his insight into his faith. With this information I can now appreciate how this form of worship threads through the minutes of everyday existence.

After Osane leaves, I return to my book. After several days of study, I am finally ready to return my books to the library. Now it is time to decide if I can declare myself a Muslim. As I ponder, I have two main reservations. First of all, the fanaticism of the Wahhabi sector of Islam is worrisome. The concern is increased because Islam is a faith without an established hierarchy. There is no Pope to excommunicate zealots. Each individual is free to interpret the Word of God in his or her own way. Sura 111:7 of the Koran acknowledges this dilemma: "Some... verses are precise in meaning—they are the foundation of the Book—and others ambiguous. Those whose hearts are infected with disbelief follow the ambiguous part, so as to create dissension... no one knows its meaning except God."

My second concern is that the government of Saudi Arabia is based on the Sha'ria. Being an American, I was always taught the wisdom of separating church and state. Within the Kingdom, where are the checks and balances?

In turmoil, I take one-year-old Nazar to the park. I sit on a bench under a large oak tree, watching the wind swirling through the branches. Nazar is just learning to walk, and I watch him trip and tumble through the sand box. As I stare past the park to the busy traffic beyond, the same question keeps turning around in my mind. Can I declare myself a Muslim?

"I just don't know," I cry to the wind. I *have* found that Muhammad's main principles blend surprisingly into my own... and I *have* discovered that the Koran is full of love.

My mind remains in frustrated confusion, until I look down at Nazar. Laughing, he takes yet another spill into the sand. I finally decide that I am open enough to let yet another interpretation of "*love*" into my life. I will slide my new Koran into my bookshelf. It will fit nicely next to the Bible and under my picture of Buddha and other prophets. After all, each one is celebrating the same Universal Oneness.

With my decision to become a Muslim made, Osane, Nazar and I once again drive to the Mosque. As we open the door, I know I am entering his world again. Nazar and I sit on a couch at the far end of the office, while Osane pulls a chair up to the Imam's desk. Together they fill out the form to declare me a Muslim.

Everything is soon in order. The only problem is witnesses. Two male signatures are required. As the Imam and Osane root through the local barbershops and stores for Muslim males to notarize the forms, Nazar and I wait quietly. After the paper is properly signed a big seal is pounded down upon it, making it official. The next day, we mail this document to the Educational Mission, contributing yet another addition to the never-ending flow of paperwork.

Waiting now becomes our main challenge. To keep myself busy, I concentrate on processing Nazar's and my American passports. Next, I make our appointments to receive the multitude of shots required for Middle Eastern travel. Our overzealous doctor lets her imagination go wild. Not only does she administer the required cholera and smallpox shots, but she also throws in typhoid, typhus, and yellow fever just to be safe.

A few days later, I arrange to meet Osane at the Student Union for lunch. As I struggle up the steps of the Union with my baby stroller, gracious souls open the double doors so Nazar and I can enter.

Inside, I am immediately transported into the world of hustling students, clanging trays, and sandwich smells from the cafeteria. Pushing Nazar through the crowded aisles, my eye catches that of an older Arab woman. As I wonder who she is, she approaches me, holding out her hand. She introduces herself as Salha, a newly arrived Egyptian studying for her Doctorate in Women's Studies.

"Your husband Osane has been introduced to me through a mutual friend," Salha says with only a slight accent. "He tells me that you are trying to gather information on Saudi Arabia.

If that's true, perhaps you'd be interested in meeting me for coffee."

Excitedly, I shake her hand, saying, "I'd love to meet you for coffee, Salha. If it's convenient, let's meet here tomorrow at 10:00."

With that arranged, I walk away, not believing my luck. Through my excitement, however, a sudden realization knots my stomach. "Why do all Arabs I talk to about my journey into the Kingdom have trepidation in their eyes?"

The next morning I wake early. After kissing Osane goodbye as he hurries off to class, I linger at the window. The sun is shining on the new day, but I notice rain clouds gathering. The wind seems to be picking up and the branches around our apartment brush the wood siding

Leaving the window, I dress and feed Nazar, then wait for a friend who is coming over to babysit our little one. At the appropriate hour I am seated in the Student Union with pencil and pad in hand, waiting for Salha. I don't want to miss one fact. I have a feeling that her presentation is going to be highly documented and professional.

On time, she approaches the table and I stand and give her a polite hug. I have a cup of coffee already sitting on the table waiting for her. As we sip our drinks, we chat lightly for an appropriate time.

Finally she begins by saying, "Many articles and books, even in this century, have been written as though the female half of the Middle East does not exist. This has made my research incredibly frustrating. When I did discover written work on women in the Middle East, I found that many of the male authors missed the mark. This is in large part because of the complexities of the culture. Middle Eastern society is a kaleidoscope. One pattern of color appears after another. All are true, all complete, and all are made from the same stone. The challenge is to dissect the stone."

Slowly she takes a sip of coffee and her voice changes. I pick up my pencil, prepared for the historical lecture I sense will follow. She begins, "In pre-Islamic times, when some women were allowed to enjoy great prestige, Robertson Smith wrote of the ancient custom of polyandry or plural husbands. Women also fought in battles and held government positions. By the 7th Century, the time of the Prophet Muhammad, influences from the Byzantine Empire had undermined the women's position. Males held ultimate authority over women. Thus, fathers could kill unwanted daughters through exposure at birth. These same fathers could marry daughters to husbands who might take additional wives and divorce any of the women they wished. Also, brothers could divide their inheritance without provision for their sisters."

"Always through history," she continues, "There were some women who were able to rise above such lowly conditions. Khadijah, first wife of the Prophet Muhammad, was such a woman. She had outlived her male kin and inherited the estate of her late husband. Thus, she stood outside the system. It was no surprise that her second husband, The Prophet, introduced profound changes into the position held by women and children. In fact, an aim of the Koran was to improve the woman's position. The Koran gave women back many of their rights. Infanticide was prohibited. The number of legal wives a man could have at one time was reduced to four. Women could protest injustice and ill treatment. These rights were written into the Sha'ria, which still governs life within the Kingdom.

"As time went on, woman's new found rights began to fade along with the Golden Age of Islam. During the 14th Century, the Ottoman Empire conquered the area. The Turkish interpreted the Koran according to an environment in which men ruled. They imposed their own views and traditions. Veiling, seclusion, and general social segregation were thrust on an unsuspecting female population. Women were shut off from the rest of the household and placed under the charge of eunuchs. Two separate societies developed, the world of men and the world of women."

Fascinated, I bring Salha another cup of coffee. Although she has already turned the kaleidoscope several times, I am ready for new patterns. She begins by stating, "There are other elements which shape female freedoms within Muslim society. The first two are tribal customs and tribal laws. Tribal customs serve as the basis for each clan's belief systems. Tribal laws are much more restrictive for women and vary with location. The final factor regulating a woman's liberty is her communal environment. How much freedom she has is the result of her social and economic position and the composition of her family. It also depends upon her personality and her individual position within the family group."

Salha concludes by stating, "Arab women have to work out their own individual freedoms within the boundaries of the communal environment existing between the two poles of the Koran and tribal customs and law. It is the power of this balance that holds Saudi women to their roles and makes equality within their culture almost impossible."

With that, she puts down her cup. I am spellbound. I can't stop staring at her. I slowly put my pencil in my purse, thinking I have just concluded one of my upper-level sociology courses. As I hug and thank her, I wonder if I will ever see her again. As we part, she puts a small piece of paper in my hand.

I carefully fold my fingers around Salha's message and walk outside into a dark, rainy afternoon. The drops make large splashes on the sidewalk as I jump puddles to my car.

Thankful that Salha's note has remained protected in my palm, I open it.

Thoughts from a Saudi Woman

"I find, to my dismay, that I am full of conflict. I am pulled more strongly by the strings of tradition and Islam than I would have believed. I thought I was a modern woman, but what is that exactly? I am an Islamic woman first."

With the kaleidoscope changing patterns in my mind, I drive home. Three weeks later, my entry visa arrives, and the next two weeks are a blur of activity. We sell or give away most of our possessions and pack the rest.

Consciously I *run* through my days. I purposely build granite walls around my emotions and shift into a perpetual neutral state. I also put a leash on my thoughts, focusing only on departure details, leaving not even a nanosecond for contemplation. My robotic control faces short-circuiting however, when it comes time to say goodbye to friends and family.

The evening before we are scheduled to drive to my parents' home, I check Nazar in his crib and lie down beside Osane. Within minutes, we are both in a deep sleep. Sometime in the heart of the night, I gulp for air. I sit straight up, instantly awake. Fear seizes me as I try to breathe, and the cool night feels heavy and oppressive.

With a clenched stomach, I carefully get out of bed, dress quietly, open the door, and walk into the night. Almost running through winding streets, I find that no matter how quick my stride, I can't outrace my emotions.

"What am I doing?" I scream into the darkness. "Why am I jumping into the unknown, leaving my family, friends, and life behind?" I begin a frantic dialog, trying to create order out of chaos. "First," I say into the wind, "I know I am young, in love, and hungry for adventure. I am also a rebellious dreamer and want nothing to do with suburban life. My quest is for a Utopian society based on God and *honor*, and not on a *monetary* society.

"OK," I say to myself, "but you still haven't answered **why** you're doing this." Waiting for wisdom, I listen to my footsteps and the howl of a dog a few streets over. I hang in this space until I hear a Godly voice whisper in my ear. "You, dear one, always attempt to walk the path blazed by your inner voices. Intuition tells you that your feet are treading the right road. Along this narrow and rocky trail, there are two road signs. One says *faith* and the other says *trust*. Let your feet follow this ordained path and trust that you will have the faith to find your way. Know that you'll never be alone."

Pausing a moment to let my thoughts sink in, I look straight up. Suddenly I'm calmed and centered by the brilliant stars, and the awareness of personal insignificance in such a large universe. Heading for home, I conclude that I will continue this journey into the unknown. My one remaining fear is for my sanity. In this confrontation with the East, will I remain sane?

Goodbyes to our friends aren't easy. The only reason we are able to let go is our resolve to keep our feet moving forward, no matter what emotions try to tackle us.

Saying goodbye to my family is nearly impossible. I am asking them to accept an unheard-of path. It's as if I'm joining the Lewis and Clark Expedition. Without Sacajawea for female companionship, I'm embarking on an adventure into the absolute unknown, with no return date.

Finally, with our goodbyes said and our to-do list complete, we wake in the dark on departure day. Quickly we pack last-minute items. From our taxi window, we watch the sunrise over the cornfields. I keep my mind clear of all thoughts. Instead, I memorize the smell of damp American soil and the sounds of the crows as they play tag over the fresh cut hay.

By mid-morning we are at the airport and as our plane takes off, Osane recites a small portion of the Koran. The forward thrust of the plane convinces my soul there is no turning back now. We are on our way for an overnight in England, then a short stay in Beirut. The entire time, magnetic Saudi Arabia is pulling us forward. I close my eyes and hear voices repeat our pattern of struggle, persistence, flow. As our plane flies into the clouds, I say a small prayer and surrender myself to our future.

Chapter 6

Our Trip to Arabia

"The mind of man plans his way, but the Lord directs his steps."
   Proverbs 16:9

During our trans-Atlantic flight, Nazar sleeps. Osane also dozes on and off, but for me, trying to sleep is futile. I am cold. I can't get comfortable. My mind is too full to put itself to rest. Maylan French in *The Woman's World* said, "To choose a husband is to choose a life." The international life that I have chosen is sitting all around me. It feels exhilarating to be a member of this very small fraternity of overseas travelers, for in 1970 most Americans stayed home. As these thoughts filter through my mind, sleep finally takes over and I doze off. I wake as the plane lands on English soil at Heathrow Airport.

One by one our small group stumbles off the plane, weighed down by luggage and time changes. I reach into my purse and pull out passports and health certificates. We stay just long enough in England to have a good night's rest. We leave early the next morning, for our future feels tenuous. There is no time to linger.

As our plane slowly makes its way down the Heathrow taxiways, my eyes are glued to the window, for I'm taking in every detail of the airlines of the world on parade. Excited, I glimpse Air France, KLM, British Airways, Lufthansa, and Liberia Airways. On the far end of the taxiway, I spot my first Saudi airplane. Its colors are green and gold. It's covered with Arabic writing and on its tail, boldly outlined, is the Saudi emblem of palm trees and crossed swords.

We are soon in the air and after we cut through the cloud bank, I switch my attention to our Middle Eastern plane. I immediately notice a different atmosphere than I am used to on stateside flights. The decor is much more lavish. On the wall at the end of second class, an Arab village is outlined. This scene includes a mosque with towering minarets, mud houses, and large villas with arched gates. The stewardesses are dressed in green and gold. Sewn on their hats are green crepe veils, which come tapering down the side of their heads. These airy illusions of fabric twist around their chins and down their backs. Surrounding the edge of these scarves are little gold leaves, which lend style and femininity to their tailored pant suits.

My eyes keep following these striking women, for they fascinate me. Everything from the graceful way they move to their dark beauty, their Arabic language, and their intense politeness, is so different from TWA or Pan American flight attendants.

I am thoroughly enjoying this new experience until somewhere over Italy, I lean down to check Nazar and find he is burning up with fever. The cold, damp English weather coupled with time changes has been too much for him. As I wrap Nazar in his blue baby blanket, I realize that our challenges might be starting sooner than planned.

I pick up a magazine to calm my worries. Time passes and night falls. As I look out of the window, straining my eyes to see Beirut, I see one lone star shining above the Mediterranean. Just as I am wishing on it, the city appears from out of nowhere. Surrounded on one side by mountains and the other by the Mediterranean, Beirut blazes with diamond-like lights. It is a magnificent picture, which I have to pull myself away from to tend to Nazar.

The stewardesses are aware that our baby is sick. After we land, they drive us to the main airport in a special car. We are tired from our long trip and my only wish is to tuck Nazar into a safe crib in our hotel.

There is no trouble threading our way through customs, for Osane's Saudi passport and my American passport are sure entries. However, the minute we step from customs into the main airport, all order and efficiency totally vanish. We are beset by shouting, shoving, pushing, and grabbing porters. Some of these porters are young, some are old, some have teeth, and some have none. I would have taken more interest in their appearances if it hadn't been for their pushy manner, which angered me.

About four porters grab our bags and head in different directions. Osane herds them like a sheep dog and our whole party needles its way through the crowd. As we reach the parking lot, our suitcases are dumped miraculously into one pile, as porters take off in a multitude of directions to hail a taxi. The game is, the one who screams the loudest, grabs the most luggage, hails the cab, and runs back to square one first, wins the most money. The other porters simply join the fun, and we are the only losers.

Our exhausted family finally arrives at the hotel and we make our way to a top floor room. The floor plan of our temporary home is shaped like a U. In one end are the bathroom, hall, and closets. In the center of the U is the living room and at the far end are two beds. The whole outside wall is glass, which looks onto the city and then out to sea.

As I am unpacking, the crib arrives and with great relief, I finally tuck Nazar in. Settled and safe, Osane and I jump between clean sheets, and in an instant sleep closes over the activities of a very hectic day.

The next morning Nazar is still sick, and Osane telephones the hotel's doctor. Since the doctor can't see Nazar until late afternoon, we have to settle down and make do. Osane orders breakfast and, after I care for Nazar, I take what will become a well-worn seat by the window. Our position on the top floor gives me a bird's eye view into several apartments and the busy street below.

Feeling like a peeping Tom, but too curious to stop, I watch the woman of the nearest household begin her housework. Her first task is picking up the several small rugs that cover her tile floors. She hangs these rugs over the balcony and begins beating them. Then she brings out a big bucket in one hand and a large rag in the other.

Somehow I sense I am about to discover a new cleaning technique. As she drops the rag into the water, she assumes a posture difficult for chair-sitting Westerners. She squats, her feet staying flat on the floor, and she holds that locked-in position. I watch her waddle up and down the floors, dragging a wet cloth over them. She doesn't seem even a little inconvenienced by this posture, and when she becomes tired of squatting she simply uses her feet to glide the rag over the floor

Meanwhile, the five or six children of the household are shooed onto the flat roof, which is obviously their playground. Their toys consist of balls, a little house, and a blackboard. As I watch the oldest daughter hanging out laundry, surrounded by her playing brothers and sisters, I think how different their world is.

My snooping is interrupted by the porter's knock. I automatically yell, "Come in," which does absolutely no good. It is only Osane's voice saying, "fud-el," that brings our breakfast in. As the waiter spreads our meal on the cocktail table, he starts a short conversation with Osane in Arabic. I listen, trying to attach meaning to any word. Absolutely nothing makes sense but I am too hungry to care. My first meal in the Middle East introduces tahina, Lebanese olives, a tomato, onion, and egg dish, plus pita bread.

After breakfast, Osane dresses and leaves to explore the area while I take care of Nazar. After a look out the window to find out what my neighbors are doing, I slowly dress. After some time, Osane returns with an Arabic newspaper, ready for his afternoon nap. When he settles down, I give him a kiss and start for the door, prepared to do my own exploring. As I yell goodbye, he calls me back. It seems I have just walked into my first brick wall.

"Christie, you can't go down there alone," he lectures. "You don't know the city, the culture, or the language. You'd best stay up here and take care of Nazar until I can go with you."

As Osane begins his rest, I can feel the steam rising up in me. I want to blame someone for this enforced lockup, this breach of freedom. I can't blame Nazar for being sick, or this country. No one has made me come to the Arab world. My only recourse is to take responsibility for my own choices, and wait patiently for the afternoon to unfold.

Not at all sleepy, I sit down at my window seat and begin watching the traffic. Glancing over at the sleeping Osane, I feel unrest begin to bubble up in my inner world. So far our marriage has had its normal bumps, but our love remains healthy and strong. We are both free spirits committed to mutual ideals. However, the moment Osane put his feet on Arab soil I sensed a slight shift. His newly tensed jaw threw a pebble into our thriving relationship. I can only pray that this slight attitude change is only a fleeting symptom of transition.

I am suddenly pulled out of my mulling by a sharp knock at the door. As I know from experience, "come in" won't work. So I walk to the door and open it, and find the doctor standing there. He enters, examines Nazar, and gives his diagnosis to Osane in Arabic. Slowly he reaches for his prescription pad, and writes out the needed medicine. After shaking Osane's hand, he opens the door and is gone.

Frustrated, I inquire, "Osane, what did he say?"

"Don't worry, Christy," Osane replies. "Nazar has nothing serious, only a bad cold he caught in England. He is to take the prescribed medicine and get plenty of rest."

Relieved, I sing Nazar back to sleep while Osane goes out to buy Nazar's medicine.

That evening we have a lovely dinner in front of Lebanese television. Even though I understand nothing, I enjoy the programs just the same. I am pleasantly surprised by the appearance of *female* newscasters, for in "liberated America" female broadcasters haven't been allowed on the airwaves.

Easing back into my chair, I watch these Arab women with curiosity. They are beautiful, but in a much more formal manner than I am used to. Their hairdos are ratted and pulled back into tight French twists. Their earrings are bold and hang down to their shoulders, and their eye makeup is heavy and stylishly done. To me they resemble fashion plates out of Paris.

Early the next morning, Osane again goes out to buy his Arabic paper. When he returns, there is excitement in his voice. It seems he has stumbled across an almost hidden bookstore, with an English section in the far back corner. He is amazed to find several translated articles by Frank Viviano on the Saudi culture. As he hands them to me, I whisper a small prayer of gratitude, for any information is a valuable treasure.

That afternoon Osane visits some Lebanese friends and Nazar, still hot with fever, is sleeping deeply. With time on my hands, I settle down to read the articles Osane has left on the living room table.

As I skim the first translation, I note that it is about change. It states that, "Arabia had begun to see more changes in the past several decades than in the previous thirteen centuries. Since the Prophet Muhammad, the Sha'ria had governed this tribal monarchy. The Kingdom served as the keeper of the Muslim holy cities, Mecca and Medina. It served as the chief custodian of Islam and was the spiritual home of 1.3 billion Muslims worldwide. With the discovery of oil, a small rift between the ancient traditions and the modern world had begun. On March 3, 1938, in the Persian Gulf city of Dam'man, American engineers struck the first viable gusher after fifteen months of drilling. As exploration continued, it was soon confirmed that the Saudi sands held twenty-five per cent of the world's reserves. This new wealth was controlled from the capital city of Riyadh, a walled oasis town of only 60,000 people. Most of the families still lived in mud-brick houses.

The next article is short but full of religious facts. "On the Plain of Arafat, the Prophet Muhammad delivered his last sermon in 632. He stated, "No apostle will come after me, and no new faith will be born." This revelation created Saudi Arabia as Islam's historic center. The article continued by stating that a unique feature of Islam is that it is a religion without an institutionalized church, a Vatican, or formal priesthood. It relies on a direct relationship between believers and God. The religious police, or Mutawaeen, enforce a theocratic law-and-order system that dates back more than 1000 years." The article ended by simply stating that the capital city of Riyadh is the main stronghold of Wahhabism. "It is in Riyadh where the Committee for the Propagation of Virtue and the Prevention of Vice is located."

Feeling sick to my stomach, I throw the article on the floor. My cultural ignorance has created a cloud of false security around me. Now for the first time, I am staring at black-and-white reality. How can one, young, American female co-exist with the powerful Ministry of Religious Affairs? Looking out the window, I gaze down on the unveiled Lebanese women walking below. Why wasn't Osane born in Beirut? I might be able to remain sane surrounded by the cosmopolitan, educated, and exposed females of Lebanon!

Too depressed to think further, I pick up the next article. This translation deals with the thirty percent of the population, about two million people, who wander the Arabian deserts. It begins with a description of teenage boys as they make a fire for warmth against the early morning air. "In front of their tents they hammered out a drum rhythm in brass mortars, grinding coffee beans to make brain-charging Arab coffee. This free-ranging Bedouin culture remains at the center of the traditional Saudi's identity. What seem to matter most to these Bedouin are ancestors. Outside the tribe, everyone becomes suspect. Of the many deserts, the Rub al Khali or Empty Quarter is the most enormous. The Bedouin call this desert *The Sands*. One nomad states, 'His heart is at rest in the Sands.' He further comments that he knows how to read the desert winds and how to navigate at night by following the 'goat star.' Even this pure way of life is beginning to change. There is the beginning of a trend. Urbanized Bedouin have begun to work in the city but camp on the edges to retain their ancestral tribal customs."

As I finish this article, I stand up and stretch. I check Nazar and give him more medicine. Then I glance at the clock, realizing it is early. It will still be some time before Osane returns. Casually, I glance at the remaining two articles. I pick up the shorter one and am amazed at its opening statement.

"The Saudi 'majlis' serves as the Kingdom's version of democracy, with its traditions anchored in the desert." This unique concept makes me shake my head. I am glad that the next sentence defines a majlis as a social gathering for the purpose of conversation and council. It continues, "Royal majlises are held by every princely official in the Kingdom. Anyone is welcome. Some men simply want to offer greetings, while others ask about land matters, neighborhood disputes, or marriage problems. The head of state or King also presides over a majlis, where citizens can petition for help, advice or emergency cash." The article tells of a herdsman who sat down next to the King. As he patted the King on the arm to emphasize his point, he asked permission to graze his sheep on royal land. The scope of the Saudi majlis is endless, ranging from neighborhood meetings to intellectuals, businessmen, engineers, or bureaucrats.

The final article is barely half a page long, but the topic can't be more relevant. It states that, "The absolute absence of Saudi women in public is jarring. This is a half-populated country, in which fifty percent of humanity is relegated to shadows that slip silently along the edge of all activities. Even in this marginal, faceless land, there are rules. Saudi women must wear an abaya, or black cloak in public. Unrelated men must keep their distance. By law, a woman can't drive a car or travel abroad without a Mahram or male guardian from her immediate family. Most women are illiterate, with girls' schools just opening up. The chief enforcer of the constraints on Saudi females is the husband and the Mutawaee but inbred rules lie within women themselves. They are not governed by religion and ancient customs alone but also by family pressure and how the relatives perceive any action. The pressures to keep the old ways are exerted most powerfully at the family level."

Wrapped in a thick blanket of fear, I grab onto my chair for even a hint of grounding. Taking ten deep breaths, I begin to center. Finally calm enough to hear my inner voices, I once again ask the pivotal question… "Am I following my life's path?" A barely audible voice whispers that the articles are no accidents, but gifts from the far corner of a hidden bookstore. They are offerings of cold, hard reality necessary for my new life.

I close my eyes once again, centering into my empty space. As I began to sense my truth, I remember a quote from Marcel Proust. "The real voyage of discovery consists not in seeking new landscapes but in having new eyes."

The next day we are both getting itchy. With Nazar no better, we take him to the American University of Beirut Hospital. This is my first daytime excursion in the Arab world, and my eyes fly everywhere. The vegetable and fruit vendors particularly fascinate me. I watch as they push their large carts of colorful produce down narrow, winding streets.

The sidewalks are crowded, and small markets are tastefully shaded in tints and hues that catch the eye. As the taxi threads down noisy streets, I notice men holding hands. At first I cross this scene out of my mind, but as I see more male hand-holding I bring the observation up to Osane. "Christie," Osane replies, "this is cultural; male touching male is very acceptable in the Arab culture."

A short time later we arrive at the hospital, and a female Egyptian doctor treats Nazar. After a very interesting conversation, both in Arabic and English, she gives us some more medicine. Once again, we are off to our hotel. We both have renewed hope that this new prescription will quickly heal our little son.

Our departure to Arabia is only a few days away. Osane calls a family member who works in the Saudi x-ray department of the Taif Hospital. As Osane dials, he reminds me that access to phones in the Kingdom is very rare. We are fortunate that his relative works in a government hospital.

After many rings, Osane's uncle finally picks up the phone. Pacing back and forth, Osane tells him our flight number plus time of arrival in Jeddah. As he hangs up, I sense tension dripping off Osane like a winter pine covered with ice, under a hot spring sun. I notice his body posture and it scares me. I walk over to him and grab his hand, engulfing him into a comforting hug. Slowly I feel his stiff stance relax as he crumbles into my arms.

As I hug Osane, I contemplate that my trepidation came upon *leaving* my country. Now the coin has flipped. Osane is struggling to *enter* his country. Ever since we first stepped into the Arab world, Osane has been negotiating a frightful maze. Not only does he have to face the challenges of a new job and the problems of finding a new home for Nazar and me, but he is also one of only a few Saudis to bring home an American wife.

I'm sure many questions are occupying his mind. How will his family receive us? How can I possibly survive in such a different culture with absolutely no grasp of the language? How will his own re-entry into his culture go?

We both walk over to my window seat and slowly sit down. "I'm sorry Christie," Osane mutters as he looks at the floor. "I just can't stop worrying about our future. I know we both have our university degrees, but that doesn't alter the fact that we have no money. Luckily the Saudi Educational Ministry paid for our return airfare, and travel expenses came out of our savings. However, when we land in the Kingdom, we'll have to watch every penny. I have to admit I'm scared!"

With our minds drowning in apprehensions, we decide that on the last day of freedom before we take the big dive into Saudi Arabia, we'll take a day trip around the Jeweled City of Beirut. As I dress Nazar, I remember a lighthearted quote from an unknown author. "My point is, life is about balance. The good and the bad. The highs and the lows. The pina and the colada."

For the last several months, Osane and I have run headlong into one challenge after another. My hope is that today will bring hours full of laughter, joy, marvelous meals, and carefree conversation.

Early the next morning we settle into the seats of the taxi Osane has reserved for the day. Prepared for a relaxing tour of the city, my heart jumps into my throat when the driver enters the stream of traffic. It seems the Lebanese drive their cars through spaces made for bicycles, twist recklessly around corners, beep their horns constantly, and continually gesture with their hands out the windows.

We briefly cruise the city streets before winding down to the sea. Immediately we find ourselves in the country. To my Western mind, something is missing. Where are the suburbs? I ask Osane and he tells me there aren't any. In the city Lebanese live in tall apartments, while in the country the rural Lebanese live in villas surrounded by outbuildings.

The countryside seems rather barren to me, but what makes everything special is the tropical sun. This glow deepens the blues, greens, and yellows. With the light filtering through these radiant happy colors, everything appears brilliantly altered.

Nazar falls asleep in my arms as our taxi continues to weave through villages and on up into the mountains. As we climb higher, the landscape changes, and we ride by olive groves and coniferous trees. Osane explains that we are now in the Muslim Mountains, and that the Christian Mountains are on the other side of the city.

Slowly we circle back toward Beirut. As the countryside speeds by, Osane begins chatting with the Muslim driver. Out of respect for me, the conversation remains in English. I listen as the driver begins complaining about his life.

He states, "I am a fairly well-educated Muslim. I also know three or four languages, but the Christian bosses of the city won't let me climb any farther in life."

Pounding the steering wheel, he claims, "In this controlled city, the Christians and the foreigners become rich, while the Muslims are kept down."

As he becomes more emotional, his conversation slips into Arabic, leaving me time to contemplate. I conclude that his frustration, if coupled with others', could tear this "Jeweled City of the Mediterranean" apart!

Happy to be out of the hotel, seeing new sights, I refuse to dwell on religious conflict. I excitedly stare out the window as present-day Beirut passes by. I remember reading that down through the ages, Beirut's Mediterranean location has exposed it to several civilizations. The last colonizers were French. This I can believe, for the Lebanese are beautifully dressed, fashionably put together, and look like they should be strolling down the Champs Elysees instead of Beirut's Ham-ra Street. No one in the entire city looks underdressed.

Soon it is lunchtime and as a special treat, Osane takes us to one of the most famous eating spots in the city. The restaurant is located on a cliff that juts out to sea and overlooks Suicide Rock. This gigantic rock, with a hole in the middle, is one of Beirut's landmarks.

Our meal is just as fantastic as the view. It starts with humus, tahini, mint leaves, lettuce, and pickles, all eaten with pita bread. Surrounding these hors d'oeuvres are olives, cheese, and dates. Then follows the main meal of shish kabob. The dessert is usually fruit, but I choose crème caramel, a vanilla pudding covered in caramel.

After our wonderful meal we walk out of the restaurant to our waiting cab. On the way back to the hotel, Osane asks our driver to stop at a drugstore so he can purchase aspirin for the trip. While Osane is in the store, the taxi driver turns to me and asks, "Are you really going to Saudi Arabia tomorrow?"

"Yes, I am," I respond.

He stares at me in disbelief and says, "I was in the Lebanese Armed Forces and have spent time in Saudi Arabia, so I know what life is like. I label my Saudi time as pure hardship, and it's much worse for women. I'll give you one year before you break and run back home."

Talk like this, the day before I travel into the Kingdom, I don't need. I am very glad when Osane re-enters the car and the conversation stops.

The next morning as I am re-packing our clothes, I pull out my arrival dress. Many weeks ago, I'd put much deliberation into the dress I would wear into Arabia. I purposely selected what was stylish. In my American campus world of 1970, pants were simply not worn, nor were long skirts. Miniskirts were the *only* trend.

Osane had mentioned something about covering myself, but his comment had fallen on young, vain ears. What to wear, I felt, was embedded in the female realm. My only compromise was letting down the hem as far as it would go.

On a far deeper level, fashion was not my only agenda. With rebellion still a part of my psyche, I was stubbornly using this dress as my personal protest against the strict rules of an ancient Kingdom. As Yoko Ono stated, "The 1960s were about releasing ourselves from conventional society and freeing ourselves." I absorbed the era of the flower children, and on many planes I was still protesting.

With departure time quickly approaching, I slip on my short-sleeved dress, which is ironically, red, white, and blue. Carefully I draw my long, blonde hair to the side and tie it behind one ear with a jet-black ribbon. Everything considered, I feel good about myself. Osane puts on his suit and combs his long curly hair. We bundle Nazar up, pick up our bags, and Osane hails a taxi.

At the Beirut airport, the porters again pounce on us. In due time, our luggage is checked and our seats confirmed. We proceed to our gate, and after settling Nazar and Osane, I walk to the restroom to freshen up. When I return, I expect to be boarding in five or six minutes. At the end of fifteen minutes a message comes over the loudspeaker saying, "Because of engine trouble, there will be a two-hour delay."

Osane starts to complain about the inefficiencies of the Saudi Arabian airline, while I wonder what I am going to do with Nazar. Putting him on my lap, I entertain myself by studying the passengers.

As if they somehow knew our plane would be delayed, a group of Saudi women arrives. They carry their black *abayas* or cloaks, and their *mish-la* or black headscarves. None of them cover, for they are still in the freedom of Beirut.

My stomach fills with butterflies, however, when I notice that they are wearing long skirts and long sleeves. I am suddenly scared that my stubborn attempt at remaining stylish is going to expose too much of myself. With my hair uncovered, a lot of my legs showing and my arms bare, the contrast shoots off glaring red flags. Feeling immensely insecure, I also begin to feel that my vain attempt to rebel against the Saudi dress code will come at too high a price.

Resigned to my fate, I continue watching Lebanese, Syrians, Jordanians, Egyptians, and others pass through the airport. Not long ago I clumped these different nationalities under the sub-title *Arab*. My current research has begun to separate them into their rightful nations.

In my readings, I learned that the Arab world covers the northern section of Africa. Beginning with Morocco and flowing toward Egypt, this Arab world also dips down into the African nations of Ethiopia and the Sudan. Curving over to pick up Saudi Arabia and the Gulf States, it drifts north into Lebanon, Jordan, Syria, and Iraq.

These Arab nations are fused together by a common religion, language, dress, cuisine, and culture. This world stops at Iran. The Persian civilization has its own religion, language, and culture.

Saudi Arabia embodies the Arab world in its purest form. Its geographic location keeps it isolated. With no rivers o permanent bodies of water to travel, penetration is difficult. The Empty Quarter in the south and the mountains and deserts in the north kept colonization at a standstill. Only the Byzantine and Ottoman Empires had marched through the shifting sands.

Just as the desert keeps foreign colonization in Saudi Arabia at arm's length, it opens to the faithful on their pilgrimage to Mecca. As the keeper of the Great Stone, the protector of the Islamic Holy Land and traditions, the Arabian soil is sacred. In this "Holy Land" the purest form of Arabic is spoken and the Sha'ria enforces proper behavior. Even the Saudi cuisine is orthodox, for dishes originated over a Bedouin fire.

Osane's voice penetrates my drifting thoughts. "Christie," he says, "I think we're preparing to depart."

I revisit the restroom to freshen up. As I walk back to our seats, I notice people are starting to lie down. The minute I spot Osane's angry face, I know that another delay has been announced. I plop down in my chair and wrap my arms around myself. Tapping my foot, I try to gain control.

Does the Saudi Arabian airline or anyone in this entire international airport realize what internal struggles I've been through to get to this departure point? It's as if someone, after years of training and planning, is attempting to leave the final campsite to ascend Mt. Everest, and dangerous winds are preventing the summit climb!

Time crawls by and in total we wait six long hours. Ironically, the codeine in Nazar's cold medicine serves as a sedative and turns an impossible situation into a tolerable one. A final boarding is finally announced, but by this time everyone is skeptical.

With considerable effort, all the passengers find their seats. As soon as the engines turn over, I look at Osane in amazement. We have flown too many flights not to know that something is dangerously wrong. The stairs have already been pulled away, but Osane's adrenaline forces him to act. He stands up and demands to be let off the plane. He states, "There are mountains to fly over, the sea, long stretches of desert, and the way the engines sound, the plane will never make it."

Again, Osane demands the plane stop and let everyone out. Receiving no reaction, he disappears into first class and then into the cockpit. With amazement, I watch the plane roll to a halt. Osane comes back and tells me to get my things together. With everybody staring at us, we make our way up to the back door to await the stairs.

As our small family steps down the rear stairwell and into the airline bus, I notice a large black limousine pull up to the plane. One of the Saudi women I had been studying in the terminal and a male chaperon walk down the front stairs and into the limo. It seems the real reason the plane stopped, and the only reason the stairs are brought up to the plane again, is for this princess.

As I watch the plane take off from our airline bus, I silently whisper a prayer for our luggage. I keep having images of baby clothes swirling around the desert, being spread by strong, hot winds.

In the Beirut terminal, they sense Osane's frustration and handle him gingerly. We are shown into a special waiting room, where we find the princess and her chaperon. The princess is very angry and is shouting at the officials about the danger they have put her in. Airline attendants bring her coffee and tea, and try to calm her down.

Meanwhile, Osane transfers our tickets from Saudi Airlines to Middle East Airlines, which is scheduled to leave the next afternoon. With all the official business completed, we backtrack to our hotel, exhausted and completely discouraged.

Since our luggage is flying somewhere over the Arabian Desert, we clean up the best we can and fall into bed. Not beir able to sleep, Osane agonizes. "Christie, I know the male relatives will be at the airport waiting for us. If the plane is lucky enough to arrive, the only evidence of our existence will be our luggage. The family will be worried, but since phones are almost nonexistent in the Kingdom, there's no way I can get in touch with them."

"We have no choice but to let it flow," I mumble to Osane as I pull the blankets over my head, praying I can quickly escape into sleep.

The next morning I find a note from Osane saying he has already been out for coffee and a newspaper. At the newsstand, he had found an English magazine that I can enjoy until he returns. Our new flight doesn't take off until that afternoon, so I settle down to my magazine and a breakfast Osane has ordered for me.

Dipping my pita bread into my eggs, I turn to the main article. It's an interview with a source close to Mohammed Awaad bin Laden who states he would like to remain anonymous. Acknowledging that not all of the information can be independently verified, the article begins:

"Mohammed Awad bin Laden came to the kingdom from Hadramout (South Yemen) sometime around 1930. He started his life as a very poor laborer (porter in a Jeddah port), to end up as owner of the biggest construction company in the kingdom. During the reign of King Saud, Mohammed bin Laden became very close to the royal family when he took the risk of building King Saud's palaces much cheaper than the cheapest bid. He impressed King Saud with his performance but he also built good relations with other members of the royal family, especially Faisal. During the Saud-Faisal conflict in the early sixties, Mohammed bin Laden had a big role in convincing King Saud to step down in favor of Faisal. After Saud's departure, the treasury was empty and Mohammed bin Laden was so supportive of King Faisal that he literally paid all of the Kingdom's civil servants' wages for six months. King Faisal then issued a decree that construction projects should go to bin Laden. Indeed, he was appointed for a period as the Minister of Public Works.

In 1969 Mohammed bin Laden took the task of rebuilding Al-Aqsa mosque after the fire incident and later on the company took over the task of major extensions in the Mecca and Medina Mosques. Mohammed also built up the TV infrastructure in the 1960s, against violent protests form the Wahabbis.

Mohammed bin Laden was a fairly devoted Muslim, very humble and generous. He was so proud of the bag he used when he was a porter that he kept it as a trophy in the main reception room in his palace.

Mohammed had a very dominating personality. He had a tough discipline standard and exposed his children to a strict religious and social code. He maintained a special daily program and obliged his children to follow it. At the same time he entertained them with trips to the sea and desert. He dealt with his children as big men and demanded that they show confidence at a young age. He was very keen not to show any differences in the treatment of his children.

Born in 1957 to a Syrian mother, Osama bin Laden was the seventh son among fifty brothers and sisters. Osama lost his father when he was thirteen. He was married at the age of seventeen to a Syrian girl who was a relative. He grew up as a religiously committed boy and the early marriage was another way of protecting him from corruption.

Osama had his primary, secondary, and even university education in Jeddah. He earned a degree in public administration from King Abdul-Aziz University. After his higher education, he spent much of his time in Pakistan and Afghanistan."

Osane's return interrupts my reading. I throw the magazine aside, mentally noting to keep track of the bin Laden family in the future. We dress in the clothes of the previous day, but all enthusiasm for our appearance is gone.

Seeing the airport again puts us both into a negative space. But since we have no luggage, at least we can escape the fervent battling of the porters. As the afternoon passes smoothly, we begin to relax. In the hands of the efficient crew of the Middle East Airlines, we check in, board the plane, and take off with no problems. Soon we are in the air, heading straight toward the Kingdom of Saudi Arabia.

Chapter 7

Our Arrival in Saudi Arabia

"It's not the load that breaks you down, it's the way you carry it."
   Anonymous

Through most of the flight I am glued to the window, studying the desert terrain. There really isn't much to see, but I am fascinated just the same. Soon we are approaching Jeddah, the commercial hub, busiest port, and most cosmopolitan city of the Kingdom..

Nervously, I fidget in my seat and once again review the relatives I will meet. Adjusting Nazar's blanket, I think of Big Bird on <u>Sesame Street</u>. I am sure that Osane's extended family would short-circuit the yellow bird's brain.

To survive my mental flow-charting, I quickly categorize the faceless names under the main topic, "relatives," and further group them into pods.

The head of the Taif household I am visiting is Saeed. I am told he is approximately forty. The females of this household are sisters. Zora is an unmarried woman in her thirties, and Mina is a young girl around sixteen. Their brother Osama is studying economics at a college in Jeddah, and is a frequent visitor.

Osane has picked this household because of its exposure to the West and its openness. He had spent the last few years before coming to the States with this section of his family. If my transition from the West to the East is possible, these relatives will serve as my best conduits.

Our plane effortlessly touches down on Saudi soil and as I say a prayer, our family makes its way toward the departure door. At about the third step, the humidity and heat come crashing down on my body like a load of bricks. It feels as if the air surrounding me is pressing and squeezing me from all sides, making it hard to breathe. As I gasp for breath I think, this is only October; what can the heat possibly be like in August? Making our way into the terminal, we have to step over stacks of lumber with nails sticking out. I have a nervous impulse to clean up the clutter and make everything neat and tidy, but the crowd pushes me onward.

Upon entering the small Jeddah terminal, the first thing I notice is a gigantic picture of King Faisal. I then focus on the men in their native dress. I have seen pictures of Osane in his gown or *thobe*, and his headdress or *otra*. Now, I see these long nightgowns in different shapes, sizes, and colors.

My observations are cut short by a cold, clammy feeling, as I feel stares piercing my body. A male crowd circles close by, leering at my body. It doesn't take long to realize the reason for this special attention. There are only two women in this gigantic room. The other woman is also a Westerner, but she is clad in a pantsuit that covers her completely. She is married to an Englishmen and is quickly hustled through customs and out the door into a waiting car. That leaves me, inappropriately dressed and accompanied by an Arab.

Our family is also rushed through customs, but Nazar and I are left standing under the big picture of King Faisal, as Osane disappears to locate our missing luggage. Absolutely exposed, I feel like a fragile deer being hemmed in by wolves. Only anger at myself for not listening to Osane about apparel keeps me rooted to my spot. My only recourse is to hold Nazar and wait. Soon a barefoot, short man from Yemen arrives with our black suitcase on top of his head. He is wearing an open T-shirt, plaid skirt, and a matching turban.

Praying that Osane will return and end my ordeal, I finally spot him at the far end of the room, arguing with an older man. This man resembles one of Jesus' disciples, but his face and body language do not fit any of my church pictures. He looks angry, rigid, and deaf to reason. I can tell by Osane's gestures that he is also getting angry. Soon quite a crowd has gathered in the office. I can only assume they are arguing over our missing suitcase full of Nazar's baby clothes. I am therefore mystified when Osane finally arrives carrying the missing suitcase.

Breathing heavily, my incensed husband explains that a red flag was raised when I put Muslim on my airline entry card. Osane had showed them my certificate from the American Muslim Center. They studied the certificate and said it wasn't valid. The only way I can become a "true Muslim" is to go before the Muslim Court in Saudi Arabia. Until I do this, customs officials will keep my American passport!

Still fighting for control, Osane states, "To make matters worse, Christie, they're forcing us to drive the Christian road from coastal Jeddah, all the way through the mountains to Taif. Their issue is that Mecca happens to be right between Jeddah and Taif, and since you aren't an official Muslim, they demand that we take the much longer and little-used Christian road."

By this time, I don't care what road we take or when I retrieve my passport. I simply want to get away from the stares. Six lifetimes later, a taxi is hailed. We fight our way through the thick male crowd. With relief, Nazar and I take refuge in the back seat, as Osane and the cab driver load the baggage in the trunk. Inside the taxi, I look up to find a sea of male faces, with their noses plastered against the window. They are staring at me!

As the taxi speeds away I begin laughing nervously. A stiff and tense Osane looks over at me with questioning eyes. "Oh, Osane," I murmur. "If I don't laugh I'll crack into a million pieces. That whole airport scene was excessively weird and Hitchcock-like! Did that really happen?"

My raw nerves begin to unwind, as the vastness of the desert encompasses us in soothing isolation. As the miles pass by, it begins to grow dark. I keep asking how far Taif is. Osane, trying to keep my spirits high, tells me not very far. So I rearrange my hair, check my makeup, straighten my dress and watch a few more sand hills go by. A short time later I once again arrange myself, but as more miles speed by I give up on my appearance. In a trance, I watch the dark desert, and listen to Osane talk to the taxicab driver. After the bantering has gone on for some time, I ask Osane what they are talking about.

"Not much, Christie," he replies. "I simply want to keep the taxi driver awake."

An hour later, the driver pulls down a small dirt road that ends at an isolated desert cafe. Instead of pulling up to the entrance, he drives his taxi to the back of the building, parking beside an empty water truck. The driver gets out and spreads a small rug on the desert, beside the back tire. He places a small thermos and cups beside the rug and, looking at Osane, walks off to the cafe for some tea.

"Osane," I ask, "why are we in the back of the parking lot instead of in front, with the other travelers?"

Osane gives me one of his sly looks. "Cafes are for men only. If we want refreshment we can sit on the rug by the back tire, where you will be out of sight."

"What?!" I scream.

Then Osane smiles at me, and we both begin laughing. We continue giggling for some time. Our experiences in Saudi Arabia so far can definitely be labeled the "Theater of the Absurd."

After the laughter comes the peace. We sit together on our rug, looking out over the wide, expansive desert. Beside us a donkey is grazing, trying to pick a few pieces of grass out of hard soil. After such a hot day, the cool desert night air is a relief. For a short moment, on our rug by the back tire, we are sequestered enough to feel secure.

The driver returns and we bounce back onto the empty Christian road. A very short time later we reach the mountains. As soon as we begin climbing, I can feel the air getting cooler. With the refreshing air however, comes tension.

There is only one route up the mountains and this road winds around hairpin curves, like a chain of rubber bands linked together. Osane once again begins his chattering to the taxi driver to keep him awake and focused. I need no encouragement to stay alert, for my heart is in my throat. Not only is the road narrow and the turns sharp, but the driver completely ignores the white dividing line. Even on the blindest curves, he darts into the opposite lane, oblivious to the fact that a car might be coming in the opposite direction.

To make this harrowing drive even more interesting, the motor keeps acting up. After we have been climbing for about half an hour, the driver stops the car. As he gets out, he asks Osane to sit behind the wheel so he can check the engine. While he is opening the hood, the car begins rolling backwards. Osane automatically presses on the brakes, but there are no brakes. He then quickly grabs for the hand brake, and finds no hand brake. As we are on a very sharp incline, the car starts gaining backward momentum, and Osane does the only thing that can save us. Before our speed becomes too excessive, he backs into the side railing. Miraculously, we bump to a stop.

The taxi driver comes running down the hill and after he exchanges stern words with Osane, we once again begin climbing up the mountains. Somehow we live through fifteen more minutes of climbing before the road levels off, and we enter the city of Taif.

I make a final attempt to freshen up, while Osane remarks, "Christie, I can't believe how much this town has changed. It's only been six years since my last visit, but in that time expansion has occurred." Meanwhile, I casually wonder how this *village* can be labeled a *town,* but by this time, I am too exhausted to care.

When we finally pull up to his relatives' villa, it is close to 2 am. The only souls to be seen in the darkness are cats. I sit in the cab, while Osane pounds on the gate. Finally, someone answers the door. After an involved conversation, Osane returns to the car.

He informs me that about a year ago his relatives moved. "The man at the gate thinks they now live in an apartment around the corner, but he isn't sure."

Still determined to find his family, we drive to the suggested apartment. Osane once again gets out of the car and bangs on the gate, but pound as he does, no one answers. Osane is not ready to give up. He walks back to the taxi, reaches through the window, and starts honking its horn. Finally, one of the windows opens and Osane asks its occupant questions. It seems that no one knows where Osane's relatives live.

With no options left, Osane re-enters the taxi and sits silently looking out the window. His silence reeks of disgust and discouragement. As I check the sleeping Nazar, I think of the irony of us in Taif looking for his relatives, while his male relatives are in Jeddah looking for us.

We finally pull up to a hotel, and Osane tells me to wait in the car until he makes the necessary arrangements. When he returns he whispers, "Christie, be sure to walk quickly behind me."

It seems I am the first woman to stay at this hotel. Few Saudi women travel and when they do, they stay at the homes of relatives. Trying to digest this information I scurry up the stairs, trying not to wake the sleeping Nazar.

We open the door into a very primitive room. There are two iron-frame beds and one window with wire mesh over it. A bare light bulb hangs down from the ceiling, and a large prayer rug is nailed to the far wall. Realizing no cribs will be available in these quarters, we push the beds together and shed our soiled clothes. Depleted, we slip between the scratchy but clean sheets. As I kiss Osane goodnight, his eyes reflect how miserable he feels. What a way to bring his new American bride home. Although he has verbalized his apology, the look in his eyes is worth a thousand words.

Sleeping that night is next to impossible, for mosquitoes keep bombarding us. The mesh on the window turns out to be more for atmosphere than effectiveness. The only option is to hide under the sheets and try to get a little rest.

Early the next morning, I roll over and notice that Osane is already up and out. He has left a note saying he is searching for his relatives. Silently I wish him luck, as I slip out of bed and into what is now my hated dress.

As Nazar and I sit dressed, waiting for Osane, a bit of mischievousness bubbles to the surface of my unoccupied mind. If I am the only woman customer this hotel has ever experienced, then I must leave my calling card. Just as I am slipping a few bobby pins on the bathroom sink, Osane comes rushing into the room. His face is beaming, which means he has finally found his relatives.

While we gather our belongings Osane excitably relates, "The men are still at the airport waiting for us, but the women are at the apartment expecting our arrival."

Quickly we climb into a waiting taxi, and as the car pulls away, butterflies flutter into my stomach. The inevitable meeting between East and West is finally about to take place.

Chapter 8

The Relatives

"Often the right path may be the hardest for you to follow. But the hard path is also the one that will make you grow as a human being."

    Karen Mueller Coombs

We return to the apartment building we had been in front of the night before. I can feel my heart skip beats as we climb two flights of stairs. While Osane knocks on the door, I hold onto the door frame and remind myself to keep breathing. It seems to take an eternity, but the door finally opens to a smiling Mina. She greets Osane with animated excitement, and shyly but warmly welcomes me. Her main exuberance, however, is saved for Nazar, and she fusses over him all the way into the *majlis* or the Arab version of a Victorian parlor. I remember Osane telling me that it is in the palace's majlis or parlor that the King hears various petitions and requests.

We are just sitting down when Mina's sister Zora walks in. Once again there is hugging, kissing, and squealing over Nazar, who is thriving on all the attention.

As the conversation between Osane and Zora continues, Mina leaves the room and returns with an elegant silver tray and an etched teakettle. Also on the tray are four miniature teacups, on saucers with small spoons. Each tea setting is delicately decorated with gold and silver leaves. Zora pours the tea and I can smell the fresh mint, which combines with raw sugar to create an excellent brew.

A short time later Mina again leaves for the kitchen, returning this time with sharp-smelling Arabian coffee. In one hand she carries a long-spouted brass coffee pot and in the other hand, she holds four china cups, one stacked into the other. She pours one cup of coffee and hands it to Osane, and the next cup becomes free. She then pours coffee into it and hands it to me, and continues to Zora.

The fresh mint tea is very pleasant in contrast to the cardamom coffee, which is very bitter and strong. When I involuntarily make a face while attempting to swallow my first sip of Arabian coffee, everybody starts laughing. I'm thankful when Mina takes the cup from my hand, still full.

After the customary trays of tea and coffee are cleared away, Osane settles down to share the stories of the past six years. While the relatives chat, I take in the details of the *majlis*. I expected the Oriental rug, but I did not anticipate the fine set of Italian furniture. The large couch and the four chairs are covered in light and dark green tweed. In between each of these chairs is a small table with a white doily on top. Along the accent wall is a stereo and record rack sitting on a dark, oak table. In the far corner sits an ancient ship chest and on top of that rests an intricately carved wooden ship. The room lacks wall decorations or curtains, but cleanliness and taste enhance its feel. This room's similarity to a Western home mirrors an openness in this family's consciousness, and is undoubtedly the reason Osane has chosen this for my transition home.

As the storytelling continues around me, I turn my attention to the two sisters. They are very similar. The main difference is that Mina is 16 while Zora seems to be in her 30's. Their faces are attractive, with classic features that speak of strong character, and their dark eyes reflect quick minds and kind souls. They are several inches shorter than I, but average by Saudi standards. Their well-proportioned, thin figures are clothed in long skirts and long-sleeved blouses, and their thick black hair is pulled back. They both wear gold earrings, bracelets, rings and necklaces, which accentuate the beauty of their olive skin.

The sisters move with slow grace. There is something about their proud carriage and self-contained manner which I admire. My first impression is that they have come to terms with their world, and have transposed restlessness into simple acceptance. With a deep sigh of relief, I realize I like them. I feel welcome and comfortable. Intuitively I know that these are good people. With this realization I join in their laughter, even though I don't know what's being said.

Sensing that Nazar and I are tired from traveling and time changes, Zora asks through Osane, "Do you care to rest?"

Silently thankful for her sensitivity, I nod my head and she leads me into another room across the hall. The minute I walk into this typical Arab room, my eyes bounce from detail to detail. The entire floor surface is covered with two large Oriental rugs. On top of these rugs, multicolored floor pads hug the walls. Perching on top of these pads are Arab pillows, filled with straw and measuring one yard wide and half a yard tall. Their rectangular shapes are covered with red and white velvet material, featuring patterns of flowers, swords, and leaves. There are no wall coverings, and two bare lights hang down from the ceiling. It seems the Arabs believe there is no need to look up with so much color on the floor, and there is indeed color! The different designs of the Oriental rugs combine with the patterns of the padding and cushions to create a brilliant hodge podge that somehow fits together.

After settling down for a quick nap, I wake when I hear Osane open the door. When he sees I have opened my eyes he smiles and asks, "How about a tour of your new surroundings?"

"Sure," I reply, eager to learn anything about my new Saudi life.

I had already discovered the parlor and the Arab room that both exited off a large, marble hallway. The real tour begins when we walk through this hallway. The sounds of our footsteps remind me of walking in the Capitol building in Washington, D.C.

The first room we enter is the family room. As soon as we step through the doorway I know we have found the main living area, for every corner radiates heavy usage. Again, I find two oriental rugs on the floor and the Arab cushions, but these quarters lack the floor padding. In the corner, on a covered orange crate, is a sewing machine, and at the far end of the wall is a newly acquired television. Near the entrance is a clothing tree filled with male pajamas, gowns, and headscarves.

Osane then leads me into Mina and Zora's bedroom. Along the far side of the wall are two freestanding wooden closets. The rest of the room is completely empty except for two oriental rugs. As I wonder where the beds are, we move on to what Osane calls the Arab bathroom.

As he opens the door I am expecting a shower with a colorful shower curtain, a sink and a counter where I can spread out my toiletries. Instead I gaze at an empty room with a hole in the floor, a bare light bulb hanging from the ceiling and a shower nozzle sticking out of the wall. Prison cell comes to mind, as I slam the door shut.

Clenching my stomach, I follow Osane to the next room. To my great relief, this turns out to be a Western bathroom. With a smile, Osane explains, "Uncle Saeed has gone to a lot of time, trouble, and money to fix this room up especially for you, Christie. As you can see, he has installed a Western toilet, sink, and shower. He feels an Arab bathroom will be too difficult for you to use."

"How absolutely sensitive and considerate," I reply to Osane. "I'm very touched."

Our tour moves on to the kitchen. Attempting to keep an open mind, I am still startled when we enter this room. I have seen campsites with more cooking equipment. Along one side of the wall runs a long marble counter with a small sink. Under this slab the relatives have built two storage shelves, with curtains substituting for doors. Next to this shelf is a small propane gas stove, and on the far side of the wall is a standard refrigerator. The cement walls are painted a drab gray and the only light source is from a bare light bulb hanging from the ceiling. I'm happy to see that multicolored trays, kettles, and straw bread baskets brighten up the space.

The final room on our tour is the storage and washing room, which is off the kitchen. This space stores leftover oriental rugs, pads for sleeping, a turn-of-the-century washing machine, clotheslines, and miscellaneous items. Since the relatives' apartment is on the top floor, the upper quarter of the far wall is open to the outside. From this room I can glimpse the sky, and I can also hear noises from the rest of the apartment dwellers.

The tour finally over, Osane leads me back to the Arab room and closes the door.

"Well Christie," Osane asks, "Do you feel comfortable in your new home?"

"I do," I reply. "The rooms are wonderfully clean and more than adequate, but I am confused by the floor plan. So many rooms lead off one hallway, and the traffic patterns seem chopped, with no real flow."

"Well," Osane says, moving closer. "Remember I told you that you have to change lenses, and understand life through Arab eyes. The relatives' floor plan is cultural. It is functional for female and male visiting. Saudi homes are partitioned into separate male and female rooms, which feed off one main hallway. Doors off this hallway can be closed for seclusion, keeping females hidden from the view of men."

"Oh," I reply, with a blank look in my eyes.

"Christie, are you okay?" Osane asks.

"I just need some time to digest all of these cultural differences," I reply. Osane squeezes my hand and kisses Nazar before leaving the room. When the door closes, a claustrophobic fear claws at my soul and begins to overpower me. I blindly pace the small room, noting that it is ten paces wide. My steps quickens as "cage" reverberates through my mind. Calm down, I warn myself. Take one moment at a time.

Starting to panic, I grab my sides and slump into the corner. How can I live with such non-negotiable boundaries, I scream to myself. I'm trapped in a small room, in a small apartment in the middle of a whole Kingdom, that denies women even exist!

Suddenly, a vindictive voice pierces my mind. "You're a fool! You knew all about the woman's role in Saudi Arabia before you left!"

"Yes," I refute, "but being *told* is different than actually experiencing confinement. Just realizing that I am the only educated, Christian, American female within hundreds and hundreds of miles terrifies me!"

Wanting to bolt into a blind run to escape my inner turmoil, I grab Nazar to save myself. He smiles up at me, and gently rubs the tears of frustration off my face. Hugging each other, we lie down and Nazar's calm breathing settles me down. As I listen to the sounds of the house, I'm tired enough to escape into sleep.

About an hour later, I wake. Feeling re-centered, I quietly leave our bedroom and follow the food smells to the kitchen, where I find Zora completing the afternoon meal. I know from past conversations with Osane that the Saudis eat breakfast around 7 am. The main meal of the day is around 2 pm, and a light lunch is served between 10 and 11 pm. My American stomach can join the Saudis at breakfast, but I will have to adjust my meal schedules for the rest of the day.

With a smile, Zora motions me to follow her to the family room. On the floor, in the middle of a plastic tablecloth, is a large plate of rice and lamb (*cupsa*). There are also small dishes of lamb-bean stew (*fusolea*), an onion, tomato, and parsley salad, pita bread plus small homemade loaves. For dessert, there is a cream custard (*mahalabea*). The Saudis consider the guests' first meal the most important. So, while Nazar and I slept, Zora and Mina spent their time in the kitchen preparing these wonderful dishes.

I am directed to my place on the floor, where I find a plate and silverware. In contrast, the others are using one large spoon to dip into the different dishes. While I wait, the relatives fill my plate with the tenderest pieces of lamb and generously dish out large portions of stew, salad, and flat bread. My plate is soon overflowing.

I am the honored guest. The sisters have cooked a special meal, and the least I can do is to reciprocate with graciousness. However, all I can do is squirm. My problem is my miniskirt. The only way I can sit on the floor with any degree of comfort is in a cross-legged position, which certainly won't do. Therefore, I try to kneel on the floor, but my feet fall asleep. I attempt the side positions with my legs together, but my hips begin to cramp. Mina saves me. She brings a sheet and with this protection covering my legs, I can finally enjoy my first Saudi meal.

After dinner is over, I help the sisters carry the dishes back to the kitchen. Zora and Mina fight over each plate I pick up. As a guest, I am not supposed to help. Finally accepting my role, I am just walking back to the family room when I hear the awakening cries of Nazar.

A short time later I return to the kitchen, carrying my sleepy little one. I am amazed to find the dishes already done. My one plate and full set of silverware have been quickly scrubbed. The only other items to wash are the pans and trays. Eating with only one spoon or hands certainly has advantages.

While I watch Zora and Mina in their kitchen, a smiling Osane walks into the room.

"I hope you enjoyed your dinner, Christie, because I certainly did. It might interest you to know that Saudi food differs slightly according to the region. The cuisine of the Hijaz, the Najd, and the al-Hasa areas each has its own uniqueness. Different histories equal slightly different taste buds," he explains.

"Please continue, Osane. You know how fascinated I am with everyday Saudi living."

"OK, you asked for it," he replies. "There is more unity than diversity in our food, for all regions base their meals on rice (aish), which means life. Another similarity is the tomato-onion-garlic-olive oil foundation for most dishes. Fruits of the season provide desserts, while dates, figs, and apricots satisfy everyone's sweet tooth. The harshness of our environment forces reliance on hardy sheep and goats for meat and milk, and religion removes pork and wine from the menu. Finally, cardamom coffee and sweet mint tea serve as foundations of the ritual of hospitality. Universally, the Arabs show respect for food, for the ceremony of eating is the basis for our hospitality.

"One more point, Christie. Genuine Saudi food is rarely found in restaurants. Arabian food is food of the home, where cooking and eating are social activities."

"Thanks so much, Osane. That was fascinating!" I reply.

Mina, carrying a laughing Nazar, interrupts our conversation. She motions us into the family room, where we find

Zora serving tea. I scoop up my very necessary sheet, and sit back down on the floor. Unable to enter into the conversation, I watch a happy Nazar crawl from lap to lap. I then attempt to familiarize myself with the different phonic sounds of the Arabic language. I search for any patterns, word combinations, or any foothold into this mysterious language.

Noticing my stillness, Osane looks up and flashes me a warm smile. Suddenly I become the center of attention, for the relatives want me to feel a part of the conversation. Zora begins asking questions about my family. I am aware that this will be the beginning of many translations for Osane. I only hope he has the patience.

When the conversation quiets, Zora rises and takes the tea tray to the kitchen. This is the signal for afternoon naps. I watch the sisters disappear behind their bedroom door. I leave Nazar and Osane in the family room and wander into the parlor, which contains the only chairs in the house. Surmising that this room is saved for guests only, I walk across the hallway to the Arab room where our suitcases are placed.

I sit down on the floor and pull my sheet around me, wondering how I am going to sit politely when I only packed short skirts? I start rummaging through my suitcase and what I find is very depressing. "Christie, how can you be so stupid!" I say aloud. If only I hadn't turned a deaf ear to Osane's comments about covering up. My only recourse is to change into my one pair of worn-out slacks that I threw in at the last moment.

After retrieving Nazar from the family room, I re-arrange my belongings and the afternoon passes. Soon the household begins to stir. Wondering what the next family ritual will be, I return to the living room and find it is Saudi TV time. Osane welcomes us, noticing with approval that I have changed into my slacks. He motions me to sit beside him, mentioning that Saudi TV comes on in the evenings only.

Full of curiosity, I watch the government station open at 6:00 pm with the reading of the Koran. A Mahudthan or holy man sits cross-legged on an Arab prayer rug. He is dressed in a long, gray robe with a white turban wrapped tightly around his head. In front of him, on a beautifully carved wooden stand, is the Koran. He takes his two hands and covers his ears. As he rocks back and forth, he chants verses. He sings in an excellent tenor voice and uses articulation and timing to roll words off his tongue. At the end of each stanza, he bows his head and pauses. He then takes a deep breath, puts his hands up to his ears, and again starts rocking through another verse.

After the holy man finishes his verses, a picture of the Great Stone in Mecca flashes on the TV screen. I patiently wait for the picture to change, but it's as if the screen has locked. I sit still, wondering and waiting for the next step in this evening routine.

Suddenly, the whole town bursts into a call for prayer. From the TV and from the minarets surrounding the apartment, the call to worship is sounded. "God is good. God is great. There is only One God, and Mohammed is his Prophet," is the Arabic phrase that echoes throughout.

After prayers, Zora brings tea into the family room. When the TV comes on again, my education on the singers of the Arab world begins. The first song is by a popular Saudi singer, Muhammad Abdo. He sits on a rug with his ude, which is similar to a guitar but with more strings and a rounder shape. The inlaid stones and designs of this instrument make it quite beautiful, and its medieval sounds complement the minor key songs.

The next tune is instrumental. Three musicians play a hand drum, lute, and ude. Then we are then entertained by Tha-lal, another Saudi singer. Finally Farouse, a very popular female singer from Beirut, follows Mina, who sings from Jordan. I quickly conclude that female singers from other Arab countries are permitted, as long as they aren't from within the Kingdom.

Wanting more out of Saudi TV, I whisper to Osane, "Is there any way we can change the channel?" He looks at me and translates my statement to the others. They all laugh. Still smiling, Osane explains that there is only one government station.

Somewhere during Mohammed Abdo's third song, my mind goes into overload. I marvel at Mina and Zora's ability to *just be.* They have somehow internalized the essence of Zen, while my restless, active mind is beginning to drive me mad. I glance over at Osane and see him also squirming.

We are both saved from our boredom when the songs end, and marching music blares onto the screen.

"What is that?" I whisper to Osane.

"Just wait, it gets better," he replies.

It seems it is time for the evening news, which consists of a half-hour of following the travels of the male Royal Family. As I watch King Faisal reviewing the guards—again—my eyes begin to close.

Just as I'm falling asleep, the theme song of *The Virginian* shocks me awake. I can't believe my ears. In disbelief, I stare at the TV and see scenes from the American West. Desperately needing a lifeline to my world, I almost scream *"no"* when Mina stands up and turns the TV off. Instantly my link to the English language is cut off!

Seeing my distress, Osane leans over and says, "Don't worry, Christie. Many western shows such as *Wagon Train, It Takes a Thief, Leave it to Beaver,* and *Donna Reed* will sometime air late at night.

I give Osane my hand and he pulls me up. He leads Nazar and me into the Arab room which serves as our bedroom. As I am dressing Nazar in his pajamas, Zora brings in our mattresses. They're thin, cotton-stuffed pads covered with flower material. Over these pads Zora tucks a light blue bottom-sheet, and then a top sheet and blanket. The final touches are three light blue pillowcases embroidered with colorful flowers. These are obviously Zora's best linens, and it's as if we're sleeping in a garden.

As I kiss a tired Nazar goodnight, I notice that Osane is standing by the window. Sleep seems far from his mind. I walk over and put my arms around him. "What's wrong, Osane?" I ask.

"I have no right to complain," Osane replies. "My transition from free America into the mazes of Saudi Arabian society is nothing, compared to the changes you're facing. But while you're a stranger and still above behavioral patterns, I'm expected to conform immediately. There are exact manners for every situation and these rules have evolved through centuries. They're rigid and unbending. The do's and don'ts can fill a book the size of Webster's Dictionary."

"It's been a very long day for us all," I reply as I lead Osane to bed. After a kiss goodnight, we curl up together and let sleep filter into our troubled minds.

Early the next morning I wake feeling ill. It's as if my stomach and small intestines have dropped through my back, and I am totally nauseated. As the rest of the household isn't up yet, I quietly walk to the kitchen and fix Nazar's breakfast. Then I give our little one to Osane, saying that I'm not feeling well. I can't face one more minute on the thin floor mat, so I take my blanket and lie down on the couch in the guest parlor.

As the sun rises, I begin to hear sounds in the kitchen. Feeling better, I roll up my blanket and cross the hall to our bedroom. I dress in my one pair of blue pants and walk into the family room. Osane and Nazar are already there. They are sitting in front of a breakfast of eggs, olives, white cheese, and dates. The meal is on a large, circular tray and the relatives are using their flat bread as a scoop. As I am sitting down I hear poundings on the door, and enough screams to signal the arrival of the male relatives.

I quietly enter the hall and stand against the wall. I watch, while Osane is enveloped in an Arab greeting. Hands grab onto arms as each person kisses the other person's cheek two to three times. In between, questions are muttered. "How are you? How is your wife? How are your children?" This whole process continues until the proper amount of time passes.

Throughout the commotion, no one notices me standing in the corner. This gives me an opportunity to hurriedly connect names to faces, before attention inevitably turns my way.

It is easy to recognize Uncle Saeed, for he is unusually tall. Brother Osama is also easy to pick out, because he resembles his sisters Mina and Zora. However, I do not have any idea who the short man is. My only clue is his resemblance to the teenage boy who is standing beside him.

Pleased with my deductions, I smile at them as they shyly but warmly approach me. Automatically I extend my hand, which they accept in a warm handshake. This western greeting lacks the customary warmth. Therefore, through Osane they continue their welcome by saying: "Thank God, you're here. Thank God, you're safe. May God be with you."

Then it's Nazar's turn. He passes from one relative to another, until Uncle Saeed picks him up and walks into the family room.

As the men take off their camelhair cloaks and headscarves plus ropes and hang them on the clothing tree, questions are shot back and forth.

"Osane, where have you been? We have been waiting for three days. Your luggage came through, but you didn't. We were very worried about you."

While Osane explains the story, the relatives respond with laughter and clever comments. Not understanding the words, I watch their dramatic gestures, which are large, defined, and universal. I slowly conclude that, after getting acquainted with the standard gesture patterns, I might be able to follow the gist of many conversations.

With the blur of Arabic sounding in the background, I begin piecing together the genealogy puzzle. I remember Osane telling me that Uncle Saeed's father and Osane's father were brothers. The family resemblance between the two lines had detoured somewhere. Uncle Saeed, at age forty, bore no resemblance to Osane.

Uncle Saeed is a very tall man, much taller than the average Saudi. He has straight, dark, thinning hair and a full mustache. His complexion is fair. Because of his height and skin color, he could be mistaken for a Westerner. His face is pleasant and his eyes are shy but kind. Osane had told me that Uncle Saeed had traveled to Egypt when he was in high school, and studied to become an x-ray technician. He then spent six years in Italy studying art, and is now working in the X-ray department of the Taif military hospital. Because of his European exposure, he speaks a little English, which is very rare.

Next to Saeed sits Ali, his older brother by a different mother. He is the small man I couldn't identify in the hallway. Ali's face is thin, covered by a silver beard; he wears thick glasses. Almost because of his height, Ali carries himself with a dignity that portrays a mighty presence. I detect a quick mind, an authoritarian personality, and a small streak of mischievousness. Because he is the oldest male, he is the head of the family. He lives in southern Arabia with his wife Madia and their eight children. Ali has the important position of being the administrator of the local hospital.

Ali's oldest son, Walid, sits next to him. Walid will be living in the Taif household while he attends high school. I sense that his personality and certainly his short build resembles his father. After two more years of high school in Taif, he plans to go to the States for higher education.

Finally, next to Walid sits Osama, Zora and Mina's brother. He has that same quick laughter, curly hair, eyes, and olive complexion. Osama is studying economics at a college in Jeddah. Because of his advanced education, he also understands a *few* words of English.

The sisters have long ago left the family room, for it is their duty to prepare the afternoon meal. Nazar and I walk into the kitchen to join them. We find them squatting on the floor, cleaning and cutting vegetables over one of their colorful trays. Since there are no chairs in sight and the tile floor is cold, I also try to assume their squatting position.

It is impossible. Every time I try to crouch down, my heels go up and I find myself balancing on my toes. If I try to keep my feet flat on the ground, I can't bend down far enough. In frustration I force my feet to the ground, resulting in a backward somersault. Our laughter brings young Walid into the kitchen. I motion for him to squat, hoping his attempts will be as fruitless as mine. When he effortlessly bends down and locks in, I give up. With no other option, I sit down on the cold floor in a cross-legged position.

When dinner is ready, I watch Mina spread the tablecloth on the family room floor. Zora brings in a big tray, full of dishes similar to the afternoon before. I am again given a plate and silverware, with the addition of two pillows piled one on top of another. Upon this homemade chair I thankfully sit. After a day and a half of floor living, my joints are stiff and aching.

Nazar, on the other hand, is totally ecstatic to find all the adults on the floor within easy reach. I feed him his junior foods before the main meal, leaving him free to pound on one back after the other while munching on pita bread.

After the meal Zora cleans up, Mina serves tea, and I put Nazar to bed for a nap. When I return to the family room, I notice that all the men have left.

When they return, I find out that the relatives have taken Osane to the *suq* or marketplace to "*Arabize*" him. The initial items purchased are three long white robes, or *thobes*. Next on the shopping list are white boxer shorts and white t-shirts, which are worn under *thobes*. White handkerchiefs are then purchased, along with gold and silver cuff links, and a white embroidered skullcap called a *gaba*. Next, a checkered white-and-red *otra*, (or headscarf) is added to the pile, along with an *e-gal* or two connected rope-like black strands. The e-gal keeps the headdress in place.

The final stop on this shopping trip is the barbershop, for it is against the law to have long hair or sideburns. If the Religious Police or *Mutawaeen* catch Osane with his long hair, they will forcefully drag him into the nearest shop and shave his head bald as a punishment. To prevent such an embarrassing scene, Osane walks into the barber's and is given three pictures on the wall to choose from. If his hair is cut in any other way, the barber is liable to end up in prison.

The men return to find Zora, Mina, and me in the family room. As they enter the room, they glance at me with sheepish smiles. When Osane steps through the threshold, I know why. There stands my husband—transformed into a Saudi male. The real surprise, however, is waiting for me seconds later. When Osane takes off his Arabic headdress, I see that his beautiful long curly hair has been sheared. In its place are short, bristly stubs. The Saudi culture has taken its first toll.

While the men play with Nazar, the sisters walk into the kitchen to brew some tea. Zora carries the tea tray back and Mina picks up the silver teapot and pours tea into each one of the delicate teacups. The conversation is light and easy, for there is so much to discuss. Carefree laughter fills the room, accompanied by warm smiles. I study the faces and take in the joy of this loving family reunion.

After tea, the men leave to visit Osane's Aunt Sara, leaving Zora, Mina, Nazar, and me to pick up the teacups. After prayer time, the women once again settle down for an evening of TV. Wondering if I can possibly sit through another series of Arabic songs, I sink into my corner of the floor.

We are halfway into Samera Tofuk's first song when Zora walks into the room carrying a sheet and blanket. I watch as she spreads the blanket out on the floor. Leaning over the blanket, she spreads the sheet. She then leaves the room and returns carrying an iron and a bundle of laundry. As she sits down and plugs in the iron, Mina brings in a pan of water. Zora spreads a *thobe* or robe flat on the sheet, sprinkles it with water from the pan, and begins to iron. She starts from the bottom of the *thobe*. As soon as that is ironed, she loosely gathers it onto her lap and pulls some more of the un-ironed *thobe* toward her. After Zora is through with the *thobe*, she begins ironing the *otra*, or the large headscarf. Next she irons the white skullcaps, the *gaba*, and finishes off with the handkerchiefs.

The process is very time-consuming and the phrase "ignorance is bliss" pops into my mind. I wonder how frustrated Zora would be if she realized that half of the world wears wash and wear. I, however, am not ignorant. I fully realize that maintaining Osane's 100% cotton wardrobe will be my responsibility. Dismissing the thought, I walk into our bedroom and begin preparing Nazar for bed.

Waiting for Osane to return from his visiting, I lie down in bed and allow my mind to wander aimlessly. While I am grateful for the love and acceptance every member of Osane's family has given me, I am also unsettled. It has been a day full of strain. My body aches from sitting and sleeping on the floor, and I find myself picking at the foreign food rather than eating it. Determined not to dwell deeply, I neutralize my thoughts and in an instant I am asleep.

The next morning, Nazar and I are once again the first ones up. I silently creep into the kitchen and fry him an egg. I use these early morning hours to concentrate on our son. After Nazar's harsh sickness in Beirut, he has forgotten how to walk. So back and forth across the kitchen we go, one successful step after the other.

Chapter 9

Our Visit with Aunt Sarah

"In my garden, love grows."
Anonymous

At about 10 am, the house begins to stir. Nazar and I are invited to our second breakfast. After the meal, Osane tells me to get ready to visit Aunt Sarah's house.

While I am preparing for the visit, Osane walks into the room and says, "A quick family update, Christie. Remember I told you that after my mother died during my birth, I went to live with my grandmother on my mother's side? In her house I was brought up by my grandmother, Aunt Sarah, Aunt Zainab, and Uncle Hamid—the male influence in my life."

"I recall the rest," I tell Osane. "Aunt Sarah married and moved to Taif. Aunt Zainab stayed in southern Arabia with

Uncle Hamid and his family. You have always been special to Aunt Zainab, who loves you deeply. Every day she prays for you, and ever since our wedding she has carried a picture of me in her bosom. When Aunt Zainab found out we were traveling from America, she came from southern Arabia to Aunt Sarah's house to greet us."

"Very good, Christie," Osane says with a smile. "One more thing to remember is that you will soon be leaving a less traditional home to step into mainstream Arabia."

Pondering Osane's last words, I shuffle through my suitcase. I have been in the Kingdom long enough to realize that no matter what I do, I will not be properly dressed. Doing the best I can, I take off my old pair of pants and put on my best miniskirt. As Saeed pulls his car in front of the apartment, I comb my hair, pick up Nazar and we're off.

It feels wonderful to be out of the apartment and into the fresh air. Because we are in the mountains, it is very pleasant weather during the day and just a little chilly at night. The temperate October sun shines off the villa walls as we make our way through town and down a long driveway with a large gate. As we approach the gate, the guard stops us. He looks into the car. Recognizing Saeed, he waves us through. As we drive down the lane, Osane explains that Sarah's husband is the head secretary to one of the Princes. Saeed's car pulls to a stop in front of a small villa, while down the drive I glimpse the Prince's palace in the distance.

We knock, and Sarah's son opens the gate. He warmly lets us in, and runs to tell his mother of our arrival. As we enter the garden, two women walk toward us, smiling broadly and repeating Arabic greetings.

Nothing in my life experience has prepared me for the next thirty seconds. I stand as still as a rock. Barely breathing, I try to absorb the overwhelming welcoming energy, and the alien appearance of the two females moving toward me.

The first detail that stands out is the henna or darkish red dye that stains the palms of their hands and the bottom of their feet. Next, I focus on their clothing. The material is not subtle like Zora or Mina's, but bold and silky. The style is not European but traditional. These long dresses drop to the wrists and down to the ankles. Over their hair they both wear a double-layer, black, gauze scarf. These scarves are long enough to wind completely around their faces once and tuck in around the cheek area. The rest of the scarf hangs over the top of their dresses. Finally, I hear the jiggling of heavy gold bracelets that cover their wrists and necks. Long earrings hang down from their ears, and the older woman wears a pearl stuck through a hole in the side of her nose.

Suddenly my thirty seconds end, and henna hands grab me in an Arabic greeting. I stand there as Aunt Sarah kisses one cheek two or three times then the other cheek two or three times. She then weaves back and forth from cheek to cheek, muttering traditional words of welcome. Still swirling, I hold out my hand to Aunt Zainab, but it goes unnoticed. Instead, I find myself in another kissing and hugging Arabic greeting. I am then introduced to Aunt Sarah's seven children. After the third introduction, I give up trying to memorize their names. In my present state, I can't even remember my own name.

After the preliminaries, Aunt Sarah takes my hand and guides me into the *majlis* or Arab parlor to meet her husband. After this final introduction, everyone sits down on the floor. This is easy enough for the relatives to do in their long thobes and skirts, but very awkward for me. I assume the one polite position I have figured out, knowing that in a matter of minutes my legs will fall asleep.

I glance over at Osane. It is obvious he feels at home. Nazar is in a similar state of ecstasy, as he has found a completely new group of people who think his every movement is a wonder. Seeing my family at ease, I relax a bit and start looking around.

This living room is similar to Mina and Zora's Arab room, consisting of the typical Oriental rugs, Arab pads, and cushions. My observations are interrupted when Osane leans over and whispers, "Christie, follow my two aunts."

The relatives lead me along a hallway, through a garden and into a small room. This is obviously the family room, and looks warm and comfortable. Aunt Zainab motions me to sit down, and Aunt Sarah sits on my other side. In the traditional atmosphere of welcome, Zainab picks up my hand and begins stroking my hair. I know from Osane that it is acceptable in the Saudi world for men to touch and hold hands with men, and for women to hold hands with women. However, I feel awkward and queasy with such familiarity. It takes inward control to continue the hand holding, and to sit still while the aunts examine me. I remind myself that I am the first American female they have ever seen. This increases my patience and tolerance of the situation.

I sense their first remarks are about my hair. Since length and thickness is a sign of beauty, I hope I have scored points. Next Sarah holds up my hand and examines my long fingers and fingernails. They're well groomed and shorter than usual because of our moving and packing. Again their heads nod in approval, but they both conclude that my hands would be much more beautiful if I dyed the palms with henna. They keep pointing to their palms and smiling. I keep shaking my head back and forth. Then we all laugh in the realization that we are communicating.

My blue eyes are a fascination point for them and so is my light skin. Zainab keeps picking up my arm and laying it next to hers, pointing out the difference. I also appear much too thin, as most mature Saudi women are heavy. My height is another peculiarity. By the end of an hour however, I sense that I have passed their test. Slowly the aunts rise and Sarah smiles, motioning me to follow her into the garden.

As we walk into the courtyard, I notice a slight breeze. A pleasant sun reflects off the twelve-foot tall, three-foot wide cement wall that encloses the villa. Along the borders of the white walls and the house are beautiful flowers. Daisies, lavender, verbena, sage, lantana, salvia, and sunflowers blossom in the soil beds, while bougainvillea, jasmine, and ivy climb the walls. Winding through the center of the garden are small, stoned-in paths. These cinder strips serve as the children's play spaces, while the bordering flowers create a cool and aesthetic atmosphere. Gazing around the garden at the beautiful space Sarah has created for her family, my respect for her grows. She certainly has cultivated a fine collection of nature's best.

While we are walking at the far end of the garden, the children run down the paths to meet us. Nazar, of course, is right in the middle of things. Suddenly, he crawls through a small door at the end of the women's courtyard. I dart trough the door after him, hearing giggles from the older girls.

Instantly I sense I have done something wrong. Quickly I grab Nazar and jump back through the door. Looking at the girls, my questioning expression relays the message that I want to know how I blundered. There are more giggles. Sarah slowly walks over and pats my arm as if saying, "Don't worry, everything is still okay."

Sarah quietly leads me back through the house and down the hall to the closed door of the living room. She motions me to be silent while she opens the door just a crack. I peek in and see that while I have been with her, male visitors have arrived. She then takes me down the hall and back to the far end of the women's garden, and the door I had walked through to retrieve Nazar. She opens that door just a crack, and again motions me to peek through it.

Suddenly it dawns on me what I have done wrong. I have trespassed into the male domain and have shown myself to male visitors, who are forbidden to see me. Quickly I conclude that the instant any male (other than immediate family) enters, the household automatically divides into two sections. Until these male visitors leave, the men's living room and garden are out of bounds.

With my mouth open and my hands held wide in disbelief, my face loses some color. The relatives respond to my demeanor with laughter. Their eyes relay a message: "You've learned your first lesson on becoming a Saudi woman."

Slowly Sarah takes my hand and leads me over to a large rug that is spread in the garden next to the kitchen. As the women and the older girls prepare dinner, I sit in the warm sun watching the smaller children play with Nazar.

Disciplining myself to sit still, I focus on the children. They are so beautiful. Their large brown eyes, olive skin, and curly black hair are enchanting. There is something else about them. Is it their sense of total acceptance of life within defined walls? Within these barriers, they have found their own version of freedom. I also note the respect they have for one another, and their calm and flowing interactions. It seems strange that they have no toys. They simply play with what nature provides or with each other.

Finally, Osane walks into the women's quarters. I am overwhelmed with joy to see him. He joins me on the rug. With an intense need to express myself, I tell him about Aunt Zainab and Aunt Sarah's inspection of me, and my first lesson in female protocol.

When I finish my stories, Osane says it is necessary for him to rejoin the men. Suddenly wilted by the different environment and all the unfamiliar stimulation, I ask Osane if I can rest until dinner. He responds by settling me into a room. Just before closing my eyes, I wonder where Nazar is. With seven attentive babysitters around, I know he will be well entertained. He is probably continuing to chase the cats and many kittens that use the flowerbeds as hiding places.

When I wake up, I find that the male guests have left. This means the family can eat together. Once again, my special needs are anticipated. Sarah's oldest daughter sets a plate and a full set of silverware at my place. Another of her daughters piles up two pillows, so I can be more comfortable.

As I sit down, I look around the room and count thirteen of us at this afternoon meal. I think to myself how much easier it is to find thirteen spots around a cloth on the floor than to try to fit thirteen chairs and silverware settings around a table.

After dinner, the older girls clean up and the children run out to play. That leaves the adults in the family room, engaging in more conversation. While tea is being served, Zainab stands up and walks over to sit next to me. She pulls my much-worn college graduation picture from her bosom. This is her way of saying how glad she is to finally meet me, and that she carries me close to her heart.

During a break in the conversation, Osane turns to me and says, "Christie, Aunt Sarah wants you to follow her."

"Okay," I whisper to Osane, "but can we please leave soon? My endurance is really starting to wear down."

Sarah guides me into her bedroom, and digs into an old sea chest. I watch her curiously, as she pulls out a tape measure. She then stands up and proceeds to measure everything she can find on me to measure. My excitement grows as I realize that Sarah has sensed what I need most: clothes that will allow me to sit comfortably on the floor.

With the dimensions of my figure recorded, Sarah and I return to the living room. Excitedly I tell Osane about my measuring session, and ask him where Sarah bought her daughters' dresses. Osane translates my question, which sends laughter throughout the room. It seems that Sarah and the older girls sew their own clothes. There are very few (if any) ready-made clothes in the Kingdom and since tailors are expensive, dresses are made at home.

After an appropriate amount of time, Osane signals to everyone that it is time to go. As Saeed rises to leave, a great commotion follows. The relatives don't want us to go, yet Osane insists that we have to leave. Soon everyone is engaged in what appears to be a heated argument, full of stern expressions and raised voices. Becoming agitated myself, all I can do is look from one group to the other and wait for an outcome. Little do I realize that this is simply a customary end to a visit. Underneath all this noise, no one is actually upset; they are simply following traditional rules of visitation.

Arguing continues all the way to the gate, where there is finally a lull. Before we are allowed to leave, Sarah pours large quantities of cologne into the palms of our hands. I questioningly look at Osane, while Saeed shows me how to rub my hands together and spread the scent through my hair and my neck. With more smiles, shouts of goodbye, and warm departure kisses, we are finally driving down the driveway.

I close my eyes over what is now a splitting headache. I marvel that I made it through such a strange visit. With different rules and customs constantly bombarding me, my resolve was tested on all levels.

Little do I realize that in the future, as I blend more into the Saudi culture, Sarah will become like a mother to me.

Chapter 10

Our Trip to the Muslim Court

"The only way 'round is through."
Robert Frost

Upon returning to Zora and Mina's house, we settle around cups of tea. As Nazar jumps from lap to lap, renewing old acquaintances, I change into my familiar pants. With a great sigh of relief, I tuck myself into a safe corner with my book.

Meanwhile, the men begin discussing the situation surrounding my American passport, which was confiscated at the Jeddah Airport. Osane explains that the officials stipulated that I appear before the Muslim Court to be declared a Muslim. When these signed papers are handed to customs, they will return my passport.

After more conversation, the relatives decide that Osane, Ali, and I will leave for Jeddah early the next morning, before the sun becomes too hot. Since I will have to go before the Muslim Court, they begin asking me questions about their religion. Looking up from my book, I repeat the Five Pillars of the Muslim faith, the history of Muhammed, and so forth. As Osane translates my answers, they nod their approval.

After our religious discussion, Zora enters the room carrying an *abaya* or black cloak. She places this silky material in my lap. With immense effort, I attempt to control the anger and rebellion stirring within me. If I put on this covering I will be sliding into the world of the invisible with the other faceless Saudi women. Concealing myself in black represents my first step toward non-existence. The next compromise down this slippery slope will be to cover my face with two or three layers of a gauze scarf, called a *sha-la,* and the only skin remaining will be my two hands.

With all the relatives in the room watching my reaction, my pride in womanhood won't let me take this black silk cloak of suppression. Sensing my turmoil, dear Zora does the only thing that will allow me to put on the *abaya.* She starts to laugh, and the situation turns into comedy.

The whole family gets into the act, as Mina tries to stretch Zora's *short* abaya onto *tall* me. Finally draped, I don't know how to move, sit, or stand. In a fit of giggles, the women lead me into the hall and attempt to teach me how to walk. The silky material of the abaya keeps slipping off my shoulders; my feet, used to miniskirts and slacks, trip over the long folds of material.

The sisters conclude that since the abaya will never fit, it is permissible to slip some of the folds over my forearms. This slight modification will make it easier for me to move, while hiding the incorrect length. They also decide that it will not be sinful to skip the *hub-wa,* or the veil that goes over my face. They instead tie the black *sha-la* or scarf, tightly around my head and lay the abaya over my shoulders. As I stand in front of Zora's full-length mirror, I hardly recognize my own image. In a matter of seconds, I have transformed into a semi-covered woman. As I look into Zora and Mina's eyes, I notice glimmers of approval; the external remaking of an American into a Saudi has begun.

The next few hours pass quickly and soon it's time for bed. With the constant foreign stimuli bombarding my days, most nights I am asleep the second my head touches the pillow. Tonight however, I take time to ponder before slipping into my dreams. As I take my emotional temperature, I wonder why I am still sane. Then I turn over and hug my anchor Osane, and listen to the soft breathing of our little son. They are the center of my world. With them surrounding me, I am safe.

With my arms still around him, Osane snuggles closer to me. As he settles back into sleep, I dig down another emotional layer. Closing my eyes, I remember all the expressions of disbelief scarring my soul, every time I mentioned marrying a Saudi and living in his Kingdom.

Gradually all these negative comments transformed into branches, that were thrown onto my slash pile of determination. Once ignited, this roaring flame becomes a smoldering motivator. Its force constantly assists me in overcoming the enormous obstacles Saudi Arabia keeps pelting into my psyche. This fervor to succeed grounds, centers, and keeps me from dropping into the world of dismay.

The next morning when Nazar wakes me, I find the rest of the household already up. I am told to hurry, because even though it is October, the desert sun is to be respected. Ali wants us to drive down the cool mountains and through the low desert to Jeddah before the sun is too high in the sky. I quickly dress and kiss Nazar goodbye. After giving last-minute instructions to the sisters, Osane, Ali, and I run down the stairs to the waiting taxi.

My spirits are high this morning, for this seems a great adventure. I am actually sitting in an *abaya* in a taxicab full of Saudis. Arabic music is blaring from the radio and high-wall mud houses are passing by outside. I hum, "If My Friends Could See Me Now" under my breath and look out the window.

Slowly we wind down the mountains of Taif and onto the Jeddah plateau. Beginning to see through "desert eyes," I find the scenery much more appealing. The early morning sun also enhances the landscape and I settle back and let the vast, unoccupied stretches of desert pass through my senses.

A few hours later our party enters Jeddah. Our taxi winds through the city streets and finally turns into the Muslim Courthouse parking lot. It is Osane's job to stay with me, for a woman is never left alone. Meanwhile, Ali exits the taxi and enters the courthouse to set up an appointment. We are hoping to appear before the court later that same day. As time passes without Ali's return, however, it becomes obvious that he has run into difficulties.

The sun rises in the sky. It becomes hotter and very uncomfortable in the car. Osane and I open all the windows, both doors, and put pillows along the back window to block out the sun. Nevertheless, the car has turned into a furnace. Long ago, the taxicab driver has stepped out and is squatting in the shadows beside the rear wheel. Since I am a woman, I have to stay inside. Since Osane is guarding me, he also has to stay put.

At first, there is enough activity outside the cab to hold my interest. Soon however, my eyes tire from the sun. I let them rest by studying the interior decorations of the taxicab. Used to the bare and cold insides of a Yellow Cab, my senses explode every time I open the door of a Saudi taxi.

Mighty splashes of different textures and colors bombard me. Some of the dashboards have long, furry red carpeting with birds or flowers hanging from the rear view mirrors. Other taxis have curtains on the rear windows, with shiny beads hanging from the tops and the sides of the car's interior. This cab has four bold-shaded pillows in the back seat, three of which are being used as sun blocks.

Gazing out the window again, I conclude that these colorful patterns on top of patterns brighten the insides of Saudi taxicabs, the interior of Arab homes, as well as Bedouin tents. These bold decorative statements seem very balancing and necessary in such a bare, hot land.

Hot, tired of waiting, and bored, I inwardly yell. "Where are you, Ali?" To curb the beginning signs of claustrophobia, I pick up my book. After a while, it becomes too sultry to concentrate. The asphalt is baking and I feel angry and sick. The intensity of the heat, even with a slight breeze, is raising my body temperature to a critical level.

Finally, after four hours, Ali returns. He explains that after much effort, he has managed to secure an appointment for us two months from today. Osane and I look at each other in boiling frustration. Coming from the efficient West, we find it unbearable to accept such ineffectiveness. As is becoming clear yet again, this country will not bend or magically westernize to suit our needs.

Putting discouragement aside, present matters become more pressing. It is imperative to get me out of the sun. I am drenched in sweat, weak, dizzy, and am in the first stages of sunstroke. Osane and Ali hold an intense conversation. Ali disappears again, this time returning with water and some papers he hands the taxi driver.

The atmosphere in the cab is serious as we head out of the city. Feeling slightly refreshed from the water, I look out the window and notice that this is not the Christian road back to Taif. The streets are much wider and densely inhabited. I watch children herd goats and sheep in the mid-day sun, and I notice Bedouin families dotting the desert on either side of the road. These nomads live in black tents. They have staked up the sides of their homes, allowing protection from the overhead sun and air ventilation from all four directions.

Osane's voice pierces my observations. His urgency startles me. "Christie," Osane whispers, "quickly veil." Swiftly I cover myself, just as we are pulling up to some kind of security station. In front of us is a lowered gate and an armed guard is asking to see the taxi's papers. When the guard gazes into the car to check out the passengers, my backbone stiffens. I suddenly feel like a disguised East Berlin refugee trying to escape through Checkpoint Charlie.

Since everything appears to be in order, the guard waves us through. As soon as we are out of sight of the checkpoint, I turn to a very somber Osane.

"Osane," I ask. "What's going on?"

"We are on the Muslim Road," Osane replies. "Ali and I have made the decision to take the shortest route to the mountains and cooler air. You are our responsibility and we take your discomfort very seriously. We feel strongly enough to risk our lives, for you are an un-papered infidel who will soon be driving through Mecca."

My thoughts are interrupted by the approach of another checkpoint. This time, as I pull the veil over my face, apprehension glues me to the car seat. A very young Bedouin soldier with a sub-machine gun looks into the cab. Can he see through the thin mesh of my veil? Can he smell my fear? He leans his gun on the cab and slowly inspects the papers. Finding everything in order, he finally waives us on.

Afraid to uncover, I live through one more checkpoint and soon we are driving through the Holy City of Mecca. My veiled eyes are glued to the window, for I know I will never see this city again. The streets are not crowded for luckily it isn't *Hajj*, or the month of the Pilgrimage to Mecca. During the *Hajj* more than two million Muslims prostrate themselves at the Grand Mosque. Their goal is to walk in the footsteps of Abraham, Hagar, Ishmael and Muhammad and to circle the

Kaaba, or the Great Stone. As these Pilgrims walk, they worship Allah, the One. With more than a billion people (roughly one-sixth of humanity) being Muslim, I am glad that Mecca is at rest.

Almost through the city, I note that everything is incredibly clean. The buildings, the bridges, the road signs, everything seems to be aesthetically decorated and has blossomed into art. Soon we are on the other side of Mecca, beginning the climb into the mountains. As the air becomes cooler I unveil and begin to breathe, thankful I still have my head in place.

With the back window open, the cool mountain air dries the mixture of sweat and dust I have collected under the sun's relentless rays. Slowly, I allow my tense muscles to unwind. The weakness and nausea also begin to dissipate.

As our taxi begins its climb to Taif, the air becomes even cooler. Unfortunately, I quickly realize that this driver is playing a dangerously familiar game. He also is driving around blind curves on the wrong side of the road. Every time we come to a hairpin curve, I find my foot unconsciously braking and my heart falls into my nervous stomach. Osane is also watching the driver. With his patience long gone, he sternly tells the driver to stay on his side of the road. As we drive up to Zora and Mina's apartment, I am one happy person to reach what I now consider *home.*

Chapter 11

Life in Taif

"Life is like playing a violin solo in public, and learning the instrument as life goes on."
    Samuel Butler

The homecoming is quite a celebration. As Zora and Mina welcome us, I find myself in the middle of a traditional greeting and am astonished to find that it is coming naturally to me. The sisters and Saeed are full of questions about what happened, while I am only interested in how Nazar behaved.

The relatives make their way into the family room, busy with the talk of the day. Meanwhile I slip into the Western bathroom, and literally peel off my clothes. As I step into the cold, refreshing shower, I wonder how anyone can survive the constant heat and humidity of seaside Jeddah.

After my cleansing, it is time to clean up the bathroom. Shower curtains are an unheard-of commodity. No matter how hard I attempt to make my body the only thing in the room to get wet, the rest of the bathroom is inevitably drenched.

Feeling refreshed, but still weak from sun exposure, I wander into the kitchen to see what the sisters are preparing for dinner. I find Zora squatting on the floor, cleaning parsley onto her big tray. Meanwhile, Mina is at the sink washing tomatoes. I gesture to them that I want to help, but they smile at me and point to the family room. It seems my continuous chore as a guest is to remain comfortable.

Banished to the family room, I enter and sit next to Osane in what is becoming my mute fashion. By the sternness of the conversation, and the look each of the male relatives give me as I sit down, I know that they are talking about me. Curiosity overcomes me, and I ask Osane what they are discussing.

"Well, Christie," Osane says. "Ali, as head of this family, is lecturing me. He is very aware that you have left your country, family, and the things that are familiar to you, to be with me in Saudi Arabia. Since a new culture, family, and language now surround you, it is my duty to protect and take care of you. Because of your sacrifices, I must be good and Godly to you always."

I look up at dear Ali, and the rest of the male relatives sitting around that small circle. My heart goes out to each one of them. I realize that somehow, I have just been accepted into their family. I am no longer a strange American woman but a Saudi wife, to be cared for by the entire family. It is a good feeling. It is a warm feeling, and as I smile back my comprehension, the bond is cemented.

The next morning I wake up before Nazar. Lingering in the twilight between awake and asleep, my ears catch the sounds of the early morning. Even though it must be around 5:30, the many hoof beats on the pavement signal life below. Quietly I stand up, and open the shutters at the far end of the room. Carefully I peak out. I have been in Arabia long enough to know that women are never to be seen.

The scene below is a flashback into the past. There are many white asses, too big to be donkeys and too small to be mules, pulling water wagons. Many of these animals are decorated with orange henna. These designs are sometimes applied around their feet, while other times the henna circles their eyes or covers their chests. The asses wear plain harnesses, and young boys weave the wagons through traffic. The speed and direction of each wagon is directed by the boy's stick, and by special chanted words.

Horses, pulling larger wagons, make the other hoof beats. These horses wear tassels on their harnesses and look well cared for. Up and down the streets, the hoof beats clatter, and I wonder how I ever slept through this noise on previous mornings.

As the sun rises higher in the sky, I watch the shops open in the cool morning air. Soon men and boys fill the streets. It is their job to do the daily food shopping before going to work or school.

In a land time has forgotten, I watch a pockmarked man casually walk down the alley and relieve himself. Startled, I draw in a breath, smelling earthy and natural odors. Animal dung, spices, sweat, exotic incense, perfumes, and fresh cut meat combine to create the unique smell of an Arabian *suq* or marketplace. While I listen to the donkeys' braying, the jiggling of harness bells and the mewling of sheep, I think what a privilege it is to experience the primeval. Somehow, I sense that the whole culture will soon be shot at warp speed into the future.

Nazar interrupts my observations. I say goodbye to the *suq*, close the shutter and carry him to the kitchen for breakfast. A while later, Zora and Mina appear. Nazar smiles in anticipation of the greeting he knows he will receive. After the relatives are done eating, I show Zora one of Nazar's diapers, and shake my head. Her return nod signals comprehension, and what follows is my first Saudi washing day.

I follow the sisters into the back room, and watch as they pull out the washing equipment. The first step in this scrubbing ritual is the lighting of a kerosene burner. On top of it Zora places a large rectangular tin, filled to the top with water. She then pulls out an old 1890s wringer washer, which makes me think of my great- grandmother Hoag on her washing day.

While the tin of water is heating on the kerosene burner, Mina leads me over to a large tub that is filled with soaking white *thobes* (robes), *otras* (head scarves), underwear, t-shirts, and handkerchiefs. It is obvious that this overnight soak contains Clorox, for the fumes make my head swim. Using a large spoon, she swishes around the soaking clothes.

A few moments later, Zora motions to Mina that the water in the tin burner is hot. It is Mina's job to bucket in the cold water, and Zora's to scoop in the hot. As I throw in the diapers, a familiar Tide box, covered in Arabic writing, is pulled off the shelf.

While the machine is beating the diapers clean, Mina walks over to the corner and pulls out a large oval washing tin. She fills it with water plus Tide, and squats down to begin her hand washing. After watching for a time I decide to try. My novice attempts run into nothing but trouble. My first problem is the squat, which I soon give up for the more familiar kneeling position. I then pick up the wet clothes, but as I attempt to squeeze, all my fingers turn into thumbs. Soon I am getting sopping wet, and accomplishing nothing. Mina laughingly steps in. She makes washing look so easy. Her hands never seem to tire, and her technique plus rhythm make it fascinating to watch. After her clothes are washed and rinsed three times, they come out sparkling clean.

Meanwhile, Zora is draining the washing machine and guiding the diapers through the hand wringer. The large, oblong tin sitting on the kerosene burner is again filled with water and heated up for a second wash. As the last diapers makes their way through the wringer, Mina takes up her station. Once again she throws buckets of water into the washer as Zora scoops in the hot water, diapers, and Tide. Finally we work our way through the wash, wringer, and third rinse cycle one final time. As I hang each diaper to dry, I can't erase mental pictures of our college Laundromat. Just a few months ago, I simply threw Nazar's diapers in one machine, his baby clothes in another, and Osane's and my clothes in another. It took a minute to fill the machines, put in quarters, and walk out the door.

With Nazar's diapers finished, Zora and Mina begin to heat water for the family wash. There are five men living with them now, and the sisters are responsible for taking care of their clothes. Because it is dusty and hot, the men change their clothes often. Each time they do, they throw aside six pieces of clothing, mostly white. These clothes have to be soaked overnight in bleach, and washed and rinsed three times. Then they are put through a special bluing process, before they are hung to dry.

Once a week, the women start their wash early in the morning. They only stop to prepare the men's breakfast, and later on the main meal. The amount of work for the sisters is incredible, but not one complaint is ever uttered.

The next afternoon, Osane leans into the family room where I am reading my book, to tell me that he and Saeed are going shopping for baby food. The abrupt change to Saudi food has been too much for Nazar. He is refusing to eat. So we've reverted to bottled junior foods. My main concern is to keep our little one healthy, for I know he needs all his strength to fight off the germs in his new environment.

The afternoon wears on. Nazar has his nap and Zora and Mina have their tea, and still the men haven't returned. I am just beginning to worry when they walk through the door, their arms full of boxes and packages. Instead of buying one or two jars of baby food, they have purchased a crate.

Curious, I pick up a peach jar and notice Arabic writing scrawled over the label. As I trace the flowing letters with my finger, I remember reading about the ancient Middle Eastern civilization. This enlightened culture developed and spread science, art, philosophy, and medicine throughout Europe and Northern Africa during the era of the Muslim Empire.

Over time, the Middle East was slowly stripped of its creative outlets. With only language left as an acceptable religious expression, the Arabs began decorating their Mosques with breathtaking mosaics. Their songs and poetry also became incredibly complex and their written language slowly evolved into an intricate form of acceptable ingenuity.

My thoughts are interrupted by Osane, who is busy spreading out Nazar's new winter clothes. My eyes scan three suits. They are striped around the neck, ankles, and wrists. They look like a cross between a jogging outfit and long underwear. Adjusting to the bright colors of green, blue, and red, I am having a difficult time accepting their style. I do, however, have to agree with their practicality. The material is warm and soft.

When I look at the label to see where they are made, I find only Arabic writing with a small "Made in China" written in the corner. The thought that my American-Arab son is wearing Nationalist Chinese clothing strikes me funny. As I put the clothes away, Osane tells me to get dressed. It seems we are visiting his sister, Hannah.

Again, I am presented with the problem of what to wear. Already my height, blue eyes, and white skin make me blatantly obvious. My nontraditional clothing compounds my nonconformity, and turns me into a bright red flag. Unfortunately,

I am slowly finding that every second I appear in public turns into pure drama.

With no options, I reluctantly dress in my best blouse and a short skirt. Then I put on my London Fog raincoat and cover my head with a black scarf. Since my raincoat only comes down to my knees I am not covering much, but it's at least an attempt at being presentable.

As Saeed drives us to Hannah's house, my mind wanders back to a stateside morning several months ago. It was right after sunrise and I was sitting in front of the earliest edition of *Good Morning America*, nursing Nazar. Half asleep, I wasn't paying much attention. Suddenly the program mentioned something about Saudi Arabia. Immediately I was awake, for in 1969 Saudi Arabia was *never* on the news.

Listening intently, I heard the broadcaster say that in the desert Kingdom of Arabia there had been a mid-air helicopter collision, killing every soldier on board. I ran in to wake Osane. We watched the program throughout the morning, but the news item was never mentioned again. Osane immediately said a prayer for his sister Hannah, whose husband was a helicopter pilot.

We found out on our return to Saudi Arabia that tragically, Hannah's husband was killed in the accident, leaving Hannah to raise her son and two young daughters. Traditionally, family assists grieving widows. Therefore, her husband's brother and Hannah's mother had moved into the household for support.

Our car suddenly stops at a corner house, which is bordered on two sides by dirt roads. A black iron door creaks open, and down uneven clay steps runs Hannah's son. A handsome child, with a white complexion and a constant smile, he welcomes us warmly. With enthusiasm he leads us up the stairs and into his house, loudly announcing our arrival.

From down the hall runs Hannah, right into Osane's comforting arms. After the siblings greet, the family erupts into a grand welcoming. Nazar is being hugged, Osane is hugging and being hugged, and so are the rest of us.

Hannah takes Zora and Mina's black *abayas* and my strange raincoat, guiding us into her *majlis*. In this living room I am overjoyed to find chairs. Quickly I glance around the room, catching hints of sophistication and travel abroad.

As the relatives converse, I study Hannah. She is of average height for a Saudi woman. Her thick black hair is tied back, and her eyes are a deep brown. What keeps my attention and makes her stand out however, is her smile. The Arabs have a saying. They say a person is "like sugar or honey." This is a perfect description of Osane's sister, who radiates gentleness and goodness.

After tea, Arab coffee, pistachios, cashew nuts, and popcorn are served. While the rest of the family converses, Hannah takes me on a tour of her home. She guides me down a large hallway, and past a traditional Arab room. The kitchen tells its own story for it is spotless, neat, and well organized.

The bedroom holds the big surprise—*a bed*. This is the first time I've actually seen a bed. Against the wall stands a matching cupboard and dressing table. The most noticeable item in the room is a large picture of Hannah's husband, which hangs over her bed.

Under the glass of the dressing table are pictures of the family in Italy, where they had accompanied Hannah's husband for flight training. In these shots, Hannah is wearing a western-style dress and her hair is wrapped in a French twist. The pictures glow with happiness and a peace of mind that has obviously been lost. Instead, emanating from the entire home is a feeling of great sadness. My heart goes out to Hannah. To be able to have a smile on her face while patiently accepting long-term suffering, is indeed admirable.

Our tour ends back in the *majlis,* where we join the rest of the relatives. As Osane rises to leave, our departure is met with resistance. The same exit ritual that had played out at Aunt Sarah's house is being re-run.

Finally, Hannah walks to her bedroom. She collects the relatives' *abayas*, and hands me my raincoat and black scarf. She patiently watches as I put it on, and is way too polite to allow any "crazy American" thoughts to show on her face. After many warm kisses, we are on our way.

Chapter 12

The American Embassy, a Quick Step into my Old World

"The worse the Passage, the more welcome the Port."
   Tomas Fuller

That evening while I am resting, the men gather over tea. The topic of conversation, once again, is my American passport. The appointment with the Muslim Court is months away. None of the family approves of my official papers being locked away in the Ministry during all that time. It is decided that the next day, Osane and I will tell our story to the American Embassy and ask them to intervene. My passport, as a legal document, needs to be returned to me.

Osane and I rise before the sun the next morning. While dressing, I notice that my emotions are mixed. I'm always ready for an adventure, but I haven't forgotten the blazing sun of Jeddah. However, with no choice, I surrender to the trip and enjoy the drive down the Taif Mountains.

In the cool early morning air, I watch the sun play on the landscape. I note that the horribly barren mountains that not long ago resembled the moon to me, are becoming more appealing each time I travel this road. Since Osane is riding in the front seat with the taxicab driver, I have the whole back seat to myself. I open the windows and breathe in the invigorating breezes. I discover that this wind blends perfectly with my own body temperature, and creates a feeling of oneness around me. I remain in this half-dozing condition the whole way down the mountains.

By the time we reach Jeddah, the air is much warmer. As we weave through the streets, I can feel myself covering with sweat in the humid air. With the recent experience of sunstroke fresh in my mind, I stare out the window to control feelings of claustrophobia.

Driving down narrow dirt roads, we suddenly turn into a neighborhood with wider streets, larger villas, and center strips planted with royal palms. Without warning, our taxi turns right, through large unmarked gates, and into the American Embassy.

The instant I touch American soil, waves of buried emotions well up within me. Tears sting at the back of my eyes as I notice brilliant green lawns. The garden beds scream orderliness, cleanliness, and beauty. The walks are lined with pink bougainvillea and oleander, and there is actually a paved parking lot with yellow parking stripes. Standing with one foot in a Third World country, I now understand why underdeveloped countries have such a mixture of respect and jealousy for the might of the United States.

As we proceed through the embassy entrance, we are a strange sight. Osane walks in front of me in his native dress, while I follow in my white raincoat and black scarf. Before we can enter the main headquarters, we are stopped by an American guard, who asks Osane the reason for his visit.

Taking control, I step out from behind Osane and state, "I am an American citizen and this is my husband. We have come to see someone in the Embassy about my American passport." The guard gives us a strange look and lets us by.

Osane follows me to the front desk, where I explain in detail the reason for our visit. The male secretary asks us to be seated and leaves the room, but I cannot sit. Glancing around, my eyes settle on a picture at the far end of the room. This large portrait draws me in. Suddenly I find my feet planted directly in front of the Nixon family. Staring back at me are Julie, Tricia, Pat, and Richard Nixon.

Completely without warning, the picture triggers an invisible land mine. The inward blast explodes my emotional being into warring fractions. My American self resonates pride and homesickness. The females in the painting appear so independent and free. It is obvious they stand in their own female power, full of an open strength and beauty.

My newly-acquired Saudi identity registers irrational anger towards these uncovered women. Caught off-guard, I am amazed that the Arabian culture has already invaded my personal belief system. The blackened out Western women in Newsweek and Time keep flashing in front of my mind. I have to grab both my hands to prevent a subconscious urge to scribble over Julie, Tricia and Pat Nixon's features with flat, black magic marker.

As I fight for control, my final persona surfaces. This new shard of my being, the *self caught between two worlds*, is appearing much more often lately. This sliver is full of anger and frustration that the Nixon females remain free, while I am forced to cover.

Overwhelmed, my eyes brim with tears and I force myself away from the picture. Mental caution beacons shoot off, reminding me that institutions lock people up for schizophrenia. Am I going insane? With that fear foremost in my mind, I quickly click my splinters back into a controlled whole and shift my emotions firmly into neutral. I return to Osane, just as he is following the male secretary down a long hallway into a back office.

Upon entering the room, we are introduced to the Embassy Officer assigned to us. The secretary has already explained our situation to him. The Embassy Officer also feels it is inappropriate for the Saudi government to hold my American passport. After a quick call, it is decided that he will accompany us to the Ministry of the Interior. We make our way back down the long hall. As we pass the Nixon portrait, I give the uncovered women one last look and walk back into Saudi Arabia.

During our ride to the Ministry, I ask the Embassy Officer how long he has lived here. He replies that he and his family have been here for two unhappy years. This is his first assignment overseas and since he is black, he feels he has been assigned to a very harsh and unimportant country. He resents being thrown into a far corner of the world. He also feels that his service to insignificant Saudi Arabia won't look good on his record.

We exit the car at the Ministry. Once again, I encounter the stares that greet my every outside appearance. As we walk through the gate, my mind flashes on an analogy. I propose that a western female in a male Saudi ministry must feel as out-of-place as our black Embassy Officer in an all-white American suburb.

Soon our party is inside. As we make our way down the halls, I realize that all conversation stops until I am scrutinized and pass by. We finally reach the larger offices and as we enter, Arab hospitality takes over.

Osane and the Embassy Officer shake hands with the Ministry Official, and a chair is pulled out for me. While the men discuss my passport, we are served Arab coffee followed by a refreshing orange juice. In between many apologies and handshakes, my American passport is finally handed over to me. Our business is finished. Before we leave however, it is customary to hold a more general conversation. Since this is conducted in Arabic, I am left to observe my surroundings.

I am impressed by the dignity of the Ministry Official. I also notice that an obvious class structure is firmly in place. It is clear who the head of the office is, and which are the male secretaries. The male servants are less distinguished. They keep the energy swirling, by serving different beverages and running documents from office to office.

As I scan the area, I notice stacks of paper scattered all over the room. Some papers are signed and others are waiting to be signed. It seems obvious to my female organizational mind that a government run by such an enormous amount of paperwork is destined to bog down.

Finally, the proper amount of time has lapsed. After traditional handshakes we walk out of the building, my passport in hand. Osane and I say goodbye to our Embassy Officer and thank him for his help. As he drives off, I wish him luck. He looks back at me with an unreadable emotion, and wishes me the same. I watch his car drive back into Little America, as I step into a Saudi taxi. With a sigh, I wonder when my next brush with my own people will be.

With my American passport in our possession, the main issue holding Osane in Taif has been solved. This means that within the next few days, he will be traveling to Riyadh. It is time for him to report to the Educational Ministry and be assigned a job. Since Osane has been educated on a four-year government scholarship, he now owes the Ministry of the Interior four years of work in return.

The established plan is that Nazar and I will remain with the relatives in Taif, while Osane settles into a job in Riyadh. This solution seemed very logical when we were discussing it in the States. However, with his departure imminent, I feel sick, literally nauseous. I think of Sara Young's words, "Do not hide from your fear or pretend it isn't there. Anxiety that you hide in the recesses of your heart will give birth to fear of fear: a monstrous stepchild."

Knowing that I am supposed to bring my anxieties out into the light, I try to surrender to the fact that I am being left with non-English speaking relatives I barely know.

It is only fair to remember that these dear family members will be given the responsibility of keeping a young American bride stable and happy, while attempting to Arabize her. There is only one certainty. The next few months will be challenging for us all.

Chapter 13

Osane's Departure and My Solo Visit During Ramadan

"It is easy in the world to live after the world's opinion; it is easy in solitude to live after our own; but the great man is he who in the midst of the crowd keeps with perfect sweetness the independence of solitude."
   Ralph Waldo Emerson

With the tension building up around Osane's departure, I am not surprised when he announces that he is leaving early the next day. In the same breath, he also tells me that tomorrow is the beginning of the religious holiday called Ramadan.

At the mention of Ramadan, my mind darts back to a long article I had read in *Aramco World*. I remember that each year the Muslims fasted for the month of Ramadan, and because this holiday was based on the moon, it was celebrated at different seasons of the year. The fast began with the sighting of the new moon and ended thirty days later with the appearance of the new crescent moon. During this month, Muslims were not permitted to eat or drink anything from the time the sun came up until it set. The reasoning behind this was that Muhammad wanted the rich to experience what the poor had to live with. By exposing themselves to hunger, it was thought that Muslims would become more sympathetic and giving to the have-nots.

During Ramadan, Muslims renewed their relationship with God through prayer, reflection, worship, purification, and charity. Their lives revolved around the sun. As soon as it set, cannons would go off. Minarets over the entire city would sound the call to prayer signaling the end of that day's fast. The Muslims would then sit down to a large dinner, and to late night TV, or wander through the markets that were full of socializing and shopping. The next meal was served around the 4 am call to prayers. The families enjoyed this meal until the cannons once again went off, signaling the rising of the sun and the beginning of the next day's fast. At the end of Ramadan was a three-day celebration called Eid ul-Fitr, which means "feast of fast-breaking." This holiday consisted of parties, family gatherings, and gift giving.

Running this information through my mind keeps it off the reality that Osane will be gone tomorrow and I will be alone. My lifeline to anything familiar, to anything that makes sense in our new life, will mercilessly vanish.

After a sleepless night Osane simply closes the door on us, and in an instant he's gone. Nazar and I sit looking at the closed bedroom door. A hollow fear creeps into my stomach, as I realize we are all alone. Totally alone. The space Osane, our anchor, occupied is nothing but still air.

I want to slide into the protection of sleep, but I know from experience that once Nazar stirs, he is awake until his afternoon nap. Having lost all concept of time, I open the door and peek at the big hall clock. Confusion is the only thing that registers, for it is set in Arabic time. I had tried to figure out this time before. I hadn't put much effort into it, for Osane had always been there to transpose it into Western time.

Needing a mainstay to my day I rack my mind. Finally I remember Osane telling me that when it is 12 o'clock American time, it is 6 o'clock Arabian time. However, at this point I am too tired and depressed to figure Western time. Besides, Nazar is already halfway down the hall towards the kitchen, so I figure the next event will be breakfast.

While the rest of the household is deep in sleep, we eat. Not wanting to disturb the relatives, on the first day of Ramadan, we quietly walk back to our bedroom and close the door. Sitting down on the Arab pads, I consider the obvious problem Ramadan will create for us. The family, along with the rest of the country, has been up until 4 am. The Kingdom will slowly rise around noon or 1 pm. Meanwhile, Nazar and I will go to bed at our regular time and my little rooster will sound at around 6 am.

The only logical solution to this time warp, is to become a night owl with the rest of the Muslims. I know the family will warmly welcome us into their Ramadan ritual. The problem lies with me. Without Osane as a buffer, I simply don't feel strong enough to participate. I therefore choose solitude. This means that for six hours every morning I will remain sequestered, attempting to keep a two-year-old quiet and entertained.

With those thoughts swirling through my mind, I sink into the corner, feeling homesick and alienated. As tears flow onto my cheeks, I remember that three lifetimes ago I had been a college coed—jumping from class to class—free as a bird. Now at the age of twenty-three, my physical body and my energy are being confined in a thick concrete cage.

Waves of doubt roll over me like a tidal wave, pounding at my self-confidence. Osane's departure has shifted all my emotional weight and balance. My fear of losing my mind hovers over me like a bad dream. Am I strong enough to remain balanced through this month of Ramadan and the weeks that follow?

I spiral deeper and deeper into the abyss. My thread of hope, which holds my head up high, is unraveling, and my faith is taking a nose-dive into bottomless darkness. Before all is lost, I suddenly jump to my feet. *Anger* wells up deep within and saves me. Of course I am going to make it!!

All the new stimuli in my life will serve as a catalyst, and will propel me forward. Everyday I will learn. Each day I will change. The relatives' humor, wisdom, and warmth will guide me on my journey through this new landscape. The fuel will be my youth, determination, and months of study. Those haunting words of *"I told you so"* will strengthen my resolve. Making a fist, I strike the rug. I will survive, because I have to survive. I simply have no choice!

Drying my tears, I pick up a squirming Nazar, who is crawling all over me. I realize my trump card is that my son is too young to transform our room into a cell. He is happy and healthy. As I hug him, my mood brightens. We spend the morning playing with the few toys Osane has been able to find at the market. We pile Arab pillows up and make houses and platforms. Then I watch a giggling Nazar run through our creations, scattering red and white pillows all over the room.

Finally I hear movement in the far bedroom, signaling that the sisters are getting up. I glance at the Arabic clock and note that it is 6 o'clock. Now I have a temporal benchmark. After the bedroom noises, I hear washing sounds in the kitchen. I sense it is permissible to let Nazar into the hall. He is so sick of being confined that he screams all the way to the kitchen, waking up the rest of the house.

After the men dress, they leave for work and school. Meanwhile, the sisters begin cleaning the house. When my stomach starts telling me it's lunchtime, the next Ramadan quandary begins to formulate. With the household fasting, how can Nazar and I eat?

Sensing my dilemma, Zora points to my stomach. With smiles and the nodding of her head, she signals to me that it is OK for us to eat. I smile back, pleased that our non-verbal communication skills allow us to impart our needs.

After lunch, Nazar and I are both tired, and we retire to our bedroom for a nap. I wake before Nazar, to wonderful strange smells. I follow my nose to the kitchen, wondering what exotic foods can be casting such foreign aromas. I stare in amazement at the sisters, who are busy creating a Ramadan feast.

When the males return home from work and school, I can sense excitement in the air. At the end of a full day of fasting, everyone is hungry. Naturally, we all gravitate toward the kitchen to watch the food being prepared.

Mina is squeezing lemons and pouring sugar into a lemonade drink, while Zora kneads dough. We all watch her pound and twirl the dough into the air to shape one round circle. From this large circle, she cuts out many small circular shapes. Into these she spoons a mixture of cooked ground lamb, onions, tomatoes, parsley, and cooked rice. She then folds the dough over the meat mixture and seals it with her thumbs. Finally she cuts around it with a pastry cutter, forming a crescent-shaped sambusa. She lowers each sambusa into hot fat until it becomes golden brown. Meanwhile, Mina is dipping into a large tin of dates, sent from relatives who live on a date plantation. Soup is also being prepared, along with salads and other meat dishes.

A sense of exhilaration fills the apartment. You can feel the whole Kingdom focusing on the countdown until sunset. The Ma-hud-thans or religious criers are readying themselves, waiting for the time when it is too dark to tell the difference between a white and a black thread. When this moment comes, the cannons will boom, which will set off the call to prayer. From all over Arabia the cry "Alla-hu-akbar" (God is good) will be sung, signaling the end of the fasting day.

As we wait, the meal preparations continue. Mina carries the tablecloth to the family room, while Walid follows her with the silverware and Saeed opens the shutters. I stand discreetly at the window, watching the streets slowly clear as dusk sets in. Now and again, I see a white pickup truck speed home.

The emptiness in the streets is replaced by activity around the windows, as other families gather and wait for the boom. The tension and excitement of the moment is infectious. When the cannon finally does sound, cheers come from all directions. Immediately, Ma-hud-thans from all over the city start their calls to prayer. Each voice seems to have a slightly different pitch, which creates a magnificently bizarre sound.

Meanwhile, Zora and Mina are dishing traditional Ramadan foods. Soup is the first item to put into empty stomachs, followed by dates and then lemon juice. These food combinations have been passed down through the ages, as the healthiest way to break the daily fast.

At the conclusion of the first course, each of the male relatives spreads out a prayer rug. They open their Korans and are soon deep in prayer. The sisters however, have to cover first. They pick up long pieces of material and begin wrapping themselves. They start at the floor and work their way upward, tucking the last bit into the material covering their heads. Then they sit on their prayer rugs and begin their ritual.

Soon the prayer rugs, Korans, and pieces of material are put away. The whole family excitedly gathers for the main meal. We are finally able to taste the food the women have been preparing all afternoon.

The sambusa reminds me of a hamburger and I eat one after another, which pleases Zora no end. There is also flat Arab bread, rice and an Arab salad consisting of tomatoes, parsley, lemon, and onions. The main dish is a lamb, bean, and tomato combination called *fussolea*. For dessert, besides the usual fruit, Zora has prepared a special dish call *ka-taif*. This is similar to a pancake stuffed with white cheese. Over this cake she has poured sugar water. My starved sweet tooth is finally in paradise.

As usual, talk and laughter accompanies the meal. Everyone seems to be enjoying themselves except Saeed, who is exceptionally quiet. I ask him what's wrong. Through gestures and a few English words, I gather that he has a headache. It seems that it always takes a few days for his body to adjust to the Ramadan routine.

After the meal, the sisters and I carry the dishes to the kitchen. Mina cleans up and Zora makes tea. Saeed pulls out his *shisha* or hookah bubble pipe, while Walid brings in pillows, mattresses, and blankets. It is his job to prepare the family room for a long Ramadan night in front of the TV.

The days slowly fall off the calendar, wrapping our household in a continuous routine. Nazar and I wake up at 6 am, while the rest of the family rises between noon and 1 pm. The afternoons fill themselves with sewing, washing, and preparing the main meal. As evening falls, the booms sound. This is followed by the call to prayer, praying, eating, and a night in front of Saudi TV.

As time floats by, I begin feeling less and less attractive. I had always taken pride in my appearance, but my clothes have been taken away from me. I have worn my one pair of slacks so much, that they have developed holes in each knee. That leaves me squeezing into Osane's skintight jeans. They are incredibly uncomfortable and the rough material refuses to fit my female form.

The ever sensitive Zora and Mina sense my mood, and decide to take me shopping. Late one afternoon, the relatives put on their black abayas and hand me my white London Fog raincoat. At the door, Zora gives me one of her black headscarves.

Obligingly I pull it tight, flattening my normally full hair. Suddenly I feel like an acorn.

Walid, our male escort, leads the way. The instant we enter the streets, the tone of our outing is set. Curious looks follow our odd group of two covered Saudi women, a Saudi boy, a Saudi baby, and a tall American woman wearing a white raincoat. Knowing the die is cast and that bold stares will penetrate our every movement, I decide to ignore the unwanted advances and simply enjoy. After all, they look just as strange to me as I look to them.

Our party makes its way down narrow dirt paths, which wind between tightly packed market stalls. We walk by lame beggars dressed in tattered rags, cloth merchants, butchers, and dried fruit vendors selling their raisins and pine nuts. My eyes take in baskets of henna, dried apricots, rugs, and stores selling gold and dust-caked fruit. Slowly we follow Walid past cubicles selling exotic oils, spices, perfumes, and hookah or shisha tobaccos. Everywhere is the sound of animals, bustling, bartering, and conversation, along with the smell of sweat, dust, animal dung, and unwashed bodies.

Winding through the crowds of men with rosary beads trailing from their hands, I am surprised we don't stop to pick up groceries. Then I remember the food Walid and Saeed bring home every morning. Their shopping bags are always full of lamb (already chopped for cooking) and whole, plucked chickens. Tomatoes, onions, garlic, lemons, parsley, eggs, fruit, and wonderfully scented fresh bread accompany their meat bags. These daily items are supplemented by the back pantry. I recall seeing this area stocked with large burlap sacks of rice, raw sugar, tins of tea, coffee, dates, cooking oil, olive oil, and small jars of mint, cumin, saffron, salt, pepper, cinnamon sticks, cloves, pine nuts, raisins, and pistachios.

As our party walks farther into the market, I notice a roof supported by walls of caked mud bricks. In this covered section of the suq are the material shops, shoe shops, and what I have been looking for: The one stall that sells ready-made clothes.

Excitedly, I sort through the few racks. It soon becomes obvious that I am at least three sizes too tall. Nothing even comes close to fitting. I finally find a man's furry, cardigan sweater. I motion to Zora that I would like to try it on, but she shakes her head "no." It seems fitting rooms are against the culture.

After Mina helps me purchase the cardigan, I am more than ready to return to the apartment. The constant stares are wearing me down. Zora, however, is on a roll. She takes me by the hand, and firmly leads me into the material stalls.

Carefully she holds up spindles of material, her eyes asking me which ones I like. Not really caring, I point to one of the bundles. Then it dawns on me that she is buying this material to make me a dress. A revelation suddenly strikes me. In this culture the only way to be dressed is in *hand-sewn* clothes.

My spirits rekindled, I pick out two more bundles of fabric, thread, zippers, and buttons. With excited steps, the relatives and I turn homeward. Nazar occupies one of my hips. The other hand carries three bundles of material, which Zora will transform into my new Saudi wardrobe.

That evening the sisters hand me a German fashion magazine. The colorful pages are full of blonde models dressed in the highest fashions of Europe. At the end of the magazine are all the patterns. I wondered why Zora and Mina's clothes looked different from other Saudi women. The answer lies in *Burda Magazine*. The sisters' clothes are modeled after European fashions, while the women of Saudi Arabia use traditional patterns passed down from generation to generation.

With a bright smile, Zora brings over my material and sits down next to me. The rest of the evening is spent in excitement and laughter, as we decide which patterns to choose. The sisters are as excited to dress me, as I am to be dressed. The three of us communicate without a mutual language, caught up with each other, and basking in the joy of the moment.

The next morning, as usual Nazar and I are up at 6 am. After breakfast, I decide it is time to explore the roof. It is such a beautiful morning. I just can't go back into our closed-in bedroom.

Because the relatives' apartment is on the top floor, they have roof privileges. This is very important in Saudi Arabia, for roofs are extensions of the houses and are heavily used. During the suffocating heat of the summers, many families bring their mattresses up to the roof so they can sleep in the cool desert breezes. Children use the roofs for play, and some families keep animals such as pigs, sheep, or goats on the roof. Since there are no dryers in the Kingdom, the roofs are also used to dry clothes.

I take Nazar's hand, and we climb the roof stairs. We open a heavy metal door and make our escape into our own private world. Breathing in gulps of fresh air, I begin exploring. Structurally, the roof is flat and the floor is constructed of stone tiles. Around the edge of the roof are high cement walls, two to three feet thick and nine to twelve feet high.

Even with my height, I have to stand on my tiptoes to be able to peek over the wall. The only things I can see clearly are the tops of other houses and apartments. But even the highest walls can't hide the mountains from sight. The peaks flood my soul with immediate peace, for they are part of nature and they are *free*.

Meanwhile, Nazar is preoccupied with kicking a stone around the roof. He chases me, and I chase him. If it is impossible for me to see out, then no one can see in. We can therefore let our spirits fly, and become comfortable enough within these surroundings to let our true personalities soar.

Chapter 14

Revisiting Aunt Sarah

"If it is woman's function to give, she must be replenished too."
    Anne Morrow Lindbergh

Around noon, there is a knock on the door. Aunt Sarah's oldest son is led into the majlis by Walid. It seems he has come to invite Nazar and me to his mother's house. Remembering the welcome of our last visit, I feel warm inside, but also frightened. Their house is so traditionally Saudi. Knowing the invitation has to be honored, Nazar and I are soon in Sarah's Mercedes heading toward the other side of town.

It is an idyllic day. The air is crisp and revitalizing, and the sun makes everything sparkle. I open the window and watch the mountains—the ones I gazed at from the roof—get closer and closer. We turn off the main road and are soon at the big gate that protects the Prince's Palace and Sarah's small villa. The watchman lets us into the compound, and the car stops in front of Sarah's door.

As we step into the garden, Sarah's seven children appear. Each one approaches me, shakes my hand, and kisses me on each side of my face. With excited voices, they then run over to Nazar and whisk him away. Sarah and Zainab come from the other side of the house, greeting me with outstretched hands and offering to take my raincoat.

After the welcome, we settle down on a rug in the garden. Everywhere are flowers, kittens, children, laughter, and confusion. Knowing I'm not fasting, one daughter pours me tea while another brings nuts and dates. Sarah and Zainab keep up a continual conversation in Arabic. While there is no language comprehension, the body gestures of welcome and love are clearly evident.

After tea, Sarah takes my hand and leads me into her bedroom. I had stood in the middle of this room before, but I had been too overwhelmed by my first visit to be truly present.

Now that I am more absorbed into the culture, I am mesmerized by the multitude of different sights and smells of this room. I gaze upon black and maroon oriental rugs, sheets covered in bold flower patterns, and Arab pillows in their distinctive designs. These visuals create a whirlwind of color, while layers of perfume, cologne, and incense keep my senses spinning. As I am scrutinizing her bedroom, Sarah walks to the far corner and unlocks an old sea chest. As soon as the lid opens, another miasma of sweet fragrances filters throughout the room.

Carefully she hands me a full-length silk slip. Then she pulls out a floor-length orange dress, decorated at the scoop neck and wrists with sequins and stones. Suddenly, I remember her measuring me the last time I was here. The result is a much-needed dress, sewn by her oldest daughter.

Aunt Sarah quickly leaves the room. Arab women are modest, even in front of other women. As I put on my gift, I struggle with the long back zipper, but soon the dress is on. Nervously, I peek in Sarah's tall mirror. A frontier woman on her way westward stares back at me.

Trying to shake my shocking image, I begin walking awkwardly around the room. The long skirt wraps around my legs, making me unsteady on my feet. Even my best movements are stiff and jerky compared to those of Saudi females. Knowing they have to be fully covered, the Arab women make each movement graceful and sexy. Their walk, especially, is slow, smooth, twisting, and alluring. Trying to mimic them, I trip and fall on the floor. I finally decide that the only way I can be attractive is if I stand still.

When the proper amount of time has passed, Sarah, Zainab, and the girls excitedly re-enter the room and circle me. Their eyes speak their approval. To them I am beautiful. Sarah's daughters then take my hands, and I stumble off for a tour of their compound.

The freedom of Aunt Sarah's children is exceptional for Saudis. Even the girls are allowed to roam uncovered through the vast, walled-in area of the Prince's compound. Singing an Arabic song, they lead me down the driveway to the palace. When we are in front of the Prince's Palace, they stop singing and try to say something to me. After a while, I figure out that their pointing into the distance and mentioning Riyadh means that the Prince and his family aren't in residence at the moment. I conclude that this is his summer home, and he is now living in Riyadh through the winter months.

Knowing this fact, I feel a little less intrusive as we circle his large, beautiful home. We are almost back to the driveway when we come upon a fenced-off area for goats, chickens, and a few quail. Making our way among the animals, I marvel at how free-spirited Sarah's children are in their enchanted world.

We leave the Prince's Palace and walk down a small road, opening and closing gates as we go. We soon approach another large villa, surrounded by a beautiful garden. Here we meet the Indian gardener. After the children greet him, they introduce him to me.

His eyes light up. He picks a flower and gives it to me. He then motions us to follow him on a tour of his grounds. I don't recognize any of these exotic desert flowers, but I understand the love and attention the gardener has put into this bare piece of land. His nurturing has made the soil come alive, and has transformed gravel and dirt into a beautiful oasis of color and life. I shake his hand, and he tries to express in broken English how much he has enjoyed giving us a tour. He picks another flower and hands it to me. We wave goodbye and are soon heading back down the small road, opening and re-closing the gates.

When we return to Sarah's home, I am led back into the garden and served tea. Slowly I fade into the background, as the rest of the family return to the rhythm of their everyday lives. This is my opportunity to watch and absorb. There is so much to learn about day-to-day Saudi living.

While Sarah's daughters play or work around me, I note that most of them are older than ten or eleven. This means that they have crossed the line into the separate female world. Anytime they leave the house, they will be clustered into veiled groups. For the rest of their lives they will sit in woman's quarters. Upon entering a doctor's office, or an airport, or visiting a friend or relative, they will dwell in these separate quarters, cloaked in privacy.

An hour gently ticks by, as I sit breathing in the fresh air and watching the wind twirl the flowers. The Middle Eastern sun soaks my face in relaxing rays. Feeling sleepy, I gesture to one of the daughters that I would like to take a nap. Before resting, I find each member of the family and shake their hands, thanking them in English. Fully realizing they can't comprehend, I nevertheless want to show gratitude for the gracious way they have allowed me into their lives.

With the door closed behind me, I walk over to the Arab pad and lie down. Closing my eyes, I soon find myself in the space between awake and asleep, the vulnerable domain where the subconscious rules. Suddenly, without warning, my floodgates open and I begin drowning in vast feelings of emptiness. Grabbing my stomach, I gasp for breath and sit up.

I have been doggedly striving to be happy on the surface. In reality, I have been more like a vivid fall leaf caught in a swirling arctic wind. I feel *so* alone. Osane is not here. Nothing is familiar. Everything that touches my senses is strange. Even though the relatives are unbelievably loving and supportive, they are really strangers. I feel like I'm submerged in a bad dream with no way out. All I can do is wrap my arms around myself and silently sob. Finally, I fall back down on the pad and crash into the safety of sleep.

I awake to children's voices. I push the emptiness in me to one side, and come out with a smile. Sarah's face brightens when she sees me. She motions for me to sit back down on my mat, and I spend the rest of the afternoon watching the women fix the main meal. Like Zora and Mina, they do their meal preparations on the floor, balancing over big trays.

I note that half of Sarah's kitchen is inside, consisting of a sink, refrigerator, stove, and a cupboard where the serving dishes are stored. The outside kitchen contains one large gas burner, which sits on the ground. Surrounding the burner are large pans in which whole sheep can be cooked. I marvel at the fact that flies don't seem to be an issue in the mountains, making outside cooking and eating possible.

Meanwhile, I watch Sarah's three oldest daughters talking and laughing easily while they work. Their practiced hands quickly work through routine tasks, which they know will be theirs for the rest of their lives.

Somehow, they don't seem to mind walking down their mother's path. They know they will eventually marry and leave their childhood home, but it is not likely any of them will move too far away. Their days will revolve around their future husbands and children, the women of their immediate family, and their female friends. Because they accept this, their lives are full of slow, easy living, and feelings of healthy connection.

Nazar's laughter pulls my attention back into the garden. I find the younger children playing a form of jacks, with five small stones. It is a complicated game and their manual dexterity is amazing. I sit down and take a turn. My clumsy efforts result in laughter all around. Halfway through the third game, the cannons boom, and the city echoes with the call to prayers. We stand up, brush the dust from our clothes, and walk into one of the side rooms.

On the floor is a tablecloth covered with the traditional Ramadan openers of soup, lemonade, and dates. After prayers, we begin the main meal. This consists of meat and rice, a lamb and okra dish, an Arab salad, bread, and a milk pudding. On the far side of the tablecloth is a large platter filled with fruit, and a jug of water with a glass. This one glass of water passes from lip to lip, to anyone who is thirsty.

When the relatives begin eating, I make a point of restricting my vision to my place setting alone. Used to Zora, Mina, and the family's habit of eating with a tablespoon, I still find the hand-to-mouth feeding unsettling. However, there is a very strong etiquette to this form of eating. Only the right hand handles food, as the left is reserved for use in the bathroom. Small balls of rice and meat are formed and placed politely in mouths. Flat Arab bread is used to scoop salads, and tablespoons are available for soups or custards. Food is never passed, since it is divided into small serving dishes and is always accessible.

As each of the family members finishes, they utter "ca-reem a-kal-la," which means "God is generous." They then slowly rise, being careful that their greasy hand touches nothing. Next, they walk to the sink where they wash thoroughly. They then re-enter the room, sitting around the walls where they patiently wait. When everyone is finished, tea is brought in, and the family settles down for another chat.

After tea, I ask Sarah's son to take us back to Zora's apartment. It is getting late, and I long to return to familiarity. Zainab and Sarah protest our departure, but I now know that they are just being polite.

While one of the younger girls disappears and returns with my raincoat and black scarf, another daughter lights the incense burner. As the smoke billows around me, another daughter pours cologne into my hands. Finally Sarah's son opens the back door of his Mercedes, and we drive off amid much waving and good-byes.

Chapter 15

Slices of Single Saudi Living

"The current of inward life increases as it is spent."
   Ralph Waldo Emerson

We return home to find that Saeed's brother, Ali, has arrived from Jeddah. He will be spending the night before heading back to his home in Southern Arabia. Nazar and I join the relatives in the family room. As we sit down, I notice that Ali is surrounded by several large shopping bags. While the household watches, Ali digs his hands into one of the bags and pulls out eight pairs of shoes. They are all the same style, arranged in sizes from infancy to adulthood.

I look at him questioningly. Recognizing my confusion, he points to each pair of shoes, giving each a name. Since Ali has eight children, it becomes evident that he is bringing shoes to his large family. He not only has shoes but purses and other presents. As Southern Arabia is remote and shopping is limited, these items are both anticipated and necessary.

The next afternoon while Nazar and I are playing in our room, we hear a great deal of commotion. We jump up, open the door, and find the sisters in the beginning stages of cleaning day. We watch as Zora and Mina gather their equipment. I am expecting Windex, dust mops, and a Hoover to appear. Instead brooms with no handles, rags of all varieties, and a big bucket of water filled with Tide are dropped into the hall. The relatives wrap their hair with small scarves and away they go, dust flying in four directions.

They attack one room at a time, with their rags beating and snapping. When the dust settles in the first room, Mina takes out the Arab pillows and mats. Then both sisters carry out the heavy rug and throw it over a clothesline in the back room. While Zora beats the rug, Mina walks into the next room and begins snapping the shutters and the screens. When Zora is done with the rug, she mops down the empty floor with her sponge and bucket of Tide. Through the entire process, the sisters keep muttering *trop* or dust. *Trop* is their enemy and they fight it with a vengeance.

That evening, the family settles into the clean family room and begins watching TV. I notice Saeed walk over to a glassed-in bookcase, which is the only real piece of furniture in the room. I sit down beside him, and watch him thumb through old Arabic textbooks and calendars. Suddenly he hands me two worn books, yellow with age. My heart skips a beat when I realize they are written in *English*!! I hold them in my hands, fingering the covers as I would priceless pieces of art. The first book is a 1949 Readers' Digest, and the second is the novel *Love is a Many Splendored Thing*. With misty eyes, I hug Saeed and slip into the far corner with my treasures.

The next morning, I rebel at being cooped up in our little bedroom waiting for everyone else to wake up. I decide to crawl through the window that leads onto a small balcony. Sitting absolutely still I breathe in the clear, open air. Since it is an early Ramadan morning, there are few people around to notice my breach of conduct. As always, my thoughts turn to Osane. As I stare down at the streets, I find myself watching for him to come around the corner and enter our apartment building.

Unfortunately a time clock has gone off inside me, and I feel pressure building. Osane has been gone too many days, and I don't even know if he has arrived safely. Since there are no telephones, my only hope is a letter. Mail however, is very rare. Because there are no addresses, few street signs, and no post office boxes, each official letter has to be hand delivered.

The main form of communication within the Kingdom however, are informal letters delivered by male friends or relatives. These written words continually spread news throughout the Kingdom. Travelers stop by family and friends, saying that they plan to journey to a particular town or village. All the males in the family immediately gather and scribble out family news and greetings, which is then hand carried by the voyager.

Just as I'm contemplating the ramifications of women my age not being able to read or write, a shout from the street below redirects my attention. A small, male crowd has gathered. Realizing I have been caught, I crawl back into the room and shutter my window. My cheerful Nazar greets me.

That evening, instead of turning on the TV, the family decides to go shopping. Walid picks up his book, gesturing that he has a lot of homework, so he will stay home and watch Nazar. This will give me the opportunity to experience the evening market during Ramadan, which is twice as crowded as normal.

Ready for an adventure, I follow Zora, Mina and Saeed toward the town's shopping area. As we walk, Saeed moves several steps ahead of the women. Since the sisters are moving slowly and Saeed is walking at my pace, I try to catch up to him. However, every time I fall in step beside Saeed, he quickens his pace. This happens several times before it dawns on me that in Saudi Arabia men always walk ten paces in front of their women. I hear myself mutter, "Oh, my God," as I finally leave the appropriate gap.

We spend most of our time in the material market, which Zora and Mina seem to have memorized. I have to keep tight control on my patience, for their shopping pace is agonizingly slow. The three layers of fine gauze covering their faces encumbers them. This means that every article has to be pulled up to their neck. They then pull their veil out just far enough to see each object.

When they finally decide to buy an item, the bartering begins. This in itself is a lengthy drama. Zora gives the clerk an opening price, and he in turn defiantly states, "Why that price for such fine material?" Zora then offers a higher price, which is countered by the clerk. The game continues until Zora throws the material down in anger and stomps out the door, hoping the clerk will call her back and accept her last price.

With all these obstacles, it is amazing that a few hours later we head home, loaded down with thread, material, and other purchases. As we weave through the different stalls, I notice a camel in the back of a pickup truck. I study his humped silhouette and large doleful eyes, but make sure that I stay at a distance in case he pulls back his lips and spits.

The next afternoon, right at teatime, there is a knock on the door. Upon hearing excited female voices, I peek into the hall and see Mina welcoming a tall, covered female. Safely inside the apartment, her wrapping falls, exposing an exotically beautiful young woman. Her silk dress caresses her thin frame, sensually cascading onto spiked heels. Her almond-shaped eyes are outlined in charcoal, and her features touch on perfection. This desert beauty is Mina's school friend, and she has come to spend the afternoon.

After tea and excited chatter, Mina brings out a jar of henna. They apply this dye to the bottom and sides of each foot, and to the palms and fingers of each hand. After the application of this red dye, the hands and feet are bagged. Nazar can't believe that Mina and her friend are sitting in "his" family room wearing bags.

A little while later, after the *henna* has had an opportunity to soak in, the bags are removed. The final steps in this beauty ritual are the nails. The *henna* jar is put aside and bright red nail polish replaces it. Both of the girls' nails are short and when they apply the polish, they carefully paint around the moon of each nail.

When the nails dry, Mina's friend puts her gold bracelets back on and rises to leave. Fully decorated, she covers up. As she sways into a waiting car driven by her brother, I think what a shame to cloak such a blossom. In a world where women dress for women, men will never glimpse the gorgeous beauties who hide under their black silk camouflage.

The rest of the afternoon passes pleasantly, and soon it is time to begin the evening meal. I settle into my customary place of observation in the kitchen. With pen and paper in hand, I record everything Zora puts into her many dishes. For days, I have been creating my own Arab cookbook.

Zora is just finishing the main dish when I notice she needs some salt. While moving around jars in the storeroom, I stumble across a large burlap bag of popcorn. Excited to find something resembling American junk food, I run back into the kitchen and begin popping. That evening I offer the relatives a large bowl of popcorn. The generic noise of the TV is accompanied by the homey crunch of corn, which blends in nicely with the sounds of the shisha.

As the days pass, I can sense my feelings building up. The Ramadan mornings remain the hardest part of my day. Keeping Nazar quiet before everyone wakes up often reaches an unbearable point. To survive these confining moments, I spend many of them marching around the room singing from the musicals I had memorized in college. Nazar thinks this is great, and as we march and dance, we throw pillows at each other.

As I watch Nazar play, I attempt to keep my spirits high, but questions, doubts, and increasing moments of despair slip in. "Why," I ask myself, "did I marry Osane in the first place, and leave my world behind?" Since these doubts seem to be underlying my growing unrest, I sink into the corner and lose myself in thought.

I let my mind wander, seeking deep subliminal causes. Slowly my thoughts circle around to a handful of *pertinent laws* I had unknowingly internalized.

I recall that in my Cinderella Generation there was a particular female guidebook to success. I remember it stated that one must attend college, find a husband before graduation and move to the suburbs to become a full-time homemaker and mother.

I did follow the guidebook to college, and I found and married Osane before I graduated. However, on the third law I chose to part ways. It was my decision to paint my individual canvas of life in broader and bolder strokes. It was my conscious choice to marry for love and follow that love to a far-off land. It was *my* choice to swerve off the main path of life. Amazingly, once I own the responsibility for my actions, peace returns. Suddenly the sun pierces my temporary clouds, and I refocus on my present life with a deeper understanding and acceptance.

I rise from the floor and join Nazar in building pillow towers. After they are piled high, Nazar screams with joy as he topples them. While I am helping him build another pillow tower, a familiar fear again invades my thin veil of peace. "Why haven't I received a letter from Osane?" I lament. "Is he all right, or is he dead?" My worst enemy is unoccupied time, which I attempt to creatively fill. But no matter what I do, the minutes drag endlessly by.

Slowly the days blend by. Underneath everyday life, my inner spring of unrest begins twisting tighter and tighter. With ironclad determination, I shove my unrest into an interior hole. I paint a smile on my exterior persona, but a gale is brewing within.

Finally, my emotional fortitude begins to unravel. I know, even before I open my eyes the next morning, that I can cope no more. I spend the afternoon unusually somber. The relatives sense my mood but after centuries of communal living, traditions have evolved to protect the individual. Privacy is sacred, and no one is going to interfere unless I ask them to.

In blatant contrast, I am not a Saudi with centuries of communal living in my genes. I am a young American female who is used to showing and sharing her feelings. I can work out my own problems only so long, and then I need help, not privacy.

By the time I sit down to the evening meal, I am a bomb ready to explode. Zora dishes my food and I pull back, staring at it. Without warning, I burst into uncontrollable sobs. The relatives stare at me, dumbfounded. Walid stands up and hands me a box of Kleenex. Before I realize what is happening, Zora and Mina also start to cry. Saeed begins shuffling around not knowing what to do, while Zora's lovely food sits there getting cold.

Up to this point, all the drama has been wrapped in silence. Without a word spoken, the relatives don't even know what I'm upset about. That doesn't stop them from joining in on my sorrow.

I look up at Saeed and between sobs, I quietly ask if Osane is all right. "He hasn't written, so how can I know?" I question. Then I break into rapid English. Realizing I won't be understood, but desperately needing to communicate my anxieties, I continue.

"Letters," I state, "can get from Saudi Arabia to America in a week to a week and a half. I know because Osane and I have received a letter from Ali. If they can travel across the ocean in that period, certainly a letter from the capital to this apartment can make it after these many days."

Saeed looks at me with a supportive smile. He explains in broken English, "It will take twice as long to deliver a letter within the Kingdom, since each letter has to be delivered by hand. I assure you that Osane is all right. God will take care of him."

His words comfort me. In fact, just crying and communicating makes me feel so much better. Ultimately however, I realize that I have some growing up and strengthening to do. I certainly don't want to keep sabotaging the household as I have tonight. I now sense that every time I cry, Zora and Mina will also cry, and I don't want to have that responsibility.

The march of time continues and the days become colder. Because we have no heat, we snuggle beneath blankets to watch TV. One evening, I pick up one of Mina's schoolbooks, realizing that it is only during the last decade that girls have been allowed to complete elementary school. As Western contacts and conveniences slowly penetrate the Kingdom, the government has aligned with this trend and has finally introduced female education.

There was much turmoil in the Kingdom when the Ministries opened the first girls' school in 1950. Not every father thought it was proper for their daughters to leave the house to attend school. After initial violence, such as bus burning, girls' elementary schools were opened. It took courage. At night, these same schools were made available to older women who want to take advantage of elementary education. But most women my age remain illiterate.

The consequences of not being able to read or write were never real to me until I experienced them first hand. My Saudi contemporaries can't read a book, a magazine, or a cookbook. They can't comprehend sewing patterns or any instructional manuals for the new western equipment that is being sold throughout the country. An atlas is way beyond their ability, and most of them don't know where America is. Their only reality is their immediate environment. They even have to go to their husbands or male relatives to write or read any letters that are hand-passed back and forth.

Mina's generation is changing that. Most girls graduate elementary school. A few girls such as Mina continue their education through a girls' junior high and high school. A very select few even attend small university classes. Sitting in separate rooms, they watch lectures via closed circuit TV. A few more attend colleges in Egypt or Beirut.

Graduates have only a handful of careers to choose from. It is acceptable for a female to be a teacher, a doctor, or an administrator in one of the girls' schools across the Kingdom. With such a limited number of careers available to them, most girls assume their mother's role and become homemakers and mothers. However, after receiving an elementary education, they are much more prepared to raise the next generation.

Chapter 16

Osane's Return

"Joy rises in me, like as a summer's morn."
    Samuel Taylor Coleridge

Late the next afternoon, the relatives gather in the family room for tea. Mina serves, while Zora surrounds herself with freshly washed clothes and begins ironing. As she folds the pressed thobes, I marvel at the perfection of these clothes for desert wear. The robe is white, which reflects light. The sleeves and skirt are large and open, allowing just the right air circulation. The gown covers the whole body from the sun's rays, and the material is cotton so it can breathe. The large otra, or scarf, buffers male heads from the sun. These otras can also be wrapped around faces for protection during dust storms.

Idly watching Zora's iron glide over clean fabric, I recall the practicality of the coarse leather veil with eye slits the Bedouin women wear. The benefit of this type of veil is that it serves as a barrier against the constant desert wind, which pits faces with blowing sand.

After tea is served, we gather for supper. Following evening prayers, each one of us takes our customary seat for TV. Following the Saudi news, Nazar and I retire to our bedroom. Automatically I lay out our bedding, putting down Nazar's mattress and then my mattress next to his. Finally, I change his diapers and dress him in his well-used Chinese warm-up suit. Over this I tuck him into his blue jacket, bought at Penney's a few lifetimes ago. Only by wearing all these layers can Nazar stay warm through the cold desert nights in Zora's unheated apartment.

Taking off my clothes and changing into my nightwear, I snuggle under my heavy blankets. As the sheets warm, they slowly begin to reflect my body heat. I then create a nest in the exact shape of my frame, and drift off into a deep sleep.

In the wee hours of the night, I feel someone caressing my face. I open my eyes and look up into Osane's face, an illusion with a smile. I am dreaming. I have to be. All those many, many days with no word, and then he is here, kneeling over me!

We frantically grab each other and lie in an embrace of incredible relief, as waves of emotions wash over us. With tears running down our cheeks, our latent feelings explode into intense passion. Weeks of frustration peel off, as we grab at our clothes. Foreplay is for another time. The only thing we desire, the reality we *need,* is closeness. As Osane enters me, I open myself with total abandon. The power of love begins to evaporate the weariness of our many days of struggle. Our enormous challenges slowly dissolve under our unbeatable, united strength. With tremendous joy, we once again blend into our own world.

The next morning, our family of three walks out of the bedroom, happiness radiating from our beings. As we enter the family room, I can also feel the relatives' delight. The last several weeks have taken a toll on each of us. Nevertheless, we did it! Each one of us has survived, and it is now time to rejoice and celebrate.

Traditions and customs aside, Osane and I sit in the middle of the room with our arms around each other. Osane tells the relatives what has happened in Riyadh. It doesn't matter that I can't comprehend a word he's saying. The only thing that matters is that I am in Osane's presence, and that he has come safely home.

During the next couple of days, Osane and I spend a great deal of time on the roof. It is beautiful up here. The sun warms us, and the privacy enables the three of us to be alone. As we gain strength from each other, we talk about what has happened and dream about what is to come.

One evening as the stars shine down on us, Osane bares his soul. "Christie, I was challenged on absolutely every level in Riyadh, but mostly I was worried about Nazar and you. I am truly amazed and incredibly relieved to find you as intact as you are. My torn mind constantly worried about your coping ability. How could a twenty-three-year-old American girl possibly survive being left in a strange Saudi household with unfamiliar customs and no common language? The fact that it was Ramadan made the odds of your adjustment even worse! Finally, my inability to communicate with you increased my frustration even more. The only thing I could do was send letters, but I knew they might take several days or weeks to be delivered!"

I caress his worried face and give him a long hug. Then, with his hand in mine, we sit side-by-side, looking at the moon reflecting off the distant mountains.

After a long silence, Osane continues. "My job placement hasn't run smoothly, Christie. The Ministry of the Interior originally sent me to the States to study Police Administration, and I was allotted four years to graduate with a degree in Criminology. Caught up in the '60s campus scene, I decided to declare my own identity. Since my interest has always been people, as you know, I changed my major to Sociology."

"The consequence of my action," he admits, "is that I can no longer flow easily through red tape and into an army commission. I have now become one of a kind. In a traditional, rigid society where individual job placements are not easily dealt with, this makes everything much more difficult. The system doesn't know where to place me. I am not qualified for, nor do I want to go into the army. My personal focus is to become a social worker, or a professor at Riyadh University. There aren't many college-educated Saudis in the Kingdom, and I feel a responsibility to contribute."

As his narrative progresses, I silently surmise that "the system" is afraid of him. He is young, bright, and educated. What threatens a closed society the most is ambition and the desire to improve by changing the status quo. Not knowing what to do with this firecracker, they probably decided to defuse him. His Arabian elders, hoping that this young Saudi son will learn patience and conformity, likely buried his application under mountains of red tape.

Osane confirms my assumptions, saying, "Christie, I spent my time in the Ministry of the Interior, following my papers from desk to desk. This meant waiting in rooms for hours at a time. Believe me, it's a very frustrating and humiliating experience."

Getting up to pace the roof, Osane concludes. "Finally, I came to the end of my patience. Before I could spend one more day following my applications from ministry to ministry, I had to make sure you and Nazar were all right. I left a friend to follow my paper trail, hailed a cab in Riyadh, and after a ten-hour ride through the desert, I am finally in your arms."

Osane watches the worry surface in my eyes, as I absorb the news of our tenuous future. Not wanting the magic we have created since his return to fade, he gives me a quick kiss and runs off the roof. Within a few minutes, he is back. In his hand he carries a small bundle, carefully wrapped in cloth. The material alone is beautiful. It's a rich maroon velvet embroidered with gold thread. The package feels light and flexible. As I unravel it, I can't believe my eyes. There, lying in my hands, is a full set of Saudi gold jewelry, my belated wedding present from Osane.

I hold up the largest piece, a pure gold necklace. The embedded stones are turquoise in color, and the chains link together to form horizontal strips of gold that are designed to fall below the neckline. Next, I examine the earrings. The gold chain loops together in a circle at the earlobe, from which three additional gold chains with turquoise stones hang. There is also a ring and a bracelet, created from the same pattern.

As I continue to stare in bewilderment, Osane explains that this is his sister's set of jewelry, which he's arranged to pay for over the ensuing years. I turn around and he carefully hooks on the necklace and bracelet, while I slip on the earrings and ring. I then strut around the roof like royalty, curtsying here, bowing there. Osane and I laugh together, and I hug him for his wonderful wedding gift.

When we return to our bedroom, I carefully lay my new treasures on strips of cotton. I place them with the other pieces of jewelry I had received. Pure gold rings, bracelets, necklaces, and earrings with exotic and expensive stones have been showered on me as wedding presents. By now, I have quite an extraordinary collection. Osane's set is my favorite, however, for his is a gift sparkling with love.

After I put my jewelry away, Osane and I slip silently into bed next to Nazar. With a smile on my face, I feel a contentment I hadn't felt for many months. Within seconds we are both fast asleep.

The next evening after dinner, it is announced that we will visit Osane's sister, Hannah. The pace of life has certainly livened since Osane's return. As I dress for the occasion, I bypass my mini-skirts and dress in the orange dress Sarah's family has made for me. I also slip on my new set of jewelry.

Osane enters the room and can't believe my transformation. With a smile and a hug he tells me how beautiful I look. "Christie, I'm pleasantly shocked to see my All-American Girl turned into a proper Saudi wife."

Meanwhile Nazar runs from room to room, happy to be going out on evening visits again. He particularly likes to go to Hannah's house, because of the children and the goats on the roof.

We find Hannah's son sitting in the street outside his house. He climbs the stone stairs and opens the iron door for us. As soon as we enter, the rest of the family greets us. Afterward Hannah pours coffee and tea. As I sit listening to the Arabic language reverberating around me, I contemplate the theory that the only real way to learn a language is to visit the mother country and live among the people. This principle, for me, is not working. I have reached a saturation point. My brain refuses to take in one more word of Arabic, and my ears have turned off. Left to contemplate the visual dimension, I spend the rest of the visit studying expressions and enjoying the feeling of togetherness.

The next afternoon, Sarah's son arrives at the door to say that his family is coming that evening to welcome Osane back from Riyadh. So once again, after dinner I put on my one dress and my jewelry and comb Nazar's hair.

I leave the bedroom to find Zora and Mina in the kitchen. Zora is pouring sunflower seeds and cashews into bowls, while Mina is popping popcorn. Suddenly there is a commotion on the stairs. Osane hears the loud knock and opens the door to find Sarah, Zainab, and the children. Nazar is beside himself. This is the first time he has seen all of Sarah's children in his home. There is the usual hugging, kissing, and taking of abayas. Even though everyone is family, the men walk into the majlis, while I join the women in the family room.

After about fifteen minutes, Zora leaves for the kitchen and I follow her. We find Walid there, collecting the prepared coffee and tea for the men. Meanwhile Zora carries beverages to the family room for the women. Throughout the visit, Sarah's children are extremely well behaved. From a young age, the Saudi children are trained to sit quietly while their elders visit. They are to be seen, but not heard. If they take too much popcorn or nuts, their hands are slapped. Mostly they simply sit and listen to the conversation, or stare into space.

A few hours later, desiring a chair to sit on, I collect my strength and enter the male living room. I am fully aware that I am going against customs, for it is sinful to be in a majlis full of men. Since there are only male relatives present, and because I am a foreigner, I'm hoping they are willing to stretch the rules. When I enter the room I'm greeted by smiles and Saeed stands up to give me his seat next to my husband.

"Christy," Osane whispers. "What are you doing?"

"Listen Osane, if I sit on the floor one more second my body is going to crack!" He shoots me a quick smile, before returning his attention to the general conversation.

As I sit in the room next to Osane, I somehow feel I have more in common with these men than with the women. Even if they only speak a few words of English, they are still educated and more exposed to the world. A few of them have traveled as far as Beirut, Egypt, or Italy. They are also outspoken and fun, and none of the shyness prevails in this room as it does in the woman's room.

Soon it is time for everyone to leave. Both rooms empty into the communal hallway. As abayas are passed around and cologne is poured into open palms, Zainab walks up to Osane and gives him a tender hug. While watching them, I notice a special connection. As Zainab touches Osane's face with her henna hands, I see her seventy-year-old face beam and her eyes fill with love. The light reflects off her gold earrings and her pierced nose piece, as she smiles at him during their short but intimate conversation.

Then the door suddenly opens and the conglomerate of relatives squeezes through. They take their commotion and their life force energies with them, and abruptly they are gone.

Chapter 17

A Death in the Family and Osane's Second Departure

"Death plucks my ears and says, 'Live—I am coming.'"
Virgil (70-19 B.C.)

The next afternoon Sarah's son again knocks on our door. The minute we see his face we know something is wrong. He doesn't say anything until we lead him into the family room and serve him tea. Finally, he tells us that Zainab is dead. She had begun her prayers that morning, suffered a heart attack and had fallen onto her prayer rug.

Nothing more is said. A shocked Osane puts on his otra and Zora and Mina leave to put on their abayas. Suddenly they are gone, leaving the rest of us in a state of disbelief and sadness.

Time crawls by until they return, late that evening. Only silence prevails, as everyone is in mourning. Later Osane takes me aside and tells me about the burial.

It seems Zora and Mina had washed Zainab's body, and dressed and wrapped her in cloth. This completed, the male relatives took the prepared body to the burial grounds. By tradition, she was lowered into her grave by the three people who were closest to her in life. The grave faced Mecca, and she was buried on the day she died.

It was said her death was the most beautiful death a Muslim could have, for she died during prayer. It was also said that Allah had kept her alive so that she could see Nazar, Osane and me. After our reunion, the relatives felt, Zainab was satisfied. Then she peacefully passed away.

Even so, it is a sudden blow. It will take Osane some time to get over her death. It will also be hard for Osane to carry the news of Zainab's death to his Uncle Hamid. Zainab had been living with her brother in Southern Arabia, and had only left to greet us.

The next afternoon, we drive to Sarah's house to pay our respects. Osane warns me to be prepared. For one month, Sarah's home will be in mourning. Family and friends will bring meals, and professional criers will lead the women in loud, high wails. The family will spend hours rocking back and forth, physically crying out their misery.

As we pull up to Sarah's gate, I am very apprehensive. The house that had been so full of life will now be sated with death. We find the family in the majlis. Sarah looks up at us and starts crying. She pulls us down close beside her, grabs Osane's hand, and starts swaying back and forth. I take her other hand, telling her in English how sorry I am. She gazes at me through tears and nods her head, signifying she understands my words of comfort. After about twenty minutes, there is a knock on the gate. Osane has to leave the room, for female neighbors are bringing in food and want to pay their respects.

A short time later, it is time to leave. Sarah, the girls, and I come out of the female quarters. A few last words are spoken about Zainab, a few more tears are shed, and we are soon back on the street heading home.

The next day is Friday, the Saudi one-day weekend. The relatives decide it will be healing for everyone to get out of the apartment and into the fresh air of the desert. I walk into the bedroom and put on my pants and a pair of flat shoes. I come out ready for a desert romp, expecting Zora and Mina to do likewise. Instead, I find them in their usual dressy clothes plus high heels and abayas. I grab Nazar, and we are soon in the car heading out of the city and into the freedom of open space.

Everyone's spirits rise, the further we drive into the desert. We open all the windows and Zora and Mina allow their abayas to blow off. The Arabic music from the radio blares and for the moment, sadness leaves our spirits.

With my eyes accustomed to the desert, the landscape looks alive and lush. The many hills are pebbled rubble, but the valleys are full of succulents and desert trees. In many of these vales, there are also large wadis or river beds. These areas are dry now, but during rainstorms, they grow into major rivers.

Saeed turns off the paved highway and onto a dirt road, which crosses open desert. Nazar is having a ball bouncing through the dips and bumps, as we speed through the soft sand so we won't get stuck. Finally, Saeed stops the car on a level area of hard sand, under a clump of trees lining a wadi. As the perpetual wind of the desert blows through everyone's hair, Zora and Mina pull out a carpet from the trunk. It is so good to see them outside, without their abayas. There is no need for a black shroud in the privacy of the desert.

Nazar sits down on the rug, while I start to hike down the empty wadi. I breathe deeply, finding myself alone at last. I absorb the vastness of a desert that stretches unbroken as far as the eye can see. As I feel my batteries recharging, I hear sounds. It doesn't take much imagination to figure out who is fumbling and tripping over rocks behind me. With a shout of "Mommy," Nazar is in my arms and the two of us are off.

Feeling we have wandered far enough up the wadi, we turn around. After all, this land is new to me and I haven't become desert-wise. When we reach the carpet, Mina and Zora are starting out for their walk. I sit down, drink my tea, and watch their short stroll. Casually I wonder how far they can walk in sand with high heels on.

With the setting sun, Osane puts the carpet back in the car. Refreshed, we once again drive through open desert, searching for the ribbon of pavement that will lead us back into town. About twenty minutes later, I look over and find Zora and Mina completely covered. This must mean we are getting close to Taif. As we approach the apartment, it is comforting to know that wide open space is only half an hour away.

The next week passes quickly. Sprinkled through daily events is the reality that Osane will soon be leaving for Riyadh. No matter how I attempt to freeze time, the minutes tick by.

The sun inevitably rises on the day of Osane's dreaded departure. He will be traveling the first paved road to connect Riyadh to Jeddah, which was only completed in 1967. During the intense desert summer, this drive is usually made at night. Although this is winter, enabling day travel, the real danger is the driver. It is still Ramadan and these drivers are fasting, which means they spend most of the night up. I remember Osane telling me that twice during his previous 10-hour journey home, he had told his driver to pull over and take a quick nap. Three other times, he had to insist that the driver stop for tea. In between, he had created as many conversations as possible to keep the driver on the road.

On the departure morning, Osane arranges for a taxi to be waiting outside the apartment at 7 am. We are up long before anyone else. As we walk hand-in-hand through the marble hallway towards the door, I feel lonely already. Somehow, I am feeling much older than my twenty-three years, for life has suddenly become so difficult.

This parting is very hard for Osane also. So with a quick kiss and an opening and shutting of the door, he is gone. I retrace my steps through the hallway into my room, close the door, and slip into the neutrality of sleep.

I wake to the sounds of washing day. Wanting to keep busy, I join in. As we dump bucket after bucket of water into the wringer washer, I reflect that this washroom and storage area is my favorite part of the apartment. From it, you can see the sky and hear the noises from other units.

I have become quite familiar with the voices of the family living directly across the courtyard. Since the windows are staggered for optimum privacy, I have no way of catching a glimpse of this family. The only information I gather is that they are Syrian.

This gives me the literary license to concoct my own images. In my fantasy world I imagine five children, mostly male and mostly preschool age. The mother spends a great deal of time yelling at her offspring, trying to keep them under control. I sympathize with her, for it must be very difficult to raise her children within the confines of an apartment. Since she isn't living on the top floor, she doesn't have roof privileges. Because it isn't proper for good children to play in the streets, I conclude the only space she can offer her children is her small home.

That evening, Mina hands me the blue scarf I have designed as a rebellion against the black silk scarf that all females are required to wear. She has just finished sewing on the white leaves that line one edge of the scarf. Between my white raincoat and my new blue scarf, I conform to the cultural demands to be covered without wearing one thread of black. This is my stand, my own private rebellion against the abaya.

I carry my new design into the bathroom mirror. I tie it around my head, trying many different positions. The look I am searching for is one of fullness, for I hate the flat scarf look. Finally, I pull the end of the scarf with its white leaves to the middle of my forehead, allowing it to droop from ear to ear, creating an Arabian Nights effect.

When I walk out to show the relatives, they politely control their thoughts. With as much honesty as they can muster, they neutrally nod their heads and smile. Figuring I will learn my lesson from the gestures in the streets, they patiently wait to see how long I will last in my youthful revolt against their ancient culture.

A few afternoons later, Saeed leaves for Southern Arabia on business. The remaining women and one child become the responsibility of teenage Walid, the only male of our household.

With Saeed gone, transportation becomes a problem. His car sits abandoned in the parking lot below the apartment, while we are left stranded. For males there is no real driving age, and it is not unusual to see young boys driving pickup trucks, jeeps, or cars. Saeed, however, forbids Walid to drive his car, feeling he is still too young.

On the other hand, it is against the law for females to drive. If a foreign woman is found driving, her whole family will be deported. If the authorities find a Saudi woman, or a foreign woman married to a Saudi, behind the wheel, the husband will be put into prison.

A few days after Saeed leaves, there is a knock on the door and Mina greets a woman and her several children. Whenever

Zora and Mina have company, I am torn. Most of me doesn't want to go in and be stared at, but since I'm a family member it is considered polite to appear and greet them. I therefore dutifully enter the room and sit next to Mina.

During a break in the conversation, I quietly ask who the guests are. Mina mutters, "Syrian," pointing to the apartment across the courtyard. All of a sudden, my interest is piqued. I even become excited, for I am finally able to put faces to the voices I have heard for so many days.

As the women chat, I study our Syrian visitors. The first thing I notice is their light complexion. I have lived so long among olive-skinned Saudis that the whiteness of their skin seems exaggerated. Their faces are also broader and their hair is straighter than their Saudi counterparts. The mother is much younger and prettier than I expected and the children are sitting in the normal, well-behaved manner of Arab children.

They in turn are staring at me, judging my every feature. By now, I am used to this scrutiny. After the proper amount of time elapses, I quietly leave the room, satisfied that the voices next door finally have real faces.

Chapter 18

Further Melding into the Saudi Culture

"Things do not change; we change."
Henry David Thoreau

After the guests leave, I walk into the kitchen to prepare Nazar's meal and realize I have run out of baby food. This isn't a great obstacle, for right across the street from the apartment is a pharmacy, which carries a whole line of Gerber's baby food.

A few times before, I had asked Walid to run across the street and bring back what was needed. I therefore walk into the family room and find Walid studying. I point to Nazar's empty baby food jar, and he nods his head in comprehension.

I walk back into the kitchen and wait. This time, instead of going right away, Walid goes back to his studying. As the minutes tick by, an irrational anger begins bubbling within me, and I can feel my body tensing. Here I am, a mature adult. I'm not even permitted to go across the street for my own son's food. Once I allow myself the luxury of this thought, my mind starts to roll.

Suddenly I begin pacing. I stomp out to the storage room and scream to the sky. "Every time I turn around, my every need is dependent on other people! I can't go to the market unless the whole family goes! I can't escape into the desert unless a male drives me there! I can't even visit anyone unless the whole crew comes along!"

My patience gone, I tramp to my bedroom and slip on my raincoat and black scarf. Opening the apartment door, I walk down the stairs, shoving some money Osane had given me into my pocket. The fact that I have no idea what this Saudi money means, since the relatives or Osane have always purchased everything, doesn't deter me.

I've just reached the last step when I hear Walid come bounding down the stairs. He grabs both of my arms and goes on and on in Arabic, leading me back up the stairs and into the apartment. Then he is gone. He returns a few minutes later with not one, but a whole carton of baby food jars.

The whole family is now surrounding me. It seems I have once again caused quite a commotion. Through their words and gestures, I comprehend that Walid is sorry he hadn't gotten up right away. I also clearly understand from them that it is not permissible for me to **ever** leave the apartment alone.

As the family settles for tea, I slip into a corner, not wanting to make any further mistakes. Exasperation hangs over me like a dark rain cloud. I feel the culture suffocating me like an octopus, pulling me down farther and farther into its murky, black suppression. To keep from pacing and causing another scene, I close my eyes and meditate on huge waves crashing with mighty force onto a windy ocean beach. As the white water swirls back to sea and the wind splits palm trees with its ferocity, my breathing calms slightly. With frustrated anger still seething within me, I create a mental twister, which I set down on a deserted island. The surging wind uproots and destroys everything in its path. As wood splinters and plants fly, my anger finally dissipates enough for me to simply breathe. For long moments, I stare into a clear blue ocean pool, surrounded by coral. The cool breezes dry the sweat on my forehead, calming my whole body even more.

When I feel centered enough, I re-enter the present. Slowly I open my eyes onto my Arabian environment. Still unsettled, I pick up a pad of paper and pencil, for writing has always been therapeutic. Besides my daily journal, I have decided to record different aspects of Saudi life. On my clean sheet of paper I write, *The Complex Rules Surrounding Male and Female Interactions*. Of course the rule book changes according to what part of the Kingdom you live in.

Relieved to keep my mind occupied, I start jotting. I begin in Southern Arabia where Osane was born. This is the isolated green belt of the Kingdom. I write that it is only since the 1950s, after Saud conquers the area, that men and women are separated. When Osane was growing up, there were cafeterias on street corners where men and women mixed. Villagers used their prettiest daughters to sell their goods at the local markets and even now, the rules surrounding male-female mixing are not as extreme.

Another area of Arabia runs along the Red Sea and is called the Hejaz. This section remains independent and proud because it is the home of the holy cities of Mecca and Medina. Since ancient times, the Hejaz has served as a crossroads between Arabia, Africa, Asia, and Europe. The influx of pilgrims from all over the Muslim world plus the constant parade of traders has created a more open society. Over time, the Hejaz has developed its own music, folktales, and cuisine. It is therefore not surprising that the interaction between males and females is more liberal, especially in the seaport city of Jeddah, the cultural hub of Saudi Arabia.

In the Nazdi tribal area of central Riyadh, the rules are much stricter. In this desert area, a woman's eyes are permitted to rest only on her husband, her father, her brothers, and her sons. She cannot see male cousins, or even the husbands of married sisters. Even if they live in the same household, her sisters' husbands are never allowed to see her face.

There are also many universal codes of behavior. Throughout the Kingdom, before a door or a gate is opened, the question of "Who?" is asked. If it is an unrelated man, and there are no males at home, the visitor will be turned away. If a male is at home, the female will find him. He will then open the door and the male guests will gather in the men's living room, while the women and small children enter the women's part of the house.

When male visitors are in the home, the women of the household listen for a buzzer signaling for coffee, tea, or food. After the preparation, a female places it in front of the closed door of the men's living room, knocks quietly, and quickly leaves. The youngest male of the household opens the door, and serves whatever has been left. These roles reverse when women come to call. The men have to leave the women's side of the house, and take refuge in their quarters.

It is much simpler if you don't live in an apartment. In a villa, there are two gates, each leading into separate sides of the house. There is a big gate for the men and a small gate for the women.

By the time I finish my writing it is getting late. The relatives have turned off the TV and are getting ready for bed. I am still too unsettled to think of sleep. Still seeking refuge in reflections, I once again pick up my pen. My tone, however, has switched from analytical to therapeutic. My inner world is shifting and these changes are subtle, and submerged in mysterious shadows. Attempting to allow these nebulous feelings to surface, I give free rein to my pen as I begin scribbling, *The Tale of the Yemeni Gasman.*

I begin by noting that the only male who regularly visits the female section of any home is the Yemeni gasman. This is because large, metal propane tanks fuel Arabian stoves. Since the gas usually runs out during the critical part of cooking, most families keep two tanks, making sure one tank is full at all times.

The first time the gasman visits Zora's apartment, I answer the door and let him in. As he walks through the hallway to the kitchen to exchange propane tanks, he stares at me, and I stare back at him. Meanwhile Zora and Mina are hiding behind hall doors, and they shout at me to do likewise. I stubbornly strike a pose in the middle of the hall and wave at the small man as he leaves, empty tank in hand. "What next," I think!

Several days later, the gasman pays us another visit. As he walks down the marble hall on his way to the kitchen, I too am pressed behind a hall door. The hiding isn't that bad. The fear that is creeping throughout my being is. As I press closer to the wall, not wanting the gasman to see even a piece of my dress, I realize that I am afraid of this man, and that I am becoming afraid of all men. The worst part is that even though I am aware, I can't harness the fear. Every day that I stay in this patriarchal culture, the non-conformist part of me is slowly being suffocated. I have always been a fighter, but how much strength does one grain of sand have in an enormous desert?

Finally tired, I put my pen and paper away and walk into the bedroom to lie down next to Nazar. Within seconds I am asleep. The next morning Nazar and I rise at the regular time, and the events of the day fall into the routine of the days before.

That evening, while Osane takes care of Nazar, I decide to accompany Zora and Mina to the material market. Zora is out of thread, and I need material to sew a brown and blue skirt. I put on my raincoat and my new blue scarf. Then I wait as Zora and Mina tie the black-netted scarf around their necks and then drop, one, two, and finally three veils over their faces. Most women drop two veils, but since Zora and Mina's father had been a ruler, their behavior is carefully regulated. Their station requires the densest veils.

Soon we are out the door. As we walk closer to the market place, more males begin to gather. Through experience, I have learned some crowd survival techniques. The trick is to never make eye contact. You can look to either side, look down, but never look into eyes. This strategy erects enough of a barrier to make shopping possible.

This evening however, the glaring is more intense and is accompanied by points and snickers. Quickening my pace, I try to outrun the ridicule my blue scarf is creating. Realizing we are only halfway to our destination and knowing that the tension will only increase if I shed the scarf all together, I compromise by rearranging it. Without taking it off, I pull the material tighter around my head and knot it at my throat to create the flat look the Saudis seem to love. I then stuff the white leaves that Mina had so patiently attached, down into my raincoat. By buttoning the coat's top button and pulling the collar up around my ears, the ridicule seems to lessen, but nothing can heal my bruised ego.

Through all this drama, Zora and Mina never leave my side. Now they quicken their pace, as if speed will lighten my mood. We are soon in the material market, and they begin showing me one roll of material after another.

Carefully, I chose two wool blends. It doesn't take long to pick up the rest of the needed goods. We are soon winding our way back to the apartment, passing through the vegetable and fruit markets, the shoe section, the gold suq, and through the part of the market where old men sit on the ground in front of colorful pieces of frayed material. On this cloth, they display different kinds of incense, and gum made out of pine pitch. Among their items are branches the Saudis cut into pencil lengths. They then chew the ends loose and use them as toothbrushes.

When we enter our apartment I stomp into my bedroom, close the door, and angrily throw my blue scarf onto the floor. Each day that passes finds me more worn down. I close my eyes and sit down, tears of frustration running down my face. I dream of projecting myself into the middle of a large shopping center in the United States. It would be bliss to sit on a bench and have people walk by and not even notice me. Blending in, that's all I really want to do.

Refusing to succumb to any more depression, I force myself to accept the only logical decision. If I truly want to meld into this culture, it will be necessary to wear my black scarf. I will have to tie the black scarf tightly around my head, and tuck in my blond hair. I will also have to wear dark sunglasses to hide my blue eyes and wear no makeup. The price of invisibility no longer seems as steep as it once did. Perhaps this is the only way to remain sane in this new world of darkness.

The next morning I feel much more at peace, the inevitable lull after the storm. The days continue to slip by. With my new sense of conformity at the front of my mind, the relatives and I fall into a workable and even living pattern. I am reminded of a piece by Henry David Thoreau called *Say it Thrice*. "Our life is frittered away by detail. Simplicity, simplicity, simplicity! I say, let your affairs be as two or three, and not a hundred or a thousand."

Zora and I spend a lot of time together. She is teaching me to sew and she is quite a perfectionist. If any of my seams aren't lined up properly, she will point at them. I will then spend anywhere from a half-hour upwards tearing them out. Somehow, we have risen above the language barrier. Our needs are met through gestures and expressions.

Several evenings later, before falling to sleep, I conclude that I am doing much better through this second separation. I have learned to keep myself busier. The bonds between the relatives and me are growing stronger each day, my Arabic is slowly improving and between gestures, expressions, and elementary Arabic words, I actually find myself communicating. On a deeper level, I realize that I am adjusting to Saudi Arabia only because *I* am changing.

Early the next morning, wanting to warm up, Nazar and I climb up to the sunny roof. We throw chunks of cement I find into a pile. While Nazar is making a fort with the different cement shapes, I climb up on top of this pile and look out over the wall and onto the desert. My soul yearns for the rejuvenation I know I can find in its vastness. If only I could stand in the middle of such space, I might be able to escape from my haunting voices.

Suddenly I spot Saeed's abandoned car sitting in the parking lot. As my mind begins to spin, I realize I also know where his keys are. Fully aware I am thinking down forbidden paths, I can't stop my voices from picking up momentum.

Why can't I dress in one of Osane's thobes? I can wear his headdress, droop it over my face, and wear sunglasses. Sitting in a car, who can tell I am a woman? I quickly think of a flaw in my plan. If I am stopped, I won't be able to speak enough Arabic. But if I can talk Mina or Zora into going with me, they can speak for me. It isn't as if we would be driving on a major freeway system. Our escape route into the desert is a quiet, two-lane road.

As I jump down from my pile of cement, I tell myself the plan is not only crazy, but dangerous. As the day wears on, I find myself following Mina up onto the roof where she is studying for an exam. I watch her for a while, trying to suppress my thoughts of escape. In the end, my emotions overcome my reason. Using broken Arabic and our nonverbal language, I tell her of my plan. After my prodding she is finally more than half-convinced, and we begin giggling and laughing in anticipation of a great adventure.

Meanwhile, I run into my room and open our suitcase. I am searching for my driver's license midst the documents we keep in a plastic bag. I have these papers spread all over the floor when there is a knock on the apartment door. Angered at the interruption, I rise and run to the door, asking "Meen," or, "who is it?" To my complete amazement, I hear Osane! I open the door to find him staring back at me.

As he reaches out and grabs me, it is as if I am hugging his hologram, for I am emotionally unprepared for his arrival. With his arms and energy surrounding me, I finally feel grounded and my haunting voices vanish. From my new perspective, the craziness of our desert adventure overcomes me. It is as if Osane has arrived home just in time to save us from ourselves.

Chapter 19

Family Reunion and Eid

"The ornament of a house is the friends who frequent it. There is no event greater in life than the appearance of new persons about our hearth, except it be the progress of the character which draws them."

Ralph Waldo Emerson

After our hug, the rest of the family materializes from different directions for their greetings. Osane swings Nazar in the air and we all make our way into the family room for tea. Sitting beside Osane, I listen as he tells the relatives his adventures. As I watch his expressions, I can't help noticing a change in him. He seems older, his smile isn't as spontaneous, he is more serious, and a cloud has settled over him. After tea, we excuse ourselves and adjourn to our bedroom.

Finally alone, Osane begins pacing the room. In a frustrated voice he states, "Christie, I am at a standstill with the government! They are still passing my papers from desk to desk. No matter how patient and logical I am, no one is listening. My pleas have fallen on deaf ears. In addition, my meeting with Uncle Hamid was awful. Our initial reunion was splendid, but then I was forced to tell him about Zainab's death. Hamid was crushed. Her death was so unexpected, and the joy of our reunion vanished!"

Osane's bleak mood penetrates me. Little does he realize that I have also developed closets in my soul. In my choice to "blend in," I have inhaled the fear of men. This is now affecting me in the most private area of all, my intimacy with my own husband. Osane has just returned from a long trip and both of us are choosing talk over lovemaking.

I shake my head, physically cracking the mood that fills the room. This will not do. I take Osane's hand and place it on my heart, beginning to massage each finger slowly and sensuously. Gradually, very gradually, the dark heaviness begins to vaporize and warmth sparks between us.

As I touch his face, he begins caressing my body. Slowly a desperate passion ignites, and in a fury we reclaim each other. Within our unity a small ray of sunshine sprouts, to heal our wounded spirits. We spend the night tightly wrapped around each other. The new day finds us recommitted to our combined future.

It is no surprise when the next evening, Osane announces that we are going to pay his arrival visit to Hannah and Aunt Sarah. The household is more than eager for an evening out, for we have been home bound for far too many days.

We all walk to Saeed's car and step in, none of us realizing that Osane hasn't driven a stick shift before. The car rolls onto the street and stalls out. Osane restarts the car and we jerk here and jerk there. Zora and Mina begin reciting Arabic prayers such as, "May God be with us" or "May God look after us." As usual humor overtakes us. Soon we are all in tears of laughter, and by some miracle our car bumps all the way to Hannah's house.

Hannah is as gracious as ever. However, with the major holiday of Eid so close, there is an underlying feeling of sadness. Even though Hannah's husband is dead, you can feel his missed presence everywhere.

Since these are short visits, we leave Hannah's house and jerk our way to Sarah's. As usual, the welcome is lavish. It is obvious the house is still in mourning, for some of the children's dresses are torn, and one or two heads of hair look uncombed.

Osane tells Sarah about his visit with Uncle Hamid. Once again the Kleenex boxes are passed around, and the room fills with wet eyes and sobs. After visiting for about an hour, we also bid farewell to Sarah's family.

The next day, Zora and Mina's brother Osama comes back from his university in Jeddah. It is so wonderful to see him, for he is a ray of sunshine. He's always making jokes and causing laughter to ring throughout the rooms.

While Nazar sits on his lap, he tells the rest of the family his stories. Throughout the narrative, I keep eyeing Osama's briefcase. Knowing he is a business major, I assume he has lots of homework over the Eid vacation. Wondering if any of his textbooks are in English, I ask Osane if I can glance through any of Osama's schoolbooks.

Osane, with a devilish expression, translates this to Osama. The whole family bursts out laughing. Osama picks up his briefcase, opens it, and turns it upside down. The result is the spilling out of dirty underwear, thobes, handkerchiefs, and t-shirts. It appears the homework to be completed over vacation is to be done on Zora's washing day, not by Osama the business major.

That evening, Saeed returns from Southern Arabia. His arrival is also marked by laughter, excitement, and rapid conversation. The household is now close to overflowing with activity, chatter, and happiness. Joyously the family has gathered for the three-day celebration of Eid ul-Fitr, marking the end of Ramadan.

I am eager to learn the many traditions and rituals surrounding this festivity. I watch as Saeed leaves for the market to buy a whole assortment of special Eid candy and nuts. Zora and Mina busy themselves with beating out any dust that dares to exist in the apartment. Walid goes clothes shopping with the money that Saeed has brought from his father in the South. Meanwhile I dig down into our suitcases and pull out an outfit my mother had given Nazar before we left. I hope it still fits.

It is customary during Eid for each family to give a tenth of what they are worth to the poor. Saeed pulls out a big mat, into which Walid pours bags of flour plus gold. They both re-bag the mixture into smaller bags, and Walid carries these bags plus lamb and other foods to the poor in our neighborhood.

As the clocks tick towards Eid and the end of Ramadan, electricity fills the air and anticipation grows. The evening before Eid, Zora and Mina are busily ironing and cleaning. If they have to, they will stay up the whole night to prepare for the first day visitors.

It is difficult for Nazar to settle down and sleep that evening, for there is so much activity in the house. After awhile, I say goodnight to the relatives and climb in bed next to Nazar.

The next morning, the first day of Eid finally arrives. After a large sunrise breakfast, which traditionally breaks the Ramadan fasting, tea is served. Afterwards we dress in our new clothes and prepare to greet our first visitors. As the hours tick by, there are no visitors. Trying to keep Nazar clean in his good clothes is becoming bothersome. I finally ask Osane why, if no one is coming to visit us, don't we go visit someone else?

"Christie," he explains. "It is proper to stay at home during the first morning of Eid. We will go visiting, but later."

My logical American mind is having problems with the concept of everyone staying at home, and also visiting. Luckily, I am saved from my pondering by the arrival of our first guest.

Walid excitedly jumps up and opens the door to find one of the many relatives, wearing his Army uniform. As he walks into the family room, there is the traditional "Mabruk el Eid" greeting (Congratulations on the Eid). Then candy is passed around, and laughter and fun fill the room. After the relative leaves, several other visitors come. Again, there's congratulations on the Eid, candy is passed, and the conversation is full of humor, with the feeling of a continuing party.

That evening, Sarah arrives with her family of ten. The mourning seems to have been left behind, and smiles have replaced tears. As I take Sarah's abaya, I feel the love connection that has been developing between us. I so admire her aura of matriarchal strength. She is clearly the mainstay of this large family. She expects order and discipline, but is also a constant source of love and support.

The girls resemble miniature models with their patent leather shoes and purses. Each one of them wears a new dress and their hair is tied up with large, satin bows. Gold bracelets dangle, their earrings shine, and the henna used in washing their jet-black hair makes it sparkle with red highlights.

While I am admiring the girls, Osane pulls me aside. "Here, Christie," he says, handing me some money. "Go around to each of Sarah's girls, shake their hand, congratulate them on the Eid, open their purses, and slip in some money. They will strongly object, but be firm."

Meanwhile, Osane walks around filling up the boys' new thobe pockets with money. The children are thrilled, and the adults are having just as much fun.

All of a sudden, Nazar runs up to me, paper money flowing out of his hands. His little baby suit has no pockets, but Nazar cares more about the attention than the money anyhow. I watch as Zora and Mina pass around more candy, coffee, and tea. It is magical being a member of such a large family. I breathe in the love, and say a prayer of thanks that Sarah's family looks so happy again.

The rest of Eid passes quickly, more visits here and there, and then it is over. Life slowly falls back into its ordinary routines. My evenings once again find me in front of the TV. To keep my mind occupied, I resume writing. As the Arab singers preform their endless songs, I begin a piece on Arabian families.

Most Saudi families, I write, follow similar patterns. Saeed's schedule is very typical. He rises around 6 o'clock, prays, and walks to the market to buy the fresh fruit, vegetables, bread, and meat the women need for their day of cooking. Next, he eats breakfast and is at work by 8 o'clock. Most Saudi males are government employees, with their workdays ending at 2 pm.

After work, Saeed drives home, prays again, and eats his main meal between 2:30 and 3:00. He will then take a short nap, get up around 4:00, pray, and enter the family room for tea. The TV shows begin around 6:00. Most families settle in front of the TV, having a light supper around 9:00. This meal is usually leftovers from dinner.

Bedtime varies in each household. Since TV shuts off between 11:00 and 12:00, families usually go to bed around that time. The children have no set bedtime. They simply fall asleep wherever they run out of energy. An adult in these communal households will either put a blanket or sheet over them, or gently carry them to their rooms.

Ordinary daily schedules are sprinkled with visits. Sometimes the whole family will visit, but just as often the men will leave their women and children at home. Some women complain that their husbands never stay home. Each evening finds these husbands at their male friends' for cards, tea, and conversation. Even if the families do go together, they will enter the house by different doors, and the men will stay in their quarters while the women stay in theirs.

As the evening news blares through the TV, I turn the page in my notebook and begin a new topic. I jot the title: *The Relationship Between Husband and Wife, which is very complex indeed.* On the surface, the disadvantages of Saudi marriages seem obvious and very daunting. Couples appear distant, for any physical contact is limited to the bedroom. They are also seldom alone, since men group with men while women and children become part of the harem. The Koran and the Sha'ria states that a man can have four wives, but he must treat them fairly and equally. If a male wants to divorce his wife, he simply repeats, "I divorce thee," three times in front of male witnesses.

On the other hand, the advantages of Saudi marriages are camouflaged and very subtle, like a rainbow piercing a rainy mist. In most households there is a feeling of love, respect, and peace among couples. A major reason for this lack of friction is that the wife has a large security base. Loneliness and insecurity are seldom an issue. If a woman is divorced, she will simply go back to live with her father's family. All children under six will remain with her. When the boys become seven they will go to live with their father. Therefore she will never be forced into the job market to raise her children alone. This feeling of belonging to a strong group of family and friends enhances the wife's self-esteem.

The next evening Osane visits one of his male friends. That leaves the rest of us, as usual, gathered around the TV. Saeed with his shisha or hookah is much more interesting than Egyptian plays, so I re-focus my attention on his preparation ritual.

In his first step, Saeed painstakingly prepares coals for his pipe. He heats up these coals on the kitchen stove and then transfers them to the top of his shisha. He leaves the stem, the main part of the pipe, right outside the family room. Next, he uncoils the cord until it reaches his sitting position on the floor. The rest of the evening is spent passing the pipe from Saeed to Osama and back.

Each time the smoke is inhaled, there's a bubbling sound. As it is exhaled, a very strong tobacco odor floats through the room. At first this odor gives me a headache, and I can't spend longer than ten minutes in the family room. Even opening the windows doesn't help. As time passes, however, I become accustomed to it, even to the point where I begin to find the scent quite pleasant.

While Osama is home from University, he spends most of his evenings visiting his many male friends. After tea, he customarily walks to the clothing tree at the head of the room, right beside the TV. I watch as he takes off his pajama top, exposing the sleeveless T-shirt Saudi men wear. After pulling the thobe on, he takes off his pajama bottoms from underneath. He then puts on his skullcap or gaba, and drapes his large white scarf or otra over his head. Often he will straighten it and throw one corner over his shoulder. Finally, he grabs Saeed's car keys, says goodbye, and off he goes for another evening of fun. In a society so full of extreme modesty and rules governing female behavior, this male ritual always amuses me.

The next Friday, Zora and Osane decide we should go into the desert for an official picnic. Since this is my first Arab picnic, I immediately think of hot dogs, hamburgers, and potato salad. I quickly find out that these items are not on the menu. Instead, Arab families usually spend the day killing, skinning, and cooking a sheep. Our outing however, will only involve shish kebabs.

Once again our large household piles into the car, but this time we are loaded down with food. The radio is turned on, spirits are high, and hands are clapping. For this outing, Saeed chooses to drive farther down the main road. When we head into the desert, the terrain is hillier and thicker with vegetation.

Osane stops the car on a small rise. The family exits the car and slides down into a tree-lined wadi. It is so peaceful and isolated. I note that the vegetation appears dirty because of the continuously blowing sand. Nevertheless, flowers are budding from many succulents, and they paint the wadi in vivid colors.

The main attraction for me is the freedom of the big sky. I sit on our bluff and look past the fantastic rock formations carved out by the blowing sand, and out onto the horizon. The solitude creeps into my bones, and I sit there collecting energy. What a magnificent place to meditate.

I am pulled back to the present by shouts of "dinner" from Zora and Osane, who are almost done cooking. Ground lamb, wrapped around skewers, is cooking over an open fire and has created a wonderful aroma. Zora places this plateful of kebabs on the carpet. Beside the meat is a bowl of tomatoes and onions with lemon dressing, and plates of bread and fruit.

After the picnic, tea is served and more walks are taken. As we rest on the communal rug, we can see a puff of dust way out in the distance. This signifies a jeep or a pickup truck, and another family driving out for a relaxing afternoon in the desert.

The fresh air makes us all pleasantly sleepy. Soon we are packing up our picnic and climbing up the wadi to our car. Walid switches on the radio, and we listen to Arab singers as our car heads back to Taif and our apartment.

Chapter 20

A Saudi Christmas

"The heart of man is made to reconcile contradictions."
David Hume

The end of the Eid holiday marks a shift in our household. The first to leave is Osama. As he resumes his University studies, he takes with him his wonderful sense of humor. I remember my mother saying, "Laughter lightens your load and lifts your heart into heavenly places." These last few days of laughter have certainly allowed all of our spirits to soar.

Osane's departure time is also approaching. Each morning, I have been crossing off the days on an Arabic calendar hanging in the family room. Since the Western calendar is based on the sun and the Saudi calendar is moon based, tracking dates is difficult. I dimly realize that we are somewhere in December, and that Osane is planning to leave on the Arabic number he has circled.

It is only when I find a Western calendar buried among our official papers, that I am able to decipher which day Osane is actually leaving. I drop my pencil when I realize that his departure date is December 25, my first Christmas away from home.

Trying to stop the passage of time, I once again attempt to elongate each second. However, the minutes slip through my grasp, no matter how hard I try. Then, one early morning before dawn, Osane walks down the familiar hallway and is gone.

Once again I feel sliced in half. I retreat into our bedroom and the usual cloak of depression engulfs me. Not only is Osane gone, but today is Christmas! Remembering the decorated trees, carols, smells, gifts, and Christmas dinner of home, I sit barely moving in our small bedroom. Suddenly it dawns on me that no one within hundreds of miles even knows what Christmas means.

The house slowly comes to life. Nazar reaches up and grabs my hand, pulling me out of the bedroom. As we walk into the kitchen, the relatives greet us. In heavy accents, they wish us a Merry Christmas. Then they begin singing and clapping their hands. It seems that before Osane left, he told them about this strange Western holiday. He also explained how hard it will be for me to celebrate this Christian holiday in a country of Muslims.

Since it is Friday and the Saudi weekend, the relatives' Christmas gift to us is a picnic. The festive mood is catching as we gather the picnic supplies. As we head out into the desert, Nazar and I sing Christmas carols, as Saeed tries to find the perfect spot. He turns onto a small desert road and circles a clump of trees. My mind is saying this is fine, but my voice remains silent. Out of consideration to the relatives who are trying to make my Christmas Day a celebration, I feel the picnic destination should be theirs.

We circle three more perfectly acceptable spots, but for some reason each spot won't do. We finally approach a large rock formation. This dramatic structure rises from the flat desert floor, and is the size of a small building. The relative's eyes are focused on this splendid rock, while my eyes are riveted on the ground. Trash is piled in every direction. Somehow, we have landed in a village junkyard.

As the car stops, my insides scream no, but my mouth remains closed. We exit the car and all I can feel is nausea, for it is simply not safe to let Nazar roam over this terrain. Cut glass, cans, old Pepsi bottles, and much more are everywhere. Not knowing how I am going to survive this picnic, my spirits drop. Don't the relatives see the trash?

As my mood hits rock bottom, determination takes over. I find branches and begin breaking them off, until I have enough twigs to make a bundle. I begin sweeping a small area of the desert floor. I mimic the strokes I've seen Mina and Zora use to sweep their rugs. The relatives look over and wonder what I am doing. By this point, I don't care what anybody thinks. I have to clean up a small play area for Nazar.

When I am done, I plunk him in the middle of the clearing with a pile of rocks to play with. As Zora and Mina begin a cooking fire, I leave on a scouting trip to find a clean area. No matter how far I walk in any direction, I can't get out of the trash. Resolving to make the best of this outing, I make my way back through the mess to Nazar. He's still interested in the glitter of his pile of rocks and has stayed in the middle of his circle.

Dinner is soon heated up. On the rug Mina places a rice and lamb dish, a tomato salad, flat bread, and baskets of fruit. After dinner, as Saeed and Zora sip their tea, Nazar and I follow Mina and Walid into a narrow wadi. This small, sanded area has less trash in it, so I feel more comfortable here. Dear

Walid slips a small tape into his radio and Chubby Checker's "Let's Twist Again" blares into the open desert.

Walid turns the volume up, yelling, "Christmas Christie," and motions for me to dance. When I begin twisting, the others join in, and we all break into healing laughter. Walid turns the music up even louder, and Nazar begins jumping up and down in pure excitement.

Nazar, Walid, Mina, and I continue to twist to Chubby Checker until we drop to the desert floor in exhaustion. Our Christmas in a small wadi, in the middle of a village junkyard isn't white....but somehow my Muslim relatives innately know the true meaning of Christmas.

Chapter 21

Every Day a Lesson

"A moment's insight is sometimes worth a life's experience."
Oliver Wendell Holmes

With the holidays over, the family room turns into a sewing workshop. Fabric and patterns are spread everywhere, and the sound of the sewing machine is constant. Zora is working on three dresses. I am pinning together two skirts, while Nazar plays with leftover fabric strips.

As we sew, it begins to rain. Midwinters in Saudi Arabia are rainy months, and often-heavy drops fall for days at a time. This dampness sharpens the cold. Since Zora and Mina's apartment has no heat, the only way to warm up is to bundle under blankets. As a secondary source of heat, I learn to walk into the kitchen and turn on a gas burner. By circling my hands over the stove, I am able to warm up my whole body.

After several days of rain, the weather finally breaks. Since we are low on thread, it is decided that Zora, Mina and I will make a quick trip to the market.

Excited to get into the fresh air, I quickly follow the relatives down the stairs and into the street. As we walk into the suq, I am surprised to find that the dusty, clammy, crowded bazaar has turned into a gigantic mud flat. There is mud everywhere: on the long skirt hems, on the canvas tents, running up the legs of goats, sheep, camels, and other animals, and seeping down the narrow dirt lanes between the stalls. We weave our way around the mass of huge puddles with everyone else, attempting to straddle the standing water and stay on the few high spots.

The women find the going quite rough. They are only permitted to slightly lift their long dresses and abayas off the ground. The men however, simply take off their sandals. They then pull up their robes, and tie the material around their waist. With their legs and boxer shorts showing, they effortlessly wade in and out of puddles, right down the middle of the lane.

Our party returns from a successful day at the sewing markets with a fresh supply of threads, buttons, zippers, and accent material. After dinner, as I tuck Nazar into bed, I feel a familiar discomfort. Over the last several weeks, I have been having female problems. This situation began when I first arrived in Saudi Arabia. With no long dresses, I was often forced to wear Osane's jeans. These male pants never fit properly, and they rubbed continuously. Aggravated by the water I used to wash myself, an infection in my female parts grew.

I kept my lips sealed for weeks. In this society, this is the last part of the body that needed to become inflamed. Over time, the itch increased to a screaming state. Knowing I required medicine, with many embarrassing gestures I communicate to

Zora my plight. Understanding, she asks Saeed to drive us to a Pakistani woman doctor that evening.

I am so relieved that after so many weeks of silent suffering and worrying, I will finally get medical attention. The evening comes quickly, and soon Saeed, Zora, and I are driving through sections of Taif I have never seen before. We stop in front of a building in a residential area.

Saeed parks the car, and we climb the stairs to what appears to be another apartment. On the door is the doctor's name. When we open this door, we enter a small room divided in the middle by a curtain. Zora takes my hand and leads me into the women's waiting room, while Saeed sits in the men's section.

Overstuffed worn chairs line the women's waiting area, and in the middle is one lone table. My eyes automatically search for the magazine rack. Then I realize that none of these women can read. Instead, I watch Zora acquire a comfortable position. Accustomed to long periods of silence, she stares into space and patiently waits.

With nothing to do, I begin to fidget, but fortunately the wait is short. As Zora and I are led into the doctor's office, I rehearse a whole gesture routine to explain my problem. I am therefore amazed when I hear, "Hello, I am Doctor Kashmiri. What seems to be your problem?"

My mouth drops. I can do nothing but stare at this female Pakistani doctor. Finally I am able to say, "You speak English?"

It is beyond my comprehension that I actually share space with an English-speaking woman! I can tell by the look in her tawny eyes that she is equally surprised to see a Westerner walk in her door.

My medical problem quickly becomes secondary. Excitedly she asks me what nationality I am, and how long I have been in Taif. Her interrogation continues for quite some time. As I answer her many questions I watch the intelligence in her expressions, and her graceful movements in the colorful sari she is wearing.

Finally, she ends with the question, "As a foreigner, how do you find living in Saudi Arabia?" The joy I feel in finally sharing my feelings surprises me. Knowing I have to be diplomatic I answer, "The change from east to west has been extremely challenging, but the relatives I am living with have been supportive and loving. They have facilitated a relatively smooth transition." After answering her question, I clasp my hands and look at her.

Finally, it's my turn for probing. "Where did you learn English?" I ask.

"Well," she replies, "I learned English in England, where I was educated."

"Do you know of any other English-speaking women living in Taif?" I ask.

"No, I don't," she replies.

"Through my relatives," I say, smiling at her, "I have learned of one other foreign woman. She's German and has lived here for a long time. She has married a Saudi, raised a family, and is now living out her elderly years as an Arab among Arabs."

Gradually the conversation switches back to my medical problem. After examining me, Dr. Kashmiri gives me a prescription and tells me that it should cure my discomfort.

The goodbyes are filled with warmth, and we slowly file out through the women's waiting room and into the hall. Somehow, I feel much lighter. It seems that a small bubble of my frustrated isolation has dissipated, simply by sharing.

In the hallway, we meet Saeed. I think of him sitting there this entire time, and I wonder if the men's waiting room has magazines. As we walk down the steps, I ponder the burden it must be on Saudi men, to be so totally responsible for the females of their society.

On the way home we stop at a drugstore, and Saeed walks into the pharmacy and fills my prescription. I try to pay for my medicine with the money Osane has left me, but Saeed gives me his usual polite but final "no." It seems that anything belonging to the family, belongs to every member of the family, and that includes expenses.

As the days pass, I spend most of my afternoons in the kitchen with Zora. By now I have watched her cook most of her meals, and the routine is usually the same.
First, she lights the propane stove. Next, she pours olive oil into a large pan, blanches the onions and garlic, browns the lamb, and simmers the chopped tomatoes. Then she adds boiling water, and salt plus pepper.
While the lamb stew is simmering, Zora fills a bowl with rice and water and waits patiently for the bugs to float to the surface. After three rinses, the rice is clean and she will put it aside to drain. Half an hour before dinner, Zora will pour the rice into the lamb mixture. If guests are coming, she will include raisins and browned pine nuts. Then she will prepare the salad by chopping onions, tomatoes, and parsley. Finally, she will pour a combination of olive oil and lemon juice over the salad.
It is Mina's job to place the tablecloth on the floor in the family room. She then arranges bowls of Arab salad, freshly baked bread, and fruit for desert around the sides. In the middle she will set the cupsa, or the rice and lamb dish. Slight variations to this main theme involve adding beans or okra to the lamb stew instead of rice, and replacing lamb with chicken.

It is always fun when Zora decides to cook something new. One day she begins preparing a cake. I can hardly wait, for I have never seen a cake served in Arabia. As I watch, Zora pours flour, eggs, butter, and baking soda into a bowl and pours the mixture into a dish to bake. About half an hour later, the kitchen fills with the scents of a fine bakery. The cake comes out of the oven, golden brown and delicious looking. Meanwhile, Zora fills a large, flat pan with sugar water. Before

I understand what she is doing, she lowers the cake into this water solution. There sits my dream of a Betty Crocker cake, soaking in sugar water. When it is finally served, it is too sweet and soggy... even for me.

The next morning, I wake up with cake on my mind. I talk Walid into going to the market to buy a western cake mix. When he returns, I empty the mix into a bowl, only to find that it is infested with bugs. As I wonder how many centuries the mix has been sitting on the shelf, Mina reaches over and picks up a large sieve. She shakes the cake mixture through, ridding it of its large bug contents. With a stomach that is now queasy, I only hope that the heat of the oven kills whatever body parts slipped through.

The last step on our cake adventure is to pre-heat the oven. I quickly realize that on a propane stove there is no such thing as 325 degrees for thirty-five minutes. There is simply on and off. Any regulating of temperature has to be done very delicately, with the gas tank knob.

Crossing my fingers, I watch Mina light the propane stove with a match and we close the oven door on our two cake pans. We watch the mixture attempt to rise, but even though we pull our pans out ten minutes early, the bottoms are burnt to a crisp. Looking at each other, what can we do but laugh? Meanwhile, the whole family is waiting for my American cake. Refusing to admit defeat, I cut off the burnt bottom and shape the un-risen, heavy cake into squares. Perhaps if I play it right, the relatives will think it's normal.

Surprisingly the cake is so well received that the relatives want me to cook dinner the next evening. With a recipe for meatloaf in my head, I send Walid to the market to purchase ground lamb. Meanwhile, I search the kitchen for anything familiar, to pour into my garbage loaf. I do find eggs, milk, green pepper, salt, and pepper, but it is a challenge to make breadcrumbs out of Arab bread. Since a topping of ketchup and bacon is out of the question, I form my pseudo-meatloaf into a proper shape and slip it into the oven. I spend the next two hours adjusting the temperature and emptying grease, for this meat is far from 5% fat. The result is similar to the cake. It's far from perfect but is eaten with enthusiasm. My two attempts give us all a quick break from traditional meals, and are much appreciated.

The next day the doorbell rings, and an older woman enters. She is short, heavy, and has few remaining teeth. The cut and the material of her dress are very traditional. The universal pattern consists of long sleeves, a circular neck, a gathered waistline, and a long skirt that falls to the floor. Around her head she wears a black knitted scarf, and her gray hair is tinted red with henna, as are her hands and feet.

She walks into the kitchen and sits down on a rug next to Zora, who is preparing yogurt. She looks at me and points to herself, saying "Medina." Our new visitor spends the next two days with us on the rug in the kitchen. She has a bad cough and a runny nose that she keeps blowing into her headscarf.

During the routine of the day, each time I change Nazar's diaper I sense Medina's disapproval. This is not new. Saudi women are forever questioning me because Nazar is not yet toilet trained. My American baby books tell me to start training at eighteen months, but not to get serious until the child reaches two.

In Arabia, mothers begin toilet training at five months. Since there are no cloth diapers and Pampers are nonexistent, it seems to make sense. Osane told me that his grandmother wrapped spare material from her dressmaking around him. She then filled in a layer of sand, and put on another layer of material. With this tedious method, no wonder training begins so early.

Meanwhile, every morning I cross off another day on the Arabic calendar hanging in our room. I try not to dwell on the now-familiar feelings of restlessness that accompany me like a dark shadow. In my enforced confinement, I have many empty moments. I use all my creativity to fill these spaces. Always, before insanity sets in, I pick up my journal. As my pen glides over the paper I instantly feel centered, and relief from the rigors of the daily routine settles over me like a fresh soft blanket on a cold chilly night.

On one particularly ordinary afternoon, I decide to write about Walid. I begin my observations by noting that it is fascinating to be living with a Saudi teenage boy. Each morning, Walid greets us as he walks through the kitchen to the storage room to put his mattress away. Zora always has his breakfast of tea, cheese, and bread ready for him, which he eats quickly before dressing.

Appearance seems to be a priority with him. He regularly spends long sessions in "my" bathroom, adjusting his otra until it is just right. After he is satisfied with his reflection, he walks back into the kitchen, carrying his books wrapped in a prayer rug. With a quick smile, he walks out the door. The smaller boys balance their books on their head, but he is long past that stage.

Walid returns from school between 2:00 and 2:30, about the same time Saeed gets home from work. After they have washed and prayed, we have our main meal. Walid spends the rest of his time studying, watching TV, or napping. He does go out, but not very often, for home is the best place for boys from a good family.

As I become familiar with Walid's habits, I can't help comparing his life to his 1970 contemporaries in the West. His freedom is restricted, his extracurricular activities are limited, and the two central features of the American teen world are missing. Walid isn't even allowed to see a girl, let alone date one. In addition, the entire Arabian sports scene revolves around the game of soccer.

As I keep observing Walid, I realize that the world of the Saudi male requires a completely different training ground. These young Arabians need to develop much more discipline and self-control than their free-spirited contemporaries in the West. Their lives revolve around the honor system. From an early age, social graces are highly emphasized, friendships mean a great deal, as do generosity, hospitality, and loving warmth.

Responsibility is also stressed. A teenage boy does the family's shopping, receives the male guests, pours coffee and tea for them and cares for their bedding. In addition, he is responsible for his sisters and the smaller children. If his father dies, it is the oldest son's responsibility to care for the rest of his brothers and sisters until they are married and self-sufficient.

Finally, job openings for adult Saudi males are limited. Most Saudis work for the government. A small fraction of the male population works in businesses, hospitals, and shops; some work as teachers. Any manual labor, however, is reserved for foreigners who are given work visas to fill that slot.

By the time I finish my journal entries it is late at night. I put away my notepad and climb into bed next to Nazar. Closing my eyes on cultural differences, I begin slipping into the healing oneness of sleep. Just before I enter my dreams, I wonder where Osane is in the world. I have done my best to fill in the long days, but I can once again feel my energy reserves teetering on empty. It is time for Osane to come home!

Chapter 22

Osane's Return and Preparations for our Trip to Southern Arabia

"What we call the beginning is often the end
And to make an end is to make a beginning.
The end is where we start from."
　　T.S. Eliot

The next afternoon Osane simply walks through the door. His arrival is full of the familiar greetings, as the relatives group around him for hugs and news. During tea and amid all the excitement, I sense that a dark cloud has once again settled over Osane. I am willing, however, to cope with whatever condition he has arrived in. Just having him sit beside me allows me to feel whole again. I can finally breathe.

Much later, when we are alone, he shares a whole soliloquy of hard times. "Christie," he begins. "After an incredible amount of persistence, I finally convinced the government to give me a job as a Secretary in the Interior Ministry. This means I'm a paper pusher. It's a nothing job and the salary is awful. If converted into American dollars, my income will place us below poverty level.

"With such a low salary, it is doubly difficult to find anywhere to live. My search for housing took me around the whole city. Your request that our new home have at least one tree made it even more difficult.

After much effort, I found one possibility. This one-story apartment is very small, and it's right on the street. On the plus side, it isn't too old, it's located in the best part of town, and the landlord said it's vacant. If we like it, we can move right in"

Osane's face finally brightens as he takes my hand, saying, "At least it's a start."

I raise my eyes to his, and vulnerability, exhaustion, and fear of failure stare back at me. He has tried so hard not to disappoint us, and my heart melts as I embrace him. I reassure him that what matters is that we'll be together, and that this terrible separation period is *finally* over.

Taking Osane's hand, I lead him up the stairs to the roof. The crisp air, cleansed by the winter storms, blows briskly. Holding hands, we open our senses to the cloudless night sky and feel reborn as the wind caresses our hair. Chilled, Osane guides me to the far wall that blocks the heavy breezes, and we slide down to the floor. Silence blankets us as we watch the rays of moonlight reflecting off the distant mountains.

"Christie," Osane finally says, still holding my hand. "Before we move to Riyadh we're culturally obligated to make a trip to Southern Arabia and visit my home village. If it's OK with you, we'll leave in a few days and be gone for two weeks. When we return to Taif, we'll pack up our belongings and leave for Riyadh to start our new life."

With the decision made, preparations for our trip to Osane's village begin in earnest. Zora organizes more time for sewing, and soon finishes another dress. With Zora's two dresses, my two skirts and Sarah's two dresses, my wardrobe is finally full.

The next afternoon, Osane walks to the market. He returns home with a large bundle wrapped in white paper and tied together with a brown string. Nazar and I are in our bedroom when he hands the package to me. Mystified, I open it to find an extra tall, black, silk abaya!

I sit speechless on the floor cushion in the corner of the room. Holding the clump of material in my lap, thoughts shoot through my mind. I remember my trip to the market with my blue scarf, and I relive the stares that always accompany my white raincoat. Trapped between my pride and the need to survive, I am neutralized. Sitting stone still, an inner war wages within me.

Finally, I surrender. In retrospect, I had chosen to wear the abaya the moment I married Osane and decided to step into his Kingdom. In resignation, I unfold the cloak. Noticing this, Osane reaches into another package and pulls out a black, knit scarf. He hands this to me and I accept it. My conformity is now complete.

On departure morning, I carefully dress Nazar and choose one of my newly-made dresses. As I am putting it on, Sarah and her family arrive. The women congregate in my bedroom. I hear a buzz of approval as I pull out my abaya. Since hardly any foreigners and few if any American females have ever visited Osane's hometown, it has been decided that I fully cover. This means that the only skin showing will be my hands!

I have resigned to this fate in principle, but as soon as the black netting falls over my face the world dims. I can't see, and breathing becomes difficult because I keep inhaling the netting into my nostrils. While I struggle, Zora places my new abaya over my head. As it gracefully drops over me, she mercifully pulls the netted veil off my face and lifts it onto the top of the abaya.

As the other women effortlessly slip on their abayas and netted veils, I stand awkwardly at the door, afraid to move. Before stepping outside the apartment, Zora pulls the veil back over my face. Feeling fragile, I barely breathe. Somehow, when I move I must keep the silk abaya from slipping off my head. As I attempt to step forward I feel like an infant just learning to walk, for my movements are clumsy and uncoordinated. Furthermore, I am in constant danger of tripping over my hems, which will collapse my layers like a fallen house of cards. Somehow, I make it into the back seat of Saeed's car. Carefully I sit down, making sure that all the layers are in the right place.

The airport is quite a ways from town. The longer I sit wrapped in my imposed cocoon, the more frustrated I become. Looking out onto the passing desert, I find my eyelashes catching on the black netting, blurring my vision. I am also finding it difficult to breathe.

Our caravan of relatives finally arrives at the Taif airport, which consists of one small building and an airfield. The men walk into the spartan terminal to purchase tickets, leaving the women and the children in the back seats, chatting and moving from car to car. Everyone is having a great time. There is a party feeling in the air as Sarah passes out sunflower seeds and Pepsi to the children. Everyone is excited, except me. After a while, Osane returns and motions our party into the airport.

Since there is no women's waiting room in this simple facility, our group of women and children sit in the middle of the room on small benches. A few Saudi men walk by. When they don't bother looking at us, it becomes evident that when females wear abayas they become invisible. It also becomes clear that covered in layers of black, individual differences seem to disappear. The fat, slim, old, young, beautiful and ugly all blend into the shadows.

As we sit waiting, three American businessmen walk through the door. The moment my eyes see them, my heart starts fluttering. This is the first time I have seen my own kind in months! Everything within me yearns to be standing with them, not clumped onto a bench among covered women. I strain to hear their English, and delight in understanding every word. Suddenly, one of the men glances up and looks in my direction. I am instantaneously relieved that somehow he has recognized me as an American through my layers of black. I am crushed, however, when I realize that he is simply looking *through me*, to the clock above my head!

The reality that I don't exist suffocates my soul, and waves of emotions pound at my heart. Every part of my being wants to jump up, throw off my coverings, and proclaim myself a unique, breathing, worthwhile female. Frantically grasping for control, I bite my lips, sit on my hands, and dig my heels into the bench. I focus on emptiness. The only thing that saves me from a dramatic outburst is the Americans' quick departure onto a waiting private plane.

With the Americans' departure, my breathing gradually settles to a more regular rhythm. Our plane is delayed, allowing me more moments to center. By the time we are ready to say goodbye to the relatives, I am refocused into my present life and the upcoming adventure. Our goodbye kisses and hugs are so warm and loving, it's as if we are leaving for a lifetime instead of two weeks. Suddenly I feel their acceptance. It is as if my new Saudi family is proud of me, and I am no longer a stranger but one of their harem.

On the way up the stairs into the plane, I turn around to wave goodbye. I am juggling a diaper bag on my back and have Nazar on my hip. My veil clouds my vision and I trip on my abaya, recovering just in time to avoid a very serious fall. With my next movement, I pull off my veil. Looking directly at Osane, I angrily declare, "I will use the scarf to cover my head, but I will never veil my face again." He had seen my near fall and he nods his head in agreement.

We enter the plane and after settling Nazar, I sit down heavily. I am exhausted, for the morning has been an emotional roller coaster. As we take flight, I relax into the comfortable seats and begin looking around. I notice that the plane isn't crowded and that the friendly stewardesses make several trips up and down the aisles offering candy, food, and beverages.

Amazed that the uncovered flight attendants are dressed in miniskirts, I ask Osane about them. He answers that these women are from other parts of the Arab world, mainly Egypt, Jordan, or Lebanon. The pay for them is very good, so many competed to fly the Arabian skies.

I spend most of the flight looking out of the window, watching the land change. When we take off from Taif, I notice a few gray streaks of pavement cut through the brown desert. I can also spot the many dirt roads that wind off the main roads. On some of these dirt roads, I can even glimpse a jeep or pickup truck driving families to a desert picnic.

As we fly away from Taif, the land becomes very flat and then very mountainous. I strain my eyes to catch a village, settlement, road, river, or anything. The only thing I see is brown desert, or gray rubble mountains. This land seems so vast, so rugged, so unpopulated. I marvel that caravans ever dared to travel into Southern Arabia. I remember Osane's stories of his trips on top of Mercedes trucks following old caravan routes. Their risky journey took several days, in contrast to our air hop of today.

As we fly deeper into this primitive empty land, current reality seems farther and farther away. Am I ready to be one of the first western women to penetrate this isolated Arabia? Am I prepared for time travel into an era of no TV's or phones and just recently electricity?

Chapter 23

Our Arrival in Southern Arabia

"There is no beauty that hath not some strangeness in the proportion."
Francis Bacon

As our plane touches down, I try to control the butterflies in my stomach. I put on my abaya and scarf, but not the veil. Collecting my hand luggage and throwing the diaper bag over my shoulder, I exit the plane while whispering a small prayer. Reaching the tarmac, I look around for the terminal, but all I find is one lone airstrip lined with men and boys standing beside their jeeps or trucks.

Osane waves to one of the groups, and as soon as they see us they begin running onto the airstrip to welcome us. The greeting is like a song. They kiss both of Osane's cheeks and shake his hand, all the while chanting, "How are you?" "I'm fine, how are you?" Osane picks up the singsong and then throws it back. These two phrases are repeated back and forth, over and over again. It is different from anything I have heard in Taif, and I find it quite enchanting.

Osane's half-brothers, Fa-had and Mazin, are among the family group, along with Ali, my old friend from Taif. Mingling around us are also several sons of varying ages. When it's my turn to be welcomed, no one kisses my cheeks, but each of them shakes my hand repeatedly. They then raise the hand that I have touched to their heart or kiss their own hand, signifying an especially warm greeting.

After the welcoming, we watch as our suitcase is thrown to the side of the runway. Osane starts towards it, but Mazin sweeps in front of him. In one graceful motion, he puts our heavy trunk on his head and walks toward Ali's jeep. We follow our suitcase to the jeep, wave goodbye to the rest of the family, and head into the desert.

Mohammed, Ali's black servant, is driving. As we watch the landscape speed by Osane tells me that Mohammed is an ex-slave, who had grown up in their family's household. After he was freed, he chose to remain as a servant. I notice that Mohammed seems to have a constant smile on his face, but what catches my eye are his gold teeth.

I ask Osane about his golden grin and he replies that in Southern Arabia, dentistry is unheard of. If anyone develops a toothache they live with it for days at a time, hoping it will simply go away. If it becomes unbearable, they visit an elder in the village who will either pull the infected tooth out, or drill out the cavity and cap it with a golden tooth, creating a shining smile.

When Ali begins speaking to Osane, I turn my attention to the passing countryside. I expected to see more vegetation, for Osane has told me that the South is an agricultural center. In the few pictures I have seen, the area looks lush and green.

That's not what I see out the window. Once in awhile though, we do drive by a wadi full of yellow-green grass, broad-leafed trees, and colorful wild flowers. These bursts of unexpected greenery serve as magical surprises, sprinkled generously throughout the dry desert.

The few houses I can see from the road are captivating. These tower houses are circular and tall. They are made out of stone and mud, and are several stories high. Their roofs are flat and are outlined with mud spikes. The areas around the several small windows and the jagged roofs are whitewashed, while the rest of the house is left a natural mud brown color. These primitive homes are not only cute, cozy and practical, but they also blend into the environment.

As we approach the village, there is more magical greenery. I notice long grass and even pine trees. Not far from the main square, Mohammed turns off the one paved road and onto a very rough dirt driveway. As he off roads the jeep up the hill, everything in the car jiggles. I bounce off my seat a few times, and I can feel my teeth knocking together. The only thing I can think is, "Thank God I'm not pregnant." In between jolts, I hope this driveway is a little used back path to the home. When Mohammed stops the jeep and points up a well-used walkway to Ali's home, I realize that this is the one and only entrance.

I gather my abaya and try not to trip, as Osane, Nazar and I walk up to the entrance. Mohammed has already arrived at Ali's iron gate, and is swinging it open onto a marble courtyard and rows of smiling faces. The whole family, Ali's eight children and his wife Madia, are lined up to warmly greet us. There is much kissing and hugging and then more kissing and hugging. Finally we are led into the main majlis, where we are served coffee and tea.

After tea, Ali proudly shows us around his home. This modern concrete house is divided into two main parts. Our tour begins in the family section. As we walk by two large bedrooms, I notice the well-used family room. Near its entrance is a sunken fire pit, which looks like the only form of heat. On the walls are high shelves lined with kerosene lamps, and on the floor are the typical cushions and rugs. All these elements combine to create a very cozy room.

Right outside the family quarters is a door leading to a small outside room. This area has three walls and a roof, and I am amazed to discover that we are standing in the kitchen. As I look around, I notice no counters. Along the far wall are two large mud sinks, slightly raised from the floor. Here the girls kneel to scrub dishes or wash their clothes. Against the closest wall is a four-burner gas stove and a refrigerator, but the stove looks like it has never been used. I therefore conclude that the cooking is done on the single gas burner located in the middle of the room. I can't fathom how such a large family and their many guests are fed out of such a kitchen, but then I remember Sarah's similar kitchen.

Next Ali leads us down a path to the second section of the home, which ends in Ali's garden. This wonderful fenced area resembles a nursery, with many well cared-for plants and tiers of trees circling the hill. It is quiet on this side of the house, a needed retreat for a man with a big and growing family.

Finally, we are led into an elegant guest majlis or living room. Its charming, welcoming atmosphere attracts me immediately. Built-in benches covered with colorful pads and cushions wind around all four walls. There is a fan in the middle of the ceiling and on the far wall is a large, golden-framed picture of King Faisal.

Down the hall is the guest room, with two single beds. This means that for the first time in months I will sleep in a *bed!* This small room also feels cozy, and it is away from the noise and activity of the rest of the house. At the end of the hall is the Arab bathroom. I have never before used this type of washroom, but from now on I will have no choice.

With the tour complete Ali and Osane walk back to the main section of the house, deep in conversation. Alone at last, I put an overly excited Nazar down for a nap and begin unpacking. As I arrange our things, nature calls. Finally, it's time to face the challenge of the Arab bathroom.

I walk down the hall and open the door, finding a sink with a mirror hanging over it. On the floor, catty-corner to the sink, is the Arab toilet. It consists of an enameled hole with two large footprints on either side. Above the toilet is an iron box with a chain. Unable to resist, I pull the chain, and find that it flushes the hole, making an enormous noise. Next to the toilet, also on the floor is a watering can for your left hand, as water is used to wipe instead of paper.

I stand for quite some time, staring at the hole in the floor. Just like a jigsaw puzzle, I attempt to piece the mysterious pieces together. Some things bother me. My lack of flexibility is enough of a problem, without long skirts and slips. The forward position of the footprints on either side of the hole also mystifies me. When I place my feet on the enameled prints, enlightenment comes. I have finally solved the puzzle, and all is well.

After conquering the bathroom, I have time on my hands. Leaving the guest area behind, I walk out the front door and into the courtyard. As I follow the path around the house, I spot a stairway I haven't seen before. I climb the stairs and find myself on the roof. I am overjoyed. The wall is short enough to see over and the view is breathtaking. I breathe in the cool mountain air, and inhale the intoxicating smell of damp earth. Shielding my eyes from the sun, I spot an ancient mud fortress that must have guarded the townspeople for decades. Unleashing my imagination, I can just imagine the drama that fortress has seen.

That evening Osane, Nazar, and I snuggle under thick blankets, for it is cold in the mountains. With no TV and with electricity so new to the area, the villagers' sleep schedules are still connected to the sun. Therefore, our first night in the South finds us in bed much earlier than normal. Already affected by the slower pace of life and the pure country air, we sleep deeply.

Nazar, as usual, wakes me up early. When we walk into the main section of the house we hear children's voices. It seems that the rest of the family has already risen, the mattresses have been put away, and everyone is dressed. The females of the household are busy with their assigned morning chores. Some of the girls are sweeping out the rooms while others are hand-washing clothes. When they see Nazar, they drop what they are doing and run to him.

I walk into the kitchen and find Madia preparing breakfast. She is frying a pan of eggs on the gas burner, while the girls are chopping up Kraft cheese and white goat cheese. They are also placing olives and dates into separate bowls, and heating up round wheat bread. While everything is being put onto a large white tray, Osane walks into the kitchen with a big smile on his face. Ever since we landed on his home soil, he has relaxed and become his old self again.

Over breakfast, Osane tells me that this is going to be a busy day. We are obligated to pay the traditional greeting visits to his Uncle Hamid, his oldest brother Fa-had, and to his other brother Mazin. I can't believe that I am finally going to meet his family, and that by the end of the day they will turn from imaginary beings into real people.

Chapter 24

Introduction to the People and Places of Osane's Past

"The past is not simply the past, but a prism through which the subject filters his own changing self-image."
Doris Kearns Goodwin

After breakfast I walk back to the guest quarters, leaving Osane and Nazar with the relatives. Glad to be alone, I soak in the sublime nature that surrounds Ali's house. As I stroll through the garden, the temperate sun warms my skin, and the smell of the rich soil grounds me. With everything in my life shifting so rapidly, most days I feel like I am on a roller coaster ride. It's these special moments that center me.

I am pulled out of my walking meditation by Osane's voice, calling me. "Christie," he yells. "Mohammed is here to drive us to Uncle Hamid's house for our first visit."

Tripping on my abaya, I quickly make my way to our room., I find Nazar, and we hurry down the walkway to the jeep. Driving down the dirt driveway is as bad as going up. Needing to develop a system, I began rising up in my seat during the rough spots. This seems to cushion the jolts.

It doesn't take long to drive down the one paved street, through the square, and to the tower house where Osane spent most of his childhood. I am finally going to see the home where he lived with his grandmother, Sarah from Taif, Zainab who just died, and Grandma's only son, Uncle Hamid.

Before our car comes to a full stop, relatives are running out of the tower house to greet us. Two men, and women and children of all sizes, swarm us. The oldest boy leads us through a small door and into a stable full of goats, sheep, and donkeys. I watch as one of the children runs up the steps to the living quarters above. I try to follow, but my eyes are having trouble adjusting from the outdoor sunlight to the semi-darkness of the stable.

After tripping on the second stair, I realize that they're handmade, with each step being a slightly different height. Groping my way upward as my eyes gradually adapt, I notice that the dried mud is smooth and the stair well is painted light blue. Elated, I feel like I'm in a fairy tale house of snow.

The steps wind around into a circular main majlis, with built-in cushioned benches. On the floor are oriental rugs, and in the middle of the far wall are two small windows. Right above the benches, three colored stripes run around the room. The area above these stripes is painted a different color than the benches, and the ceiling is low and wood-beamed.

The living room is full of relatives ready to welcome us. A handsome, middle-aged man steps forward. As he takes my hand warmly in his, I sense a proud, strong, high-quality soul. This can only be Osane's Uncle Hamid. I knew there would be something special about him, and I am not disappointed. In appearance he doesn't resemble Osane, but there is something about his presence. I sense his calm confidence. Somehow he radiates feelings of peace, security, and acceptance to me. Suddenly, Nazar is in Uncle Hamid's arms. Joy and laughter follow as Osane hugs each one of his family and proudly introduces his son.

As tea and coffee are served, Osane points out Uncle Hamid's new wife Charma, who is pregnant with his fourth child. He also introduces me to Uncle Hamid's first three children. I shake hands with Hayder who looks around sixteen, and Ismail, who must be around eight. His six-year-old daughter, Sarifa, looks so clean she sparkles. Her thick black hair is pulled back into a long braid, and the large pink bow and matching dress complement her dainty appearance.

Since welcoming visits are short, after another half an hour it is time to go. Amid much protesting, I am handed my abaya. Cologne is poured into our hands, and incense burners spread a departing scent. Soon we are in Ali's car, crossing the square on the way to Osane's half brother Fa-had's home.

The jeep pulls up to a mud house, but this home isn't built in the tower shape. Instead it is a one-story, flat-roof structure. The door is opened by a smiling Fa-had, who appears to be much older than Osane. As Fa-had welcomes me, I stare into a very handsome face covered with a gray beard. His wife, daughter, and son also greet us, and we are led into the majlis and served coffee and tea.

Osane talks to his brother, while Nazar plays with Fa-had's children. Once again, the visit is short. I am soon putting on my abaya, a different brand of cologne is splashed into our hands, and the smoke from the incense burner settles down around us. We wave goodbye and turn back onto the paved road Within a few moments, Mohammed is driving up the bumpy driveway that leads to the familiar surroundings of

Ali's home. The household greets us warmly, as if we have returned from a long trip. As soon as I can, I politely retreat to my own room and the welcoming sense of privacy. My overstimulated eyes have just observed things few foreigners have ever seen. I need a short nap to assimilate and center. Half an hour later, I wake refreshed and hungry.

Walking into the family room, I find Madia laying out a special tablecloth on the floor. Ali stands over her, supervising the placement of the food. He keeps placing the choicest pieces of lamb on my plate, and then he is gone. The rest of the family is eating in another room, leaving Nazar, Osane, and me to dine in royal privacy. Once again, I marvel at the true art form of Saudi hospitality.

After dinner, I put Nazar down for his afternoon nap. Meanwhile, Osane and I drive off to visit his other half-brother, Mazin, who now occupies his father's "Big House." I am excited to see this home, for it has witnessed years of tribal history.

I remember Osane telling me that under the Ottoman Empire, the Turks had colonized and advanced to this southern village. Because the community was agriculturally based and situated in rich farmland, the villagers were able to stay in one place. They had developed progressive irrigation and sewage systems, their markets were full, and the square (which now lay barren) was full of trees and statues. The women repainted their mud houses inside and out every Eid. Each woman also took responsibility for the street in front of her house. Not only did she clean the street, but she also walked up and down it with incense.

In this tribal village, there were few restrictions against women. In fact, the Bedouin used their prettiest daughters to sell their wares. The village of Osane's birth was called the "Small Istanbul of the Arab World," and life was well organized, settled, and comfortable.

King Abdul Aziz Ibn Sa'ud wanted the village and all the fertile land for himself. During his unification wars, Sa'ud sent forces against the village, unsuccessfully, three times. On the fourth try, the King's forces proved too much. The nomadic tribesmen of the central desert were hardened by decades of harsh living and the settled villagers were simply not strong enough to withstand them. Abdul Aziz's army headquartered in Osane's father's "Big House," for it was the largest quarters in town.

Under Sa'ud's rule, everything in the village changed. The soldiers cut down the trees that occupied the square, and crumbled the statues. They covered the women, and restricted the canteens found on several street corners into "men only" establishments. For decades, the Saudi Government isolated the south, for Sa'ud's government in Riyadh didn't want the region to gain back the strength that had kept their armies at bay.

As Mohammed stops our car on the street in front of the family-owned shops, I stop my reminiscing and focus on the present. Osane leads me down a small, unpaved lane, which dead-ends in front of two gigantic gates. They are the largest gates I have ever seen, truly big enough for whole camel caravans to pass through. Thick ropes adjusted onto pulleys run above the courtyard and into the window of the family room, where they can be opened. As Mohammed pounds on the gates, they swing back, revealing a very large mud courtyard.

Suddenly I have another flashback. Osane had told me that during World War II the villagers were starving, and many ate grasshoppers to simply stay alive. Camel caravans loaded with bags of grain, wheat, and other crops from the family farms, would wind through the village to these large gates and into this mud courtyard. As the boys unloaded the food into huge storerooms at the end of the courtyard, the women spent long hours baking bread. With these supplies and the bread they baked,, Osane's family was able to keep the entire village alive.

Taking a short breath, I concentrate on the present-day courtyard where we are greeted warmly by Osane's half-brother, Mazin. He leads us through a heavy wooden door, and up crooked mud steps. We enter the family room, and sit down around its sunken charcoal fire pit. Osane leans over and says, "There's always a fire going for warmth and for a place to heat up visitors' tea and coffee."

More family members enter, and the now familiar singsong greetings fill my ears. After the family settles down for visiting, my unoccupied mind glances out the window. The three-foot thickness of the mud walls surprises me, but I suppose it provides warmth in the winter and coolness in the summer.

During a lull in the conversation, Osane introduces me to his half-sister, Rema. She approaches me with a warm smile, her dark brown eyes sparkling. As she holds out a colorful package to me, I notice that she is short with pleasant features and a kind face. I open the gift and find an absolutely stunning gold-and-pearl bracelet, which matches a ring Zainab had given me before her death. As I thank her repeatedly, I sense we will become good friends.

With tea over, it is time for Osane to show me around his father's house. As we walk from room to room, I marvel at the size of the house. I am especially impressed with his father's bedroom. It is magnificent, with built-in benches winding around all four walls. Five small windows with shutters are evenly spaced on the far wall. When these shutters are open, five separate shafts of light shine through, giving the room a heavenly aura. As my eyes study this wonderful space, I notice Osane's father's glasses sitting on a mud ledge. It's as if he had just placed them there.

The tour then continues to the outside courtyard. Osane opens a large door and takes me into the storage rooms he has told me so much about. These rooms are almost empty now, but I can just picture bags of rice, wheat, and other crops being unloaded from camels and stored in these safe, dry quarters.

After examining the storage room, we walk across the courtyard. Carefully I climb up twelve outdoor mud steps into the formal guest majlis. It is the largest Arab living room I have ever seen. This was where the young Osane had stood for hours pouring tea and coffee. It was here that he had tended to his fathers guests, laying out their beds, bringing them food and taking care of their needs.

We re-enter the courtyard and Rema hands me my abaya. With many thanks, we bid farewell to the family and to the Big House. As we walk back down the lane to the main square and our parked car, my intuition tells me that the village will soon drastically change. The historical clock is ticking and time is about up. While the rest of civilization evolved, this village is still solidly in the ancient past. However, the real world can no longer be held at bay and is slowly encroaching.

In the car, I ponder the universal urge for the excitement of the new to eradicate the charm of the old. The mud homes I have just been introduced to seem practical, climate-efficient and so homey with their wood ceilings and their brightly painted mud walls. To me it will be a crime to demolish these ancient, organic structures and replace them with generic, concrete block squares. "Progress" seems ordained to happen. When it does, at least I'll be able to recall the true magic of this village and the authenticity of its lifestyle.

Once again, our car stops at Ali's home. Elated from my quick visits with Osane's family, I slip away and climb the steps to Ali's roof. The solitude and stillness of the view is intoxicating. Built-up tension from my controlled behavior slides off my body like autumn leaves spiraling off trees on a windy day. Pure white clouds contrast with elderberry blue skies in the distance. The birds sing happily in the garden, and the air is balmy and soft, smelling of newly-turned earth.

Absolute contentment radiates from my body, as I insert a cosmic pause in my lifeline.

That evening we gather in the family room with Ali and his family. A fire is going in the fire pit and the room is comfortable and warm. Since there is no TV, everyone simply gathers and chats. Soon the whole household is tucked under thick blankets. It is during this space in time that Osane and I reunite our souls, our lives, and our plans for the future.

Chapter 25

Saudi Wedding

"The Control Center of your life is your attitude."
Anonymous

The next morning I open my eyes and can't remember where I am. Glancing around the room, I notice that Nazar is already up. Osane is gently rubbing my shoulder and when I am awake he says. "Christie, Madia wants to invite you to a neighbor's wedding. Here's your breakfast tray. She says the women of the household are leaving in about an hour."

Immediately I am up, and after a quick breakfast I dig into my suitcase. Knowing how important it is to look your best in the Middle Eastern world, I realize I have to dress carefully.

Swiftly I lay my four dresses on the bed. I hold up the aqua blue and creamy white taffeta, and decide this is my safest choice. The sleeves fall from my shoulders to my wrists, the neckline travels up to my chin, and the skirt plunges to my ankles. To be totally covered is always the goal.

My next dilemma is my long, blond hair. My blue eyes and fair skin stand out enough. With a desire to blend in, I pull my hair back. In an attempt to make it disappear, I pin it firmly to my head. Knowing that beauty is to be hidden, I then take my makeup and throw it back into my suitcase.

On the way out the bedroom door, I shut my clothes cupboard and glance into the mirror. Even though I am wearing the beautiful jewelry the relatives have given me, I am not engulfed in gold as most Saudi women are. Even their everyday wear includes thick, exotic necklaces, jangling gold bracelets, and many rings. Earrings are always worn, as is an occasional nose decoration. Instead of using banks, women wear their savings in the form of valuable stones mounted in gold jewelry and men invest their savings in rugs.

Finally, I tie my black scarf tightly around my head. Picking up my abaya, I slip the black cloak over my shoulders, letting it fall to the floor. Instead of feeling beautiful, I label myself a misfit. It's as if I'm attending a permanent costume party and the clothes belong to someone else. Resigned, I walk out the bedroom door to join Madia and her five daughters.

The second I am surrounded by the relatives, my mood shifts. I feel ashamed, for the sisterhood is fully alive and excited. Their faces are aglow with smiles, and their movements are full of ease and grace. The whole room seems a cascade of colorful fabrics, gold jewelry, exotic perfumes, and excited chatter. I watch these Saudi females effortlessly drape their abayas over themselves, material falling on material. As a group, they sensuously glide out the gate. Everything seems right in their world.

Our party leaves the house through a black iron door. We walk down marble steps and then into the desert. It's always a relief to break out from behind walls and feel the wind on my face. However, scrambling over desert pebbles in high heels soon absorbs all my attention. The others seem to glide along. Unfortunately, I keep tripping over my long skirt, slip, or abaya. Several times, I twist my ankle when I fall into dirt ruts filled with protruding stones.

Struggling to keep my composure, I shift my thoughts to what Osane has told me about Saudi weddings. Most of these conversations occurred a lifetime ago, in our favorite college coffee shop.

"Arabian weddings," Osane related, "are very large, expensive, and well-planned affairs. The event is three days long and is held at the bride's home, which is decorated with strings of white lights. The groom offers the bride's family a dowry, and many expensive presents. If anything happens to the marriage, the wife takes the dowry with her to the home of her oldest male relative.

"Marriages are arranged through families. Pictures are exchanged, business deals conducted, and guests are invited. Several sheep are killed in honor of the union, with the men dining in one part of the villa, while the women and children celebrate in a separate section. On the third day there is the wedding ceremony itself. The bride walks into the room fully covered. After the ceremony, the bride and groom go into their quarters and see each other for the first time. The marriage is considered to be consummated if the groom steps outside the bedroom door and waves a piece of material soaked in blood. This proves that his wife was a virgin."

I trip on my last rock as our party of seven reaches its destination. Madia pounds on the iron gate, and the knock is answered by the typical question, "Who, who?" We announce the name of our family, and the houseboy swings the gate wide. Out of the shadows of the home steps our hostess, smiling in the Saudi greeting, "Come in, come in, welcome, welcome."

As we all hand one of the daughters our abayas, I look around. The room is similar to other majlises I've seen. It is about ten feet square with two colorful Afghani tent rugs on the floor. Back pillows and floor cushions line the entire perimeter of the room, all in different patterns of red, black, maroon, and shades of orange.

We follow our hostess through the living room and down the back steps into a big outside garden, half of which is covered with thatching. Under the thatching sits the bride and many of the wedding party. Traditional twelve-foot high, three-foot thick walls enclose this courtyard.

The open section of the garden is full of wedding guests. Several are flowing in harmony, doing a shuffle-like dance step. The movements and chanting are incredibly catchy. I look around and find the two women who are responsible for this haunting tune. The first musician, an Ethiopian, is beating on the top of a sewing machine case. Her hands fly at top speed, each finger knowing where to beat for the proper octave and correct rhythm. Another Ethiopian is shaking and tapping a very colorful tambourine, while the rest of the guests swing and chant in unison.

I have been using these few moments to immerse myself in the scene, before the wedding party focuses its attention on me. Nothing could have prepared me for the next few moments. Suddenly I am forced to absorb the energy of 400 eyes—staring with unashamed intensity—at me! Instantly, I feel like an escaped prisoner caught in no-man's-land. All around me, floodlights and sirens slice the late night darkness.

In a panic, the only strategy my overloaded system can concoct is to avoid making eye contact. The problem is, I don't know where to cast my eyes. I look down, and very young girls are looking up at me. I look up a little further, and find older girls gazing at me. I look up some more, only to find women staring directly into my eyes. I have the choice of either looking directly at the sky or completely down at the ground. My choice is to look quickly, from person to person and pray my moment of inquisition will soon end. If only the musicians would start their chanting, but they have dropped their instruments to check out the foreigner.

Madia becomes my savior. She sees my plight, and gently directs me to a chair under the thatched roof. A group quickly gathers around me, and asks Madia the question that is in everyone's mind. "Who is she? Where did she come from? Who is her man?" Again and again, the answer is repeated. "She is Americani."

From the blank stares in their eyes, I suddenly realize that these women have no idea where America is. None of my Saudi contemporaries can read or write, they have never been exposed to TV or radio, nor traveled beyond a few miles of their village. As I attempt to assimilate this concept, I hear Madia continue. "Her husband is Osane and she has come to live in Saudi Arabia."

As the women accept this reality, the curious stares transform into more critical gazes. I sit quietly, as the multitudes scrutinize me. I can feel eyes examining my dress (thank God made by Osane's Saudi relatives), my gold (which is sparse), and my hair (which is luckily pinned tightly back). One factor in my favor is my lack of makeup, for visual emphasis belongs to the bride only. Her makeup, by contrast, is very bold. She is wearing bright red lipstick, and a charcoal pencil marks her eyes and eyebrows.

As the group appraisal continues, I feel them down-shifting into a more critical gear. It seems that my blue eyes and fair skin seem washed out and very alien to them. My 5'8' height, which has always been appealing in America, waves a red flag in Arabia. Most of the Saudi women's heads come just to my shoulders. My thin figure also appears unusual and sickly. Mature Saudi women, after many babies, lack of exercise, and high-carb diets, acquire a heavy look. This body type is considered healthy and alluring.

As my judgment continues, a path is made through the women for the young girls. They come up one by one, to get a closer look at this strange new creature. In single column they pass by, looking at the length of my nails, checking out my dress, and staring into my blue eyes. To be able to see a Western woman in detail seems to be more special than the wedding.

Finally, the last of the children files by and the attention shifts back to the music. Gradually my presence slips into the background. Always hospitable, one of the daughters serves me refreshing mint tea while some of the older women speak to me in Arabic. That is, of course useless. My attempts to reply are met by kind smiles. They are saying in non-verbal communication, "It's all right, later, you will learn Arabic later." Meanwhile, Madia stands on guard beside me like a soldier. She patiently gives out my history again and again, to all the curious.

Slowly I begin to relax. Fortunately, my lack of language skills has created an unyielding mute barrier. In contrast, my senses sharpen. Suddenly, I become aware of the exotic odors filtering all around me. Someone, in typical Saudi consideration, has placed an incense burner beside my chair. The spiraling, sweet smelling smoke blends in with the strong perfumes each woman is wearing. Penetrating all these new and mysterious smells are food odors, accompanied by the aroma of alien spices.

I am blessed with the sight of an earth-bound rainbow, twirling and swaying all around me. The new wedding dresses blow in the slight breeze of the warm winter day. Yards of brocade, chiffon, organza, and crepe flutter sensuously. In multiple hues and shades, a riot of colors splashes each garment. Currant and vermillion, platinum and fuchsia, peach, plum, and innumerable shades of greens and browns dazzle my eyes. I find the tribal dresses the most fascinating. Made of black velvet, these dresses are wide and comfortable. Hand-sewn into their fabric are intricate designs of green, red, and gold. As a final complement, these native outfits are pulled at the waist by pure gold belts.

To temper the visual input, I close my eyes. Immediately I am overwhelmed by strange new sounds. The jingle of jewelry is a constant. All the women plus the young girls, even the small baby girls, wear 21-carat gold bracelets and earrings. I also hear the rustling of long skirts, as the Saudi women walk slowly by. The most persistent din is the hum of the Arabic language, with its rolled "r", guttural sounds, and words that make little sense. Even though I have an elementary grasp of Arabic, it is beyond me how these verbal impressions can be put into words, words into meanings, and meanings into sentences.

On sensory overload, I pull into myself. Suffering from a sudden meltdown, I lose my focus. My mind begins to dart into several places, all at once. My thoughts finally settle on one major concern. It seems that the contrast between my essence, and the new lifestyle I am adopting is once again blowing my mind.

Voices spouting facts begin screaming in my ears. Like a teletype they rattle my mind, and the speed increases with each sentence.

"Saudi women," these demons bellow, "only know what goes on within a fifty-mile radius. There are few telephones and only TVs within the major cities. It is against the law for women to drive and only recently have young girls been allowed to attend school. Women of my age can not read or write.

"To Saudi women, children are their whole lives, and to me they are just a part of life. Saudis sleep on the floor, I sleep on a bed. They eat on the floor, and I eat at a table. Arabians iron on the floor, while I iron on an ironing board. Even their time is different. They are in the 13th century according to the Muslim calendar. Their main meal is at 2 o'clock instead of at 6 o'clock. They go out completely covered, while I simply open the door and go as I am. They hand-wash material that refuses to be ironed, and I am used to wash-and-wear."

"STOP," I inwardly scream. As I grab my ears, panic threatens my composure. I quietly leave my seat under the roof thatching, and walk as invisibly as possible toward the back of the garden. Searching for shadows, I am looking for any place I can be alone. I desperately need to calm the hysteria that is threatening to overtake me. I finally find an abandoned corner and sink to the ground, holding myself.

Evil voices continue to scream in my ears, "How did you possibility end up in the middle of this Saudi wedding?" they heckle.

I check my breathing and begin to inhale deeply. After about ten breaths, I feel slightly centered. "Be more gentle with yourself," I whisper to myself. "Calm down now. Remember, you intentionally came to this country to explore and experience."

Trying to create some order out of fragmentation, I repeat a poem by William Shakespeare.

> "There is a tide in the affairs of men,
> Which, taken at the flood, leads on to fortune;
> Omitted, all the voyage of their life
> Is bound in shallows and in miseries.
> On such a full sea are we now afloat,
> And we must take the current when it serves,
> Or lose our ventures."

I remind myself, "You *had* to make this voyage. Recall the predestined forces that propelled you toward this ancient culture, a way of life dating back through time!"

After allowing several moments to compose myself, I walk slowly back into the crowd to find Madia. I tap her on the shoulder and point towards her house. She nods her head in understanding. Calling over one of her daughters, she takes my hand. Her eyes thank me for coming.

Quietly I make my way back up the steps to the hostess, who hands me my abaya. After kissing her on both cheeks I slide out the door and into the desert, Madia's daughter leading the way.

As I walk back towards the safety of Ali's home and *my family*, I thank God for his support. His presence kept me sane enough to fully experience the wedding. It is his quiet voice whispering in my ear that gives me the strength to walk my path of destiny and keeps my ego voices at bay.

Chapter 26

Dinner at the Big House and a Picnic

"There are those who give with joy, and that joy is their reward."
Kahlil Gibran

The next day around noon, we leave for our formal meal at the Big House. Once again I dress with care, for this will be my first public dinner. The other meals have been for family only.

Osane tells me that this dinner is a special event. Not only is the village welcoming home one of their sons, but they are also celebrating our union. Two sheep will be offered this day. One sheep is for me, and the other will be sacrificed to honor our first-born son, Nazar.

I gather my courage as we drive to the Big House and walk down the small lane. The large gates are already open. Osane turns left and climbs the stairs to the men's majlis, while Nazar and I continue into the house and enter the family room.

I brace myself for the entrance drama, knowing that the second I walk into the room all eyes will turn towards me. As the room studies me, I sense that they aren't hostile or unfriendly stares. They're simply curious. I realize none of them has seen a Western woman this close before, and many have come just to see the new American bride.

Thankfully the gazes are also directed toward Nazar, the newest member of the family. As he runs into the middle of the room, the ice breaks. Attention is now re-directed away from me and onto this uninhibited child.

Meanwhile Rema quietly walks over and takes my hand, leading me to the far side of the room where we sit down together. I smile at everyone, and they smile their welcome back at me. With graceful gestures, Rema tells the guests my story. Each of them listens carefully. I can tell by their expressions that they are empathizing with me. They are thinking how difficult it would be to live in a strange country, far away from family, friends, and home, with no language skills. As they ask Rema their questions, they beam me smiles of support and warmth.

After my story has been told and tea and coffee served, the group returns to their original conversations. Although they look at me occasionally, I have now become almost invisible.

While they chat, I am able to study these female villagers. As I look around, I count around twenty to thirty women in the room plus children. The young girls are slim, but the women are heavyset. I know some of this weight can be attributed to the lack of birth control, and the many pregnancies each woman has endured. Diet also contributes to their wide stature, for their meals consist of large portions of bread and rice. While they do a great deal of cooking, washing, and heavy housework, they don't walk or exercise in any other way.

The most noticeable trait is their short stature. When any new guest arrives in the room, it is proper for everyone to stand up and shake hands. When my turn comes I start my ascent off the floor, get to eye level, and keep going. When I am totally extended, I am a full two heads higher than anyone else in the room. During any standing conversation, villagers actually have to raise their heads to communicate with me.

The smell of food interrupts my observations. Rema takes my hand and guides me into a large side room. In the center of the floor is a flowered tablecloth, spread with an Arab feast. Rema leads me to my place of honor, and as I sit down I am relieved to notice a plate and silverware. On this plate, the women are piling the choicest pieces of lamb. I thank them and keep my eyes lowered, seeing only my dinner and Nazar's.

The children eat quickly and leave. Many of the older women linger, eating slowly and enjoying the conversation. As the women finish their pudding and fruit deserts, they migrate back to the family room where tea and coffee are served.

Settled over beverages, their relaxed conversation continues. Meanwhile, I sit on the bench next to the window watching the families leave. Soon, only relatives and good friends remain. At the appropriate time, the men file back into the family room. As I watch their interactions, I notice that the restrictions between men and women in the south are still evident, but wonderfully diluted.

When Osane and his cousin Mohammed finally walk into the room, I'm giddy with relief. Whenever Osane is beside me, I feel much more grounded.

While they continue their conversation, I remember Osane telling me that Mohammed lives on a farm outside the village.

I notice that he is a large man. Not only is he taller than most, but very muscular. His presence speaks of a hard physical life.

In the middle of a conversation with Osane, Mohammed puts his foot across his opposite knee and balances a small teacup on his toe. This draws my attention to his feet. His soles and toes are worn into a thick leathery skin. I have heard of Bedouin walking barefoot across the rough, gravel desert. Until now, I haven't found calloused soles capable of this deed. However, I bet Mohammed's feet could walk over burning coals and not feel the flames.

Gathering up Nazar, Osane and I prepare to leave with the remaining guests. Rema passes the incense burner from person to person. The men fan the smoke into their faces, smelling its scent with satisfaction. The women lift up their robes, allowing the perfumed smoke to flow through their layers. Next Mazin pours cologne into our hands. As we walk out the large gates we wave a final thank you and goodbye to the relatives who have made us feel so welcome.

The next morning I spend on Ali's roof, basking in the warm sun. Meanwhile, Osane and Ali sit in the men's majlis, greeting guests. Some of Osane's friends don't come to pay respects, for not everyone applauds his return with an American wife. Some feel he has overstepped the bounds of traditional behavior, and that he has changed too much overseas. Understanding this, Osane rejoices in the friends who do visit.

During a quiet lunch, a smiling Mohammed arrives at the door. He's always ready to flash his golden grin. The family often calls him "Ya aswad," which means, "You black." The title holds little prejudice, for Arabia is composed of a rainbow of races. One of the first races to be introduced to the olive-skinned tribesmen were the blacks. Arab slave traders brought them to Arabia from Africa. A further blending occurred with the assimilation of the light-skinned Syrians. There is even an isolated tribe in the Southern mountains that has a pure-white complexion, blond hair, and blue eyes.

After we finish the last of our afternoon meal, Mohammed drives us to Uncle Hamid's home. Again, we meet the relatives outside their tower house, where two other jeeps are lined up. I give Osane a questioning look and he says, "Christie, Hamid wanted to surprise you with a picnic."

After the other jeeps load their passengers, our caravan weaves through the village square and out into the countryside. A few miles out, we pass a family of farmers leading two camels. They are on their way to the market, and I marvel at the distances they walk. I instantly think of Cousin Mohammed's bare feet, and the miles they must have seen.

About a half hour later we turn onto a little used sheep path that winds down into a wadi. We park the car on a hill overlooking the greenness of the river bottom. Nazar jumps out of the car first. He slides down the rocks, and stands in the soft, tall green grass. I run after him, and halfway there I am surprised to see a parked truck and some more relatives.

They are standing around an established fire, roasting slices of lamb and tending other pots full of rice and other dishes. It seems they arrived early that morning, with cooking supplies and a live sheep in the back of their truck. Meanwhile, that sheep has become the carcass I see hanging from a tree on the other side of the clearing. Thanks to their efforts, our meal is well under way.

With much commotion the two groups of relatives greet and merge with one another. Soon everyone settles down to picnic activities. Some of them cook, while others play cards. The whole time the children circle.

I am enjoying a cup of tea when Osane throws truck keys into my lap. He asks me to re-park the truck on the other side of camp. Thinking nothing of it, I am backing up the truck when I look around and find the entire camp staring at me. They peer intensely, as the first woman driver they have ever seen moves their truck twenty yards.

With the truck drama behind us, Nazar and I walk out of camp. The yellow green grass blows in the cool breeze. Always addicted to open spaces, my spirits soar as we follow the winding stream. Our wanderings bring us to a farmer's tower house surrounded by cultivated fields. A cow and donkey are staked in the front lawn, grazing on rich grass. While I listen to birds, sheep, and chickens, I remember a quote from Willa Cather. "The soil was full of sunlight and the grass underfoot had a reflection of the blue sky in it."

We continue our exploring, walking down grass paths and scrambling over rocks thrown on the banks by the river. Around a bend, we come upon three camels. Cautiously we approach, watching them eat branches off a thorn tree. Fascinated, Nazar and I quietly sit down and observe them feeding on thorns that are about an inch long and as strong as steel nails. These camels take big bites and then chew, grind, and regrind in a seesaw manner. Wondering what their mouths and tongues are made of, we sit on the side of the wadi for quite some time. Suddenly a smiling Osane appears, telling us that the relatives are going on a walk.

Osane picks up Nazar, and we race to catch up to them. As we run, freedom envelopes us. This magical visit to Osane's village has been enchanting. The natural pace of life, the easy flow among men and women, and the pure love we receive from everyone is slowly dissolving the friction that has developed between us. Coupled with our long nights under cozy blankets, our relationship is slowly being restored to its originally healthy state.

Out of breath, we catch up with the relatives. They are setting up a game. Hayder has just made a rock pile, on the top of which he has balanced a large flat stone. He then joins the rest of the men and boys, who are standing twenty feet from the pile. Each male has a handful of stones. The object of the game is to be the first one to knock the large flat stone off the pile.

Without thinking, I run up and impulsively join in their game. Transgressing into my competitive tomboy days, my only focus becomes the flat rock. Using a baseball pitch, I wind up and throw a hard ball. Luck is on my side. The stone falls. I am the winner and victory is mine.

Noticing the silence, I turn around and find everyone staring at me. I suddenly realize I am the only woman in the game. The other females are standing behind, in a large group, ready to cheer their men on. My face turns red with embarrassment. In an instant, the relatives recover from their shock and surround me. They shout their approval, laughter, and congratulations on my win.

Feeling exuberant, free, and childlike again, I race Osane to the top of the hill. We soar like hawks, our feet barely touching the ground. We are young again, outracing all of the cultural restrictions that have been forced on us.

Finally at the top of the hill we collapse into a pile, trying to catch our breath. Surrounded by this valley of solitude we calmly sit, just glad to be alone together. No words are needed. We sit in silence, simply enjoying the now. Both of us are at peace and happy.

Chapter 27

Return to Taif and Preparations for our Departure to Riyadh

"If you can risk getting lost somewhere along the day you might stumble upon openings that link you to your depths."
Anonymous

Sitting on the airplane on our return flight to Taif, I look back on our last days in the village. Never in my life have I received such unconditional love. These unpretentious souls walk in harmony with nature and understand the essence of life. Simply being in their presence is healing. I smile to myself remembering Madia washing Nazar's diapers. She hung them out to dry and then ironed each one of them.

Gathering a pillow and blanket, I settle down in my seat, and my mind continues to wander back to our visit. My thoughts randomly rest on the afternoon Madia, her eight children, Nazar, and I piled into Ali's jeep. Mohammed drove while we bounced around like a pack of sardines, traveling way out into the country. Finally, we stopped near a small stream.

As the children played around the jeep, I walked down the bank and sat on a flat rock to drink my cup of tea. Looking out over the farmer's field, I spotted two small children on a white donkey, weaving their way along a trail that followed the stream. I watched them as they approached, knowing that they hadn't noticed me. When they finally looked up and saw me, fright and surprise flashed across their faces. Having no references, they didn't know where to slot me into their realities. What was I?

When I said, "Salaam a'leikum" (greetings to you) in a soft voice, they continued to stare at me with frightened eyes; then they hurriedly turned their donkeys around. Once again, I had become the first American female these small souls had experienced.

As I rearrange my blanket and pillow and listen to the drone of the airplane engines, I leisurely re-run my bizarre tour of the village. It began when I asked Osane to see more of his childhood environment.

"Are you sure you want to drive all those dirt roads?" Osane asked. "Remember there is only one paved road. It simply runs through the square and in and out of town."

"Sure, Osane," I replied. "I've been up and down that one paved road, and I want to see more."

"OK," Osane said as he led me outside and helped me into the waiting jeep. He gave Mohammed a strange grin as we began our bounce down Ali's road.

Everything on my ride started out normally enough. I sat in the front seat, my black abaya and headscarf wrapped properly about me. Mohammed drove slowly down the paved road toward Market Square, which hosted an open-air bazaar. He circled the square, giving me an opportunity to see all the goods, arranged carefully on colorful blankets and rugs.

Suddenly our jeep braked, as a teenage Bedouin leading a camel crossed our path. He had an extremely handsome face. His long, black hair hung to his shoulders in tight, shiny ringlets. Around his waist he wore a colorful sash, and sticking out of the material was a gold-handled, curved knife. What drew my attention, however, were his eyes. They spoke of a wild, alert, untamed soul. I knew this was the closest I would ever come to an Arabian knight, and I was instantaneously awed, mesmerized, and terrified. As he proudly strolled past, I could almost hear the fierce desert winds whirl around him.

When we left the market place, Mohammed's expression became mischievous. What I quickly found out was that there was truly *one* paved road in the village. The rest of the streets were little more than goat paths that we flew over at top speed. I spent most of the ride in the air. We bumped up and down ravines, and spun out here and there. In no time, I lost my black coverings and it was all I could do to just hold on and keep breathing. In between bumps, I yelled, "That's enough, finished, I've had it," none of which Mohammed understood. My yelling must have made some impact, for he finally spun the jeep around and bounced my bruised body back to Ali's house.

Our flight to Taif seems very short, and in no time Saeed is greeting us at the airport. As we drive through town, I can't believe how cosmopolitan it appears to me. There are scores of people milling around, numerous paved streets and large covered market places. Zora and Mina warmly welcome us back into their apartment, and Nazar feels right at home among his toys and familiar surroundings.

Throughout our re-entry period, I sadly notice Osane becoming more distant, restless, nervous, and anxious. He develops a new pattern of spending most evenings out, leaving me with the rest of the women. As he isolates himself from me, I slowly begin to lose patience with his changed behavior. However, I don't want to confront him. I keep thinking that if I give him more time, he will re-balance himself.

The days pass, and Osane's new aloof behavior continues. One evening, left to myself again, I become so mad that I want to scream or throw something. I am not prepared to lose control in front of the relatives, so after I put Nazar to bed I climb the stairs to the roof.

Surrounded by the Arabian night and the stars in the distance, I pick up chunks of concrete and throw them against the wall with all my strength. As they crumble into pieces my anger also shatters, like shards of broken glass. The only presence to witness this scene is the tattered black cat that appears on most washdays. He looks through me with his yellowish eyes, and listens patiently as I share my woes.

"Black cat," I say. "My life for the last several months has pushed me to the brink. I have been on a roller coaster ride of highs and extreme lows! Everything that was once familiar has changed. But black cat, I have remained strong! My youth seems to give me strength and my natural curiosity thrives on new experiences. With that said, the truth is…well, I'm desperately lonely."

As tears stream down my face, the cat stretches and lies back down to hear some more.

"Listen, tattered black cat," I sob. "If Osane pulls away from me, whom can I communicate with? Oh, cat, I don't know if I'm going to make it. I just don't know…"

The next afternoon while I am waking from a nap, I hear someone knocking on the door. Osane walks down the hallway and stops in front of the door asking, "Who is it?" I hear a male's voice answering, "Anwar." Then the door opens to a very warm greeting.

Casually listening to the Arabic conversation, I gather that Anwar is an old friend. Losing interest, I start to doze again, until I hear a woman's voice saying, "How do you do?" I jerk rigid in my bed, not daring to trust my ears. Straining my senses, I listen to the beautiful English words explaining that Anwar is Osane's friend from his village and Mary is his new English wife.

As I jump up and dash for the bathroom, I thank God for answering my prayers of loneliness. In shock, I attempt to put myself together. I conclude that I don't care who Mary is, I love her unconditionally. In fact, she is already my very best friend.

I attempt some composure as I walk toward the living room. Osane introduces me to Anwar and his new wife. I politely shake Mary's hand and sit down on the sofa next to her. I try to catch my tongue and dilute my intensity, but soon I am bubbling over like a forceful spring stream crashing over a dam. Rules of friendship are forgotten. Everyone else in the room becomes invisible, and members of the house and the entire Kingdom are consigned to oblivion. At this point in my life, there is only Mary. I talk non-stop, and poor Mary has no recourse but to sit and listen.

After the first hour and several cups of tea and coffee, my fervor ebbs. Finally, Mary has the space to begin her own story. As she speaks, I study her. She is short and sturdy, with amber eyes and light brown, straight hair. Her features are plain but her eyes speak of intelligence, her mouth of a sense of humor; her accent is upper brow. I am not surprised when I learn she is an Oxford graduate.

During a pause in Mary's story, I glance at the other side of the room and notice Anwar. He is short and thin, with a very light complexion for a Saudi. His mouth wrinkles signifies a sarcastic smile and great humor. His face is dominated by black glasses with extra thick lenses, which blur the shape and color of his eyes.

My attention returns to Mary. She continues her story. It seems she had met Anwar in the English countryside during a University apprenticeship in a village library. They've lived in Saudi Arabia a year now. She spent the first several months with Anwar's relatives. She painted a picture of a very primitive life in a mud hut. They finally managed to find a small apartment of their own in Riyadh, and were in Taif for only a short family visit. She finishes her story by sharing that she is pregnant, and looking forward to the birth of their first child.

Mary and I continue our conversation into the early evening. Osane keeps giving me anxious looks, which I ignore. He finally calls me into our bedroom, saying that this visit is interfering with the rest of the family. Zora wants to serve dinner and proceed with their nightly routines.

The solution to this dilemma means pure elation for me. Anwar suggests that we all go out to eat in a very secluded restaurant he knows of. This means we will be leaving the apartment in couple fashion. What a treat!

The restaurant is small and out of the way. The main floor is not very crowded. The family section is on the top floor, which has a separate entrance. Upon entering the room we are forced to stoop, because of the low ceilings. The food is acceptable but the company is more than I could ask for. Unfortunately our evening out is over way too soon. As we drive Anwar and Mary back to the relatives they are visiting, we promise to have a reunion just as soon as we are settled in Riyadh.

During the next several days, I pack and we pay our goodbye visits to all the relatives. As time passes, I begin to notice that tensions are building up within me. I feel like a spring ready to snap, and I start counting the minutes until our new life in Riyadh can begin.

Finally, the day of our departure arrives. We are just having our final tea before driving to the airport when there is a knock on the door. Suddenly, among a great deal of noise and confusion, Sarah and her children walk into the family room. Before I realize what is happening, Osane calls over his shoulder that I should wait for him here. Then he walks out the door with Sarah, leaving the children behind.

As Osane and Sarah leave the apartment, I quietly excuse myself. I walk into my bedroom and close the door. Thankful that I have held myself together long enough to escape into privacy, my patience blows up like a bomb and I begin throwing pillows as I pace the room.

"I have done everything right," I rant and rave to the walls. "I have learned how to prepare Saudi food, wash clothes, and iron in the traditional way. I have learned how to sew, to make sweet mint tea and bitter Arab coffee. I have blended into communal living, harmonized with cultural norms, and shifted my shape into a Saudi woman. I have adapted to floor living. I have also acquired an elementary understanding of the Arabic language. I have accepted covering my body every time I step into fresh air. I became a Muslim and I even *silently tolerated* my husband morphing into a distant entity. All this I have done…but at what cost?"

As I pace faster and faster, my nerves become increasingly brittle. I am a guitar string ready to pop. When Sarah takes Osane out of the departure pattern, for whatever reason, she gives the last twist to my catgut cord and it is now unraveling. It doesn't matter that there are other flights to Riyadh. Intuitively I know that I only have enough strength to make *our* scheduled flight. An irrational line has been drawn in the sand, and in my mind our departure is now or never.

I have no recourse but to get myself under control. Slowly I walk back into the kitchen to help Zora and Mina prepare another pot of tea for Sarah's children. As the time ticks away, it becomes evident that Osane's return will be too late. Trying to keep calm, I calculate that the Taif airport is at least half an hour into the desert. The family room clock shows there are only forty-five minutes until take off. This means a decision has to be made. I can sit and wait for Osane's return. Or… I can somehow make my way to the airfield, surmising that Osane will be at the terminal waiting for me. As my agitation increases, it becomes insanely important to me that we catch our flight!

Suddenly, I hear a very cold and authoritarian voice ordering Sarah's oldest son to hail a cab. I am astonished when I realize that voice is mine. As the reality of my request becomes clear, the relatives begin to protest. One glance at me, however, tells them that on this issue I am uncompromising. The taxi comes and our luggage is loaded. At the last second Zora and Mina shove Aunt Sarah's children in the back seat, as my unconventional escorts to the airport.

The dark evening ride seems endless. As I struggle with my emotions I know that my behavior is inappropriate and demented, but somehow so necessary. We finally arrive at the airfield, only to find out that *our* plane has just taken off and there is no waiting Osane. The taxi driver turns our car around, and we head back to Taif.

Defeated on every level, anger is my first emotion. Suddenly I can't stand this car, this desert, the city of Taif, or the entire country of Saudi Arabia one second longer. Fury quickly shifts into vulnerability. I begin sobbing uncontrollably, burying my head into Nazar's long curls. Aunt Sarah's children look over at me, their brown eyes wide in disbelief. I sense they want to comfort me, but I don't want solace from any Saudi….no matter how small. I cry the entire way back to the apartment. As soon as the taxi stops, I grab Nazar and run up the stairs.

Upon entering the apartment, I stomp into our bedroom and slam the door. As I continue sobbing uncontrollably, Osane walks in. His face is white and pale. I look up and let him have it. All of the feelings I have been suppressing for days spill out in loud screams. I shout how alone I am, and how he is my only friend in this whole country. That ever since we returned from his village, he has become distant, cold, and aloof. I vent that I feel unsupported, frustrated, and *so* alone. Osane just stands there, letting me get it all out.

After I have calmed down, he lets silence fill the room. Then, slowly he begins to explain the circumstances behind his tardiness. It seems Aunt Sarah wanted to buy us housewarming presents for our new home in Riyadh. Planning a special surprise, she had taken him to the market and picked out blankets, sheets, and kitchen goods. During the many transactions, they were delayed.

He further clarifies. "Christie, my lack of warmth is because of my insecurities and worries about our future. I am not at all pleased with my job, and my salary means we will be living below poverty level. With hardly any money, I have found only one home that is barely decent enough to move into. If we choose this house, how are we going to furnish it?"

After he is through, I slip down in the corner. I bury my head in shame as I recall my dramatic behavior. How can I be angry with Sarah? Knowing our money situation, she is only trying to provide blankets for the coming winter. On the other hand, how can I blame Osane for worrying about his family? Finally, how can I possibly explain my uncontrollable outburst to the relatives?

Sensing my chagrin, Osane bends down and pulls me into his arms. These past several weeks have been incredibly difficult on both of us, and he knows it. We have both survived endless emotional rides, which keep throwing us up against our walls of endurance. Emotionally spent, the only recourse is to twist our arms around each other and hold on tight. Finally, we feel safe enough to let go.

Digging into our suitcases, I pull out our nightgowns and prepare Nazar and me for bedtime. Osane slips into bed next to us, and before we close our eyes we are all asleep. The next morning we feel renewed.

Osane dresses quickly and joins the relatives, but I linger. How can I possibly open the door and face the family, after my behavior of the previous day? Taking a deep breath and gathering my courage, I leave the safety of our room and walk timidly into the family room.

As I sit down in my customary corner, I notice life going on around me as usual. It is as if my outburst never occurred. I try to apologize to Zora and then Mina, but they simply give me a friendly smile and proceed with their tasks. Once again, I marvel at the finesse of Saudi communal living.

After tea, Osane drives back to the airport and buys tickets for our second attempt at leaving. Our flight is scheduled to leave two days later. Those days pass quickly. Once again, we pack our clothes plus the new housewarming presents from Aunt Sarah and prepare to leave.

Our final goodbyes to Zora, Walid, Saeed, and Mina are highly emotional. I thank each one several times, for I know they have trained me for my role as a Saudi mother, wife, and woman. We have all taken a risk and opened ourselves to a life beyond language or a common culture. The result is mutual love, respect, and an understanding of each other that extends far beyond the limiting world of words. As we walk out the door and down the steps, I realize that each one of them will be a part of me forever.

Boarding the flight with time to spare, we are soon airborne. Once again, our family is adrift in Arabia, between worlds. With an inward sigh I reach over and put Nazar on my lap, and close Osane's hand on mine. As the desert speeds by underneath, I cuddle down and close my eyes. For this second in time, all is right with my world.

Chapter 28

Arrival

"Your diamonds are not in far distant mountains or in yonder seas; they are in your own backyard, if you dig for them."
Russell H. Conwell

The wheels of our plane are lowered and after a few bounces, we land on Riyadh soil. As Osane gathers our hand luggage, I drape on my abaya and pull my black scarf tightly around my head. Meanwhile I stare through the plane's window, trying to catch a glimpse of our new home. Because of the evening hour, the only thing I can see is a barren, dark expanse. Osane's words of "let's go," pull me away from the window. The three of us walk slowly down the stairs and into the airport.

We make our way through the customs maze, and hail a cab to drive us to downtown Riyadh. Looking out the window, I search for any sights of our new city. After months in the mountainous town of Taif and a rural village in Southern Arabia, Riyadh seems like Paris to me. There is traffic everywhere; the streets are wide and lined with bright lights. A variety of desert plants grow in the center strips of most streets, and instead of the one main market square I see a variety of stores scattered here and there, European-style.

We finally arrive at our hotel, and I stay in the taxi while Osane walks in and makes arrangements. He returns to the cab with a smile. "Christie," he announces proudly. "After a long talk with the manager, I have managed to reserve one of the best rooms in the hotel for us and he's giving it to us at the standard rate."

We follow Osane to our new quarters and after fumbling with the keys, he opens the door. He has a right to be satisfied with himself, for we walk into a spacious room dominated by four large windows that overlook the street. It is a perfect space to begin our new life.

The next morning, Osane leaves for the first day at his new job. He returns that afternoon full of news. He orders dinner and while we eat, he shares his day with us.

"It was so great," Osane says with a wide grin. "At the Ministry I met Mohsen, my boyhood friend from Southern Arabia. He'll be visiting us this evening. As you know, a Saudi male is never permitted into a room with a woman. However, we're no longer living with our Saudi relatives. This is our life now, and we can bend the rules."

A few hours later, tall, good-looking Mohsen walks into our lives. His deep brown eyes and smile portray intelligence, and his carriage speaks of confidence. I am overjoyed, for he has been educated in England. After months of being tongue-tied I am finally meeting a Saudi who has not only been exposed to the West, but can converse in a smooth English accent. Containing my impulse to ask him a million questions about Riyadh, I keep my interrogation to a few sentences and let the old friends slip into Arabic.

After tea, Mohsen offers to take us on a tour of Riyadh. Stepping into the back seat of his Volkswagen bug, I am full of excitement and anticipation. Quickly I realize that Mohsen's idea of a tour includes only the Princes' villas and the King's palace. Pleased to see anything, I lean back and look up at the stars as our car drives by long walls, exquisite gates, palace guards, and glimpses of gigantic villas. At the end of our outing, I thank Mohsen warmly. As he walks out the door, he promises to come back the next evening.

The following morning after breakfast, I give Osane a kiss goodbye and settle down in a chair by the window. Before I can fully relax, I have to make sure Nazar and I aren't visible. I want to watch the population of our new city, without anyone seeing us. It seems our windows are too high to attract anyone's attention, and since there are no tall buildings across the street, we are safe.

Nazar is as much into this new game as I am, and we pass the morning studying the masses below. My first observation is that nothing seems clear in the streets, as layers of swirling sand and dust dim colors and details. I then notice that instead of a median strip between the two single-lane streets, there is a large irrigation ditch designed to catch heavy winter rains. I also observe a few cars (most of them taxis) and the usual number of bicycles, donkeys, and horse carts.

While studying the Saudis in their native dress, I also notice many short Yemeni men in white, arm-less tee shirts and skirts. They are walking barefoot, and are wearing brightly colored skullcaps on their heads. There are also Lebanese, Palestinians, Jordanians, Egyptians and other Arab men from the Middle East. They are dressed in Western pants and loose shirts. I also notice military cadets in gray or brown uniforms. Nazar particularly likes to watch the boys of different sizes as they walk or run while balancing schoolbooks on their heads.

After several hours of window gazing, it dawns on me that there is one element of the society missing. The whole morning I haven't noticed one woman, only a few small girls accompanied by brothers or fathers. After this realization, my soul shivers. Then I reassure myself that I have already learned how to live under house arrest. This is our second day in Riyadh with no books, magazines, TV and only a few toys for Nazar to play with. Yet because of our training with the Saudi relatives, neither Nazar nor I are unsettled.

Osane returns around 2 pm. As he orders our meal, I notice that his excitement has already been replaced by depression. Over our meal, I ask him what's wrong.

"Christie, I'm frustrated with this new job at the Interior Ministry. My supervisor is an old man, very set in his ways. My other male co-workers are barely educated. Any suggestions I make are met with glassy stares. All the standard routines are decades old, inflexible and unchanging."

As he peers into space, his caged discouragement bounces off the walls. In between bites I say, "Osane, I know your job seems quite grim, but look backwards and remember where we've been. We fought through our transition period and actually remained sane. Now our new home in Riyadh represents ground zero. Together we'll climb upwards in life, so please be patient. In time we will overcome this challenge."

That evening Mohsen again knocks on our door. This time he is ready to drive us to the apartment Osane had found for us while we were still in Taif. If I approve, this will become our new home.

It doesn't take long for Mohsen's Volkswagen to drive out of the middle of Riyadh, and into the foreign suburb of Malez. We soon find ourselves in a quiet and affluent area. The big villas and walled-in gardens are full of mature trees. We come to a row of small shops and, as we turn a corner, the paved road turns into dirt. At the mosque we veer left, and drive down a narrow lane that services four large villas. Our car stops in front of a black iron gate, built into the wall of the largest villa. I watch Osane and Mohsen, as they walk down the street in search of the landlord.

When Osane returns with the key, he mentions that the two small apartments behind the gate are old servants' quarters. I swallow hard, and follow him through the gate and into an enclosed hallway. To the right, stairs wind up to the roof. On the two remaining walls are apartment doors.

We enter the doorway on the left, and walk into a small, stark room. The sole source of light comes from a streetlight, which shines through the room's only window. Mohsen hands me a flashlight, and as I turn it on Osane leads me through the room and into another small hallway. Off the hallway on the left is another tiny room, also on the street, with one window. Further down the hall on the left is an undersized, oblong-shaped room that serves as the kitchen. A doorway at the end of the room leads off the kitchen, into a tiled, walled-in garden with one large eucalyptus tree.

By now, the men and Nazar have caught up to me. Osane finds me smiling. "You did it," I laughed. "I said I'd live almost anywhere, but I have to have at least one tree. Well, here's the tree!"

We re-enter the house through the kitchen, and discover a Western bathroom at the end of the hall. To the left of the bathroom is the back bedroom, with a window opening onto the garden. Osane is anxious for my opinion, but I won't give him one until I climb the stairs to the roof.

I open the roof door and the starlight illuminates my walk to the corner wall. I take a short breath and peer over. What I find are the back gardens of the large villas encircling us. It's as if I'm looking down on a secret forest. While the front of the apartment is on the street, the back enjoys complete privacy. I stand there, letting the breeze blow through my hair and reveling in the fact that I can peer over the wall without gathering a crowd of leering males. Instantly I know that this will be our first home. These walls will provide a safe space, which will shelter us as we begin our upward climb.

When I return from the roof, Osane asks. "Well Christie, What do you think?"

Keeping my face expressionless I answer. "I'm sure you realize that this apartment is small, filthy, and in horrible condition. Even in the dark you can't miss the circular crayon artwork drawn on the walls by previous children. We'll also inherit the status of paupers among the wealthy, for nothing can hide the fact that this flat used to be the servants' quarters.

"However, this apartment is available and we can afford it on your wages. Besides, it does have one tree. The roof and garden also offer outside privacy. I think in time we can make this space very comfortable. So Osane, what I think is: welcome to your new home."

The next morning finds us back at our hotel. After Osane leaves for work, I begin listing things we will need for our new house. Suddenly, I hear a knock on our hotel door. I can't imagine who it might be. I am even more shocked when I open the door and find Mary, my best and forever friend.

How good it is to see her. As I take her abaya, I recall her promise to visit once we arrive in Riyadh. When Mary is seated, she reaches into her bag and pulls out a sack of homemade cookies. Mary hands me the bag, and I take out a cookie. Biting down, I hold the ingredients in my mouth, slowly dissolving it. I feel its texture, smell its rich scent, and taste its sweetness.

Listening to English words and eating homemade cookies is pure heaven! A tiny voice whispers in my ear: perhaps we might be able to create a peaceful existence in our new city after all. Mary confirms my hope. She shares that she has met a few English friends, to whom she promises to introduce me. She further remarks that life in Riyadh can be quite nice, if you follow the rules.

Way too soon, it's time for Mary to leave. She promises she will visit us in our new apartment. She gives Nazar a kiss goodbye, and we watch out of our hotel window as she enters a car driven by her brother-in-law.

The next day is Friday, the one day off in the Saudi work week. We take a taxi to our new home and spend the day scrubbing it down. We scrape black crayon marks off the walls, beat the dust out of shutters, patch screens, and clean every inch. Then we walk through our disinfected domain. "What do you think?" Osane asks.

"Well," I reply. "I'm having problems becoming one with shocking pink walls. They make me grind my teeth. Hopefully we'll be able to paint the walls a neutral color. Other than that, I think we're ready to move in."

The next day after work, Osane goes shopping with money he has borrowed from Mohsen. He buys mattresses, one gas stove, dishes, kitchen equipment, a cupboard to stack them in, four cheap rugs and a TV. He also buys one large American refrigerator and a tiny, self-wringing Japanese washing machine.

After the goods are delivered, we move in. Osane, Nazar and I christen our new apartment with a home-cooked meal. After dinner, Mohsen comes for tea. Our first guest sits in the middle of our cheap rug, on the hard concrete floor. This will never do.

The next day Osane returns to the market. He buys Arab cushions, floor mattresses, a kerosene heater, and material for curtains. Since our front windows open onto the sidewalk, curtains mean that we will be able to open the windows for air circulation while retaining privacy.

The next Friday, Osane covers the shocking pink walls with a lime green, the only paint in our price range. Not the perfect color, but I can at least live with a greenish hue. After the paint dries, Osane and I rearrange the family room with our new purchases. Osane plugs in the TV, while I settle back on our cushions to sew our new curtain.

The following morning I hang the curtain and walk around our home. With a little effort, we've turned it into a pleasant space. However, one problem remains.

Walking into the bedroom, I look at the pile of suitcases in the corner. I am definitely sick of folding and unfolding clothes. Looking around the room, I notice an indented space meant for a freestanding clothes closet. Knowing any other purchase for our home is months away, I ponder.

Finally, I come up with a solution. Feeling like a spider weaving its web, I hang clothesline on nails I pound into the small indentation. I cross and re-cross the line, designing a section for each of us. By the time I am done, my creation is very bizarre. I know it resembles a concoction in a contemporary art museum much more than it does a closet. But it doesn't matter, because it works.

With our home finally livable, our family of three settles into it very well. The winter weeks pass by, and we submerge ourselves in refreshing sameness. We develop the pattern of visiting Mary and Anwar on Fridays. They live on the other side of town, which means a taxi ride and an excuse for Nazar and me to get out of the house.

The journey is far from scenic. We drive by dirty garages, junkyards, iron-gate welders, Mercedes truck repair and mechanic's shops. Everyone and everything that inhabits this acreage is tinted black with grease and mud. Once on the other side of this neighborhood, we enter a very crowded and busy area, and this is where our friends' apartment is located.

What makes Mary and Anwar's environment livable is their flat's location on the top floor. This means that not only are they away from the street noise, but they also have access to the roof. On many evenings we retreat to this roof, where we drink cups of tea while looking out onto the skyline of Riyadh. Often we watch the sunsets, as mosques from around the city sing out the call to evening prayer.

It is during these visits that Mary often shares historical facts about Riyadh. It seems that only a decade ago, slaves were freed. Mary also relates that it's only recently that girls have been allowed to attend elementary school, and mud brick remnants still stand as a testament to the fact that only a short time ago, the capital had been a walled-in village. Most amazingly, up until last year it was possible to fit the *entire foreign population of Riyadh* into one living room.

On other occasions, Mary and Anwar join our family for a Friday tea in the desert. On one such outing Anwar's brother drives all of us an hour out of Riyadh, to a tiny dirt road that leads into the sand dunes. The weather is perfect. The winter sun serves as our cosmic heater, the temperature is mild, and the air is clear. It has just rained, and the smell of wet sand drifts through the open windows.

When the car stops at the foot of a sand dune, Mary and I kick off our shoes and race to the top. From the tip of the dune, we both experience a feeling of freedom and space. As we glance around, our eyes view mounds of red sand for as far as we can see. In awe, we both sink our fingers into the sand. We sit in silence, for neither of us feels the need for conversation while surrounded by such striking solitude.

Suddenly, from behind our sand dune gallops a purebred black Arabian stallion. He is saddled but riderless, and his reins are flapping wildly in the wind. Almost before our minds can register this image, he disappears behind the next dune. Strain as we may, neither Mary nor I can catch a further glimpse of him. We look at each other in startled amazement. Only because both of us have witnessed this seeming illusion, do we know it is real.

It seems only right that some omen be read into this lightning appearance and disappearance of a beautiful and rebellious stallion. Not knowing whether to link this image to the beginning of a new life or the end of an old, we simply accept it as another unbelievable Saudi experience.

Meanwhile, days keep flipping off the calendar in healing normalcy. Sometime during the next month, we begin noticing sounds from the empty apartment next door. Hammering and painting can be heard in the evenings, but never in the daytime.

One night after dinner, Osane knocks on the door and meets our new neighbor, an Ethiopian by the name of Ali. It seems Ali is working for an Italian company in Addis Ababa, and has been transferred to Riyadh. Now he is readying the apartment for his wife and two children, who will be arriving in a few weeks. When Osane returns and tells me about our new neighbor's children, I am thrilled. Finally Nazar will have some playmates, which he is becoming old enough to need.

Three weeks later, we begin hearing regular movement from the apartment next door. One morning, I finally build up enough courage to knock on Ali's front door. At first I hear silence, and then the traditional "who" response. Not knowing how to say "*your neighbor*," I gently pound again.

The door opens a crack, and I see brown eyes peering out. Then the door swings wide open, revealing a beautiful Ethiopian woman. I smile at her and point to our apartment next door. As it dawns on her that we are neighbors, she shyly smiles. Then she introduces herself as Rema, and points to her two children, Usef (around five) and Samira (around three). After quick handshakes we both retreat into our homes, somehow knowing we will become friends.

As time passes, Rema and I slowly begin opening our doors after our husbands leave for work. Usef, Samira and Nazar develop a pattern of running from apartment to apartment. Luckily, our new neighbors come from the northern half of Ethiopia, which throughout history has been connected to the Arab world. They therefore speak Arabic, which means a thin line of communication is possible.

Gradually Rema and I begin spending more time with each other. I help her hang rugs on her walls, and she shares her children's baby pictures. Some afternoons I watch her dress for her outings, for she has many friends. I am always pleased when she lays out her traditional Ethiopian apparel, for it is stunning. The dress is pure white and colorfully embroidered on the short sleeves, the narrow waist, and the calf-length hemline. Over her head, she drapes a similar white and embroidered shawl, creating a picture of elegant womanhood.

Gradually the daylight begins to lengthen. Our new home, the pleasant winter weather, and most Fridays highlighted with visits from Rema and Mary make inside living tolerable. Whenever I develop cabin fever, I dash to the roof and look out over the garden of trees.

Caught up in our peaceful routine, it takes a while for my denial to wear thin. One afternoon it finally does, and I have to admit to myself that I am not well. For weeks, I have pushed myself when Osane is home. However, during the day I often suffer from a lack of energy. During these periods, Rema will often wash our dishes or sweep the floors, but I can't keep up this charade any longer.

After our afternoon meal the following day I say, "Osane, I haven't told you but I haven't been feeling well for several days. I hate to say this, but I think it's time for you to take me to a doctor for a check-up."

He looks at me, as if he was aware I was feeling poorly all along. Without hesitation, he hails a taxi. I am soon sitting in front of a female, English-speaking, Indian physician. As usual, she is more interested in my story than my health. After outlining my history and the fact that I am enjoying my new life in Riyadh, I say, "I think I have mononucleosis."

She only laughs. After her examination, she announces her prognosis. "You are simply adapting to a new environment."

Begrudgingly, I have to agree with her. I know I am breathing air with all sorts of foreign molecules, living in a strange climate, eating strange and different foods, drinking untreated water, and eating fruits and vegetables washed in that water. Physically I am deprived of any sort of exercise, and emotionally I feel a growing anger smoldering deep within. In summation, I am a mountain rose that has been transplanted into the desert and is withering.

Fortunately, Aunt Sarah's sudden arrival is just the medicine I need. Her visit keeps my mind occupied and my hands busy scrubbing the house, cooking, and entertaining. Aunt Sarah always warms my heart, for during my entry months she had become my Saudi mother.

Regrettably, she is not coming for a vacation but for medical reasons. It seems Aunt Sarah suffers from bronchial asthma and is quite sick. Her doctor insists she leaves the damp, cold, mountainous air of Taif, in order to recover in the dry climate of Riyadh.

Aunt Sarah spends most of her time lying in our bedroom playing with Nazar. Although she attempts to appear cheerful, I can hear her harsh breathing and coughing from two rooms away. One day, while Sarah is showing me how to cut up a chicken, she prophesizes, "In the future, you will live in a big villa, a grand place of your own."

I reply, "Insh allah" (If God wills), and we smile at each other.

Every week, Osane takes Aunt Sarah to the doctor where she is given a shot for her asthma. Slowly, surrounded by the dry air of Riyadh, her health begins to improve. By the middle of the second month, Sarah has healed to the point where the doctor says she can go home. Anxious to return to her family, with renewed energy and a smile she packs her belongings.

Hailing a taxi, Osane, Nazar and I take her to the airport. The only other time I had been to this airport was on our arrival to Riyadh. Now, entering this same terminal, I naturally follow Osane. Quickly, Aunt Sarah calls me back. She leads me through a door with heavy black curtains, and as I sit in the women's waiting room my smoldering anger begins to surface. I am the only foreigner in this room. Since I am married to a Saudi, the strict cultural norms of female invisibility also apply to me.

When Aunt Sarah's plane is ready to board, we are called from the waiting room. During our last hug, I reflect that even in sickness, uneducated Aunt Sarah personifies strength, generosity, and wisdom. It has been a grand visit, and our home will be lonely without her.

A footnote to Aunt Sarah's visit comes three months later. There is a knock on the gate. I go to the door and ask "meen," expecting it to be one of Rema's friends. I am therefore surprised to hear a male voice identifying himself as Aunt Sarah's husband.

I slowly open the gate and find our visitor holding a large oriental rug. My eyes open wide with surprise, as I welcome him into our home. Over tea and nuts, he relays a message from Aunt Sarah, "This rug in the beginning. Soon this rug will lie in a large, fine villa."

With a smile on my face, I bid goodbye to Sarah's husband. Spreading her new rug on the floor of our old servants' quarters, I feel that we have finally arrived in Riyadh. What lies ahead is in God's hands. However, under our feet will always remain Sarah's rug, and the reassurance that somewhere in our future is a fine villa with gardens, trees, and a hearth worthy to call home.

Chapter 29

Settling In and Meeting New Friends

"Familiar feels safe. In today's uncertain world, feeling safe and secure seems the emotional definition of sanity."
Sarah Ban Breathnach

One Friday afternoon in the early spring, there is a knock on our gate. I open it to find the daughter of our landlord, inviting us to a party at her house that evening. She says her father will be very honored if we attend.

So a few hours later, I slip on one of the dresses Zora had sewn for me. Carefully I arrange my gold, and dress Nazar in his good clothes. Our family of three walks out of our gate.

We stop a few yards away at a small side gate, which serves as the women's entrance. After Osane makes sure we are safely inside, he walks further down the wall and enters through the large, main gate.

Upon entering the women's section of the villa, I sense that once again I am stepping into a traditional situation. I feel confident that I can handle it because of the training I have received from my Saudi relatives.

Slowly Nazar and I make our way to the door of the women's majlis. I look around in amazement, for I have never seen such a large living room. The whole space is full of women and children, sitting around the padded sides sipping tea. Dominating the center of the room are three brass fire-pits filled with charcoal. Not only do these burners give off heat, but their brass lids are also beautifully shaped and engraved with intricate designs.

As we enter the room the conversation, as usual, stops. One of the girls takes my abaya and scarf, while I grab Nazar's hand and begin the customary handshaking around the room. I put forth my warmest smile, and make sure that the trailing Nazar doesn't trip over any cups of tea or coffee. I then find an empty slot along the wall's perimeter and sink down, pulling Nazar close to me, Arab style. I am served tea and after two or three more minutes of intense observation, the conversations return to normal.

Nazar has no intention of sitting quietly in front of me, and he is soon off playing with the rest of the children. That leaves me sitting in a world of my own, broken occasionally by the arrival of new guests. This means I have to rise, shake their hands, and utter a few Arabic words of greeting.

Soon the call to dinner is sounded. As I'm finding Nazar and making my way into the other room, one of the younger women grabs my hand. She motions me to follow her. I obey and find myself in a private side hallway, away from everyone else. Here I am met by the landlord and another young woman.

I shake his hand, and he points to both of the women and says, "Mine." It dawns on me that he is introducing me to his two wives, both beautiful and both pregnant. I smile back at him, thank him in Arabic for our invitation, and assure him we are enjoying ourselves.

With thoughts of overpopulation spinning in my mind, I follow his wives back into the women's section. I find myself in a room with a gigantic tablecloth spread in the middle of the floor. On this cloth are spread three cooked sheep on platters of rice, eggs, pine nuts, and raisins. Surrounding the sheep are smaller dishes of salad, pudding, bread and fruit. For some reason, Nazar and I are treated as honored guests. The women around us go out of their way to make sure we have the finest pieces of meat.

After dinner and the washing of hands, we make our way back into the large living room where tea and coffee are served. Here the women and children wait until there is a knock on the door, and their names are called.

After ten minutes I hear our name, cologne is poured into our cupped hands, the incense burner is passed, and I am handed my abaya. I shake hands goodbye, thank both of my female hosts in Arabic, and disappear out the door to a waiting Osane.

I keep my composure until we are safely behind our own gate. Then I chatter non-stop, telling Osane each experience. With every other breath, I thank the people of my husband's village and the relatives in Taif who have taught me enough etiquette to survive such a Saudi setting.

With the weather still cool, we continue to enjoy life in our humble home. At the end of each work month, Osane is paid 1,000 Saudi riyals. He brings his wages home and throws it in my lap saying, "Christie, this is yours." I take this foreign colorful money out of the envelope, give him a kiss, and throw it into the air. This delights Nazar, who loves to watch it float back down.

We are living in a transparent mist of peace, on life's simplest terms. Materialistically, we have nothing, but it doesn't seem to matter. All the Saudis around us (rich or poor) have basically the same lifestyle.

This period of tranquility, however, is destined to be short-lived. For within our beings, we both feel change in the air. There is a growing sense that Western society has been circling our lives, demanding contact. It seems that reaching this crossroad is finally inevitable.

My first introduction to another non-Saudi is through Mary. She suggests a visit to Clara, her Swiss friend. So, the next week finds Mary and me knocking at her gate. Clara invites us in and as she serves tea, I glance around her living room. This unique space seems more like a rock exhibition and greenhouse than the main living area. Everywhere are desert plants and stones of every variety, which Clara and her husband have discovered in their ramblings through the desert.

Clara immediately enchants me, for she is an extremely colorful soul. Her thin face is framed by long, curly, unruly blond hair and her blue eyes have a twinkle of rebellion in them. She tells us that many mornings she pulls on her pink boots, wraps a black abaya around herself, and visit her Bedu neighbors down the hill. During these visits, the Bedouins have covered her hands with henna and have put a bead through her nose.

As I hear these tales, I feel a jab of jealousy at her carefree existence. Being foreign and transient, Clara is able to live on the perimeters of the Saudi society. Absolute rules that apply to Mary and me do not exist for her. She is free to do what she chooses.

Two afternoons later, there is a knock on my gate. I open the door to find Clara standing there, holding a large cardboard carton. She has barely gotten in the door before the cardboard box starts to move, and out jumps a black and white kitten.

Clara says that her Bedouin neighbors' cat had kittens, and she knew that Nazar would love one. Suddenly she is gone, leaving me with the kitten. Our first chore is a bath, for the cat smells of goat straw and stable. However, the kitten doesn't like to be handled. It seems to have a wild, untamable streak, just like Clara.

A few weeks later, our exposure to the foreign population continues. Mary and Anwar invite us to dine with Jane (from Scotland) and her husband Naji (from the South Arabian Hadramaout, or Aden). Jane is a teacher at Riyadh's International School. This kindergarten through fifth grade school teaches the foreign population of Riyadh.

Over dinner and tea, I begin sharing some of my Saudi transition experiences. Jane finds my stories fascinating. That evening she appoints herself our personal guide to Western society in Riyadh. Two weeks later, she insists that I come with her to a lunch hosted by Olivia, a black American who is also a teacher at Riyadh International School.

I politely refuse Jane's invitation to go to lunch several times. Unfortunately she won't take "no" for an answer. As I ponder my refusals, I conclude that my hesitation illustrates how Saudi I have become. On many levels I have made peace with my simple Arab life. The thought of changing my path mirrors layers of insecurities. I fully acknowledge that I am only a shadow of my former self. My hair is too long and untrimmed, my old mini skirts look foreign and feel uncomfortable, and I am used to speaking in my pidgin Arabic. No matter how hard I try, I know I can't blend into American standards, physically or on a material level.

Finally, Jane's persistence wins and I accept the lunch invitation. I drop Nazar off with Rema and leave my abaya behind. I take a deep breath and walk out the gate to meet Jane and her chauffeur. We drive to a section of Malez I have never seen, full of large, modern villas.

As we arrive, other cars are also approaching Olivia's gate. Driving these new vehicles are chauffeurs, who drop their foreign employers off and then wait in the shade until they are called to drive their passengers home. Feeling I have more in common with the drivers, I get out of the car and follow Jane to Olivia's gate.

We knock, and the large iron door slowly opens. The second I step through the gate, I know I am entering America. I look around at the well-trimmed lawns, the swimming pool, and the elaborate toys that are scattered here and there. Everywhere is a reflection of upper middle-class America.

I follow Jane up the stairs and into the villa. While she smiles at everyone in the living room, I feel weak in the knees and wish I could sit down. Jane begins introducing me around the room. I have to stop myself from kissing them, Saudi-style, on each cheek. It is strange for me to simply nod my head, smile, and say hello.

After the introductions, I slip into the shadows and watch Jane work the room. Soon a lovely lunch, right off a country-club menu, is served. Sitting at a table and not on the floor, I quietly savor each spoonful, tasting familiar spices and breathing in remembered smells.

Throughout lunch I listen to the carefree banter with one ear, while the rest of me remains in reverse cultural shock. Struggling for composure, I casually listen to the soliloquy of the person sitting next to me. For some reason she has decided to give me a history lecture.

In between bites, she stares into space and begins, "My dear, did you know that the Kingdom has always kept Westerners out of the holy cities of Mecca and Medina?"

Politely I nod my head, knowing she will continue. "Well," she resumes. "Very slowly, over the years, selected foreigners penetrated the borders to teach or trade. By the late 1930s, the first oil was being extracted from the Persian Gulf town of Dhahran.

With the creation of the Arabian American Oil Company (ARAMCO), Americans begin entering the country but were kept in isolated communities surrounding the Persian Gulf. As oil brought in money, development was born and Americans began spreading to Riyadh and Jeddah.

Still, in the 1970's, each visa requires a work permit and the small numbers of American families who are allowed entry are kept inside walled compounds where they settled into their Little America.

Another breed of foreigner also began to dot the desert. Most of these early romantics are English, German, and a sprinkling of Swiss and other nationalities who chose to blend into the culture."

I'm thankful when my lunch companion finishes her history lecture and I smile at her as I watch the servants clear the dishes. Next, the desert is served. It is a vanilla pudding with a sugary caramel sauce poured over the top, and dripping over the sides. While enjoying each bite, I again listen to the general table conversations. Suddenly, I realize I am learning about coy power struggles and intricate social climbing.

It seems the source of this intrigue is an American Army base called "The Mission." The American government purposely strives to keep this small base unmarked and almost invisible. Inside The Mission, however, are the items American families yearn for. There are pools, a movie theater, and a commissary that sells American food plus culturally unacceptable pork, ham, and bacon. The base restaurant is the "in" place to go and the dances are a must on any social calendar. In a dry country, the lure of alcohol is another extremely potent Mission attraction.

Attempting to enhance the lives of U.S. soldiers in Saudi Arabia, the government allows each soldier to sponsor five families. In return for inviting the soldiers to home-cooked meals, the sponsored families are entitled to use the base facilities. It becomes very clear from the conversations around Olivia's table that if you wish to become anyone in Riyadh's foreign society, you *have* to become a sponsored family.

As I'm silently attempting to digest this new insight on social positioning, my pondering is broken by sliding chairs. It seems that the guests are adjourning to the living room.

Over coffee, I begin talking to the woman sitting next to me. Her name is Joan and she is an American married to a Palestinian. She had also taught at the Riyadh International School, but is now teaching at Riyadh School, an elite and private Saudi school. Joan and I seem to immediately connect. She, too, is married to an Arab, which necessitates balancing cultures.

When Joan rises to leave, she puts on her abaya. The rest of the women give her disapproving looks, for the traditional black cloak is threatening to these foreign women. There are a few comments, but Joan confidently states that she is on her way to work in a Saudi school and the abaya is required.

After Joan, everyone else starts to leave. Jane and I say goodbye, thank our hostess, and I am soon home. Back inside my own meager quarters, I become whole again. Here, I feel good about myself. When Nazar, Osane, the relatives, and Saudi friends surround me, I am special. I am finding that with Americans, I am a fish out of water.

Meanwhile, Jane and Naji will not leave us alone. So the next Friday evening, we are pressured into driving over to another mixed couple we just *have* to meet. Our cab stops at the villa next door to the Riyadh International School. The gate is opened by Tahar, a Jordanian. He leads us to the back of the villa, and upstairs to his top-floor flat. On the way, he tells us that he is worried about his English wife, Ella. It seems she has just been thrown off a horse, and is suffering from a back injury.

As we climb the stairs, we hear children's voices, and Nazar begins to smile. Soon Tahar's four-year-old son, plus his six- and seven-year-old daughters catch up to us. With screams and laughter they absorb Nazar into their game, while we continue up the stairs and into the living room.

Upon entering, we find Ella sitting upright in a straight back chair. She smiles a greeting, and apologizes for not standing up to welcome us. She then explains that she had been exercising a Prince's racehorse, when out of nowhere a Saudi fighter plane zoomed by at a very low altitude. The Arabian horse bolted, and she landed on the desert floor. It had been a hard fall, and she is afraid her riding days are over.

As I listen to Ella, I glance around the flat. Somehow, I immediately feel at home here. Their living quarters are adequate but not excessive. Upon hearing the happy noises of the children playing, a feeling of belonging creeps into my soul. Everyone else feels the same connection and we stay through the evening, chatting, laughing, and drinking tea.

During our visit, Jane and Naji announce that as soon as the school year is over they will be returning to Scotland. I give them both a hard stare. We have barely gotten to know them, and they are already going out of our lives. Similarly, Clara will soon be going back to Switzerland. Inwardly, I question the value of forging friendships among such a transient foreign population.

Feeling insecure, I turn to Ella and ask, "How long has your family been in Riyadh, and are you also planning to leave?"

Ella replies, "We've been here for about a year. Tahar is working for an English company that keeps renewing his contract, so we're planning to stay in Arabia indefinitely."

On our cab ride home from our visit, I snuggle my happy and exhausted son. Still mourning the loss of our new friends, I console myself with Ella's statement that their stay in Riyadh is permanent (at least for now).

A week later, I am delighted to find Ella and her small son on our doorstep. Slowly the frequency of her visits increase, until Ella and her son appear several mornings each week. Over the next month, we become best friends. Magically, the loneliness that has shadowed me since my entry into the Kingdom evaporates.

Just as we become secure in our new social patterns, the weather changes and school ends. It is finally time for Jane and Nadji to depart. So the following Friday, we hail a cab for a ride to our friends' apartment to say goodbye. As we walk into their home, we are surprised to find ourselves in the middle of a garage sale. Prices are on everything, and several customers mill about. I run off to find Jane, while Osane sits down on a couch next to a pleasant-looking Arab man from Aden. When I return, I find him deep in conversation.

As Osane introduces me to Imad, I note that he is Osane's height and has a good build. He is wearing well-tailored Western clothes, glasses, and has a kind, friendly smile. It seems Imad's Scottish wife and young daughter are traveling to Riyadh in a few months. He is at Jane's sale buying furniture to ready his apartment. Just before we leave, Osane gives Imad his number at the Interior Ministry. We promise to get together as soon as his wife arrives.

Chapter 30

Hitting Bottom in the Summer Desert

"God doesn't promise to fix things; he just promises not to go away."
Deborah Keenan

Ever since we landed in Saudi Arabia, I had been dreading the arrival of the intense, omnipresent, summer sun. I expected the transition to be gradual, but once again the desert fools me. At the end of April there is a sharp line of demarcation. One day is cool winter where several layers are required to keep warm, and the next day is hot.

Like an explosion, summer is here, and there won't be a break until mid- October. The entire Kingdom throws off layers of clothing, and digs into summer wardrobes. The men put aside their black, tan, and gray wool thobes and pull out their thin cotton ones. Meanwhile the women begin wearing light, colorful summer dresses under their abayas.

The extreme change in weather is shocking to everyone's system. One of the effects is a dwindling appetite, and I finally understand the reasoning behind government work schedules. The men and schoolchildren start work or school at 7 AM, when the heat is still reasonable. They return around 2:00 PM, allowing the whole family to eat their main meal together and spend the hottest hours of the day (from 2:00 to 4:00 pm) in their houses, napping. Life begins again as the sun's rays diminish, and evening activities occur in the coolness of night.

With the hot sun beating through the windows, our apartment becomes unbearable. After work, Osane hails a cab to the market and brings home a desert cooler. While installing the unit, he explains, "This desert cooler is the most popular unit to provide relief from the heat. The cooler will pump water into a holding tank and its fan will blow this water-cooled air through our home. By opening strategic windows and closing certain doors, we can get some relief. Unfortunately, with outside temperatures fluctuating between 100 and 130 degrees, there is only so much our new desert cooler can do. The only feasible way to cope with such intense desert heat is to leave! Each year the government moves to the mountains of Taif, and the foreign population scatters."

As soon as school is over, the exodus to escape the heat begins. One by one, families fly off to different parts of the world. It is especially difficult to say goodbye to Ella and her family. I didn't realize how dependent I had become on these new friends, nor how subtly I have slipped back into my Western ways.

Feeling like a child left out of a fabulous vacation, I brood and despair. But the days keep passing regardless of my moods. Occasionally we visit Mary and Anwar, for they have remained in the Kingdom. However, the trip across Riyadh in a taxi with no air conditioning soon becomes too wearing. That leaves Rema and her two children. So most summer mornings, we swing our front doors open and children's feet patter between apartments.

Unfortunately, Osane keeps falling deeper into an emotional abyss. Commuting to work in the summer heat is proving to be unbearable. Early morning finds him on foot, walking up to the main road where he hails a cab. Because of our money situation, he is forced to share a taxi with three or four other Saudis or Yemenis. They ride in this shared cab to the taxi junction in the middle of Riyadh. After being dumped off into a mass of dust, noise, and chaos, he hails another shared taxi to the Interior Ministry.

On his return trip, he retraces his route. At midday under a desert sun, the journey is more like an endurance trial. Every day Osane comes home hot and angry, complaining about unclean, dirty taxicabs full of body odor and dust.

During dinner, Osane will mumble about his dead-end job. When he applies himself, his superiors tell him, "Slow down, don't work so hard." When he continues to cause ripples, they offer him positions that never come through. It is a maze, and he can't find his way out.

Trying to keep my family's spirits up, I concentrate on daily routine. Nazar spends a great deal of time with our little kitten, who is now a full-grown cat. He runs around the house pulling a string, with the cat in heavy pursuit. Then he wrestles and plays with it.

Some days later, the cat is lying on a chair half-asleep. Nazar runs into the room, and pounces on him with his head. The cat reacts, and I come running into the room after hearing Nazar's frightened screams

What I find is a curtain of blood, gushing from Nazar's right eye. For a few frantic seconds I think that the cat has scratched out our son's eye. Thankfully, a closer examination reveals a deep gash in Nazar's eyelid. I grab a cold cloth, stop the bleeding, and bandage the cut as well as I can. After settling Nazar down, I grab the cat and throw him out into the street. Acknowledging that it isn't the cat's fault, I put my energies on Nazar, knowing I have to get him to a doctor for stitches.

With adrenaline pumping through my system I am ready to act, but I run into brick walls. We don't have a phone, I don't know the name or address of a doctor or the main hospital, and I have never been in a taxicab alone. I don't even know enough Arabic to communicate my plight!

With my mind shifting through options, I pick up Nazar and carry him to Rema. I then run back into our bedroom, and fumble around for a sheet of paper with Osane's office number on it. I quickly run out of our gate and across the street to a large villa I know has a phone. I pick up a stone and pound on the gate. A young girl with questioning eyes opens the door. Startled, she slams the gate shut and comes back with her mother and sisters.

Speaking in broken Arabic, I point to our quarters across the street and motion that I live there. I utter the words for baby, then cat, and try to act out what happened. Meeting blank stares, I finally end my futile charade attempts and walk past them into their house. By now, the whole harem is watching me. Their eyes tell me they are warm and sympathetic, but that they don't understand what I am saying or what I am looking for. I keep repeating "phone," until the word clicks. Finally, I am led into the living room where there is a telephone.

I am absolutely frazzled by this time, and my mind won't work. I have trouble transcribing the English numbers into Arabic. I have to re-dial several times before I manage to get the right numbers. The fact that everyone in the house is staring at me doesn't make it any easier. Ultimately, I get through. But when I have trouble communicating with the voice on the other end of the line, he hangs up! I try several more times. Eventually I am forced to give up, concluding that Osane is unreachable.

I feel like screaming, but compose myself enough to politely refuse the coffee and tea that is offered. Thanking my hostesses for the use of their telephone, I leave their house. Slowly I walk back across the street and knock on Rema's door. To my relief, a much calmed-down Nazar greets me. Rema keeps reassuring me that Nazar is all right, that I have cleaned the cut well, and have bandaged it properly.

I know differently. After cooking the afternoon meal, I climb the stairs to the roof. From this angle I can scan the street below, and I spot Osane as he walks around the corner. I run out into the street to greet him. Before Osane has time to walk through the gate, I blurt out the story, one word rapidly flowing into the next. He enters our home, has a long look at Nazar, and tells me, "Relax Christie, our son is not on his deathbed."

After dinner, Osane hails a cab and the three of us drive to a doctor. The physician examines the cut, re-cleanses it, and fastens it together with butterfly band-aids. He says it is too late to stitch and that only a small scar will remain. But I know Nazar's beautiful eye is marred by a mark that should never have been.

Memorizing the doctor's name, I take his number both in English and in Arabic. I also write down directions to and from his office. If any other incident ever occurs, I will be prepared to act. I will not be forced to rely on the neighbors or Osane.

The sun continues to bake our lives, as days turn into weeks. One afternoon while scrubbing a rice pot, I drop the sponge back into the soapy water. Depression settles over me, becoming my unwanted reality. I wander out to the garden and sit under my tree. Trying to identify what triggers my dark emotions, I decide the answer lies in our daily living. Sameness has become a gigantic snake that squeezes spontaneity and joy out of our lives. It is a suffocating blanket that forces each hour into an unwavering routine, and left unchecked it can become toxic to a young, free spirit. Unfortunately, I have begun to drown in identical moments.

Fighting my mood, I join Osane and Nazar for tea. That night before bed, I pray for a path out of my gloom. I wake the next morning pondering the natural laws of life. Just when I feel like I am going to drown in the floods of a severe rainstorm, the heaven splits for barely an instant. A splinter of sunshine slices the dark clouds, allowing me to glimpse a rainbow. That's how our entire family feels, when Uncle Hamid and his two children appear out of nowhere. Even Osane cracks a smile, and Nazar is ecstatic.

Laughter and play blesses our home for the two weeks the relatives stay. Uncle Hamid and Osane leave for work early in the morning, returning around 2:00 pm for the main meal. After dinner we all nap, as the heat dissipates. In the cool of twilight we hail taxis for a drive, a visit, or once or twice tea in the one public garden marked "families only." We arrive home in the late evening and spend the rest of our time watching TV.

The evening before they are to return to their village, Uncle Hamid takes his children to the Riyadh markets and buys them new clothes. They return quite late. Since their plane is taking off early the next morning, I wonder when they will pack. The evening passes, and they calmly go to bed without organizing one thing.

The next morning Osane, Nazar and I rise early to say goodbye. Again, the relatives leisurely wake up and calmly eat their breakfast. After the meal Uncle Hamid looks at his watch, and suddenly snaps to life. He starts yelling orders, and there is great confusion. Clothes are thrown into suitcases, beds are rolled up, children are dressed, goodbyes and thank yous said, and in moments they are gone.

Osane, Nazar and I stand at our gate. Slowly we walk back into our quiet apartment. The relatives' visit has left us refreshed, but also wondering what the next summer challenge will be.

It doesn't take long for a huge trial to present itself. The following week there is a knock on the door, and I open it to find Rema. She motions me into the hallway and points to the hazan, which is our submerged water-pit. Rema has already pulled up the two iron doors covering the pit in the hallway floor.

Into this cement hole run our water pipes. Normally the water level is up to the top, but now it is only one-quarter full. If the water level goes much lower, there won't be enough suction for the pump to push the water up to the roof water tank, where it gravity-feeds back down into our homes.

This lack of water in a mid-July desert is very serious. Without enough water in the hazan there will be no water to cook, wash dishes, take baths, wash clothes, or fill up the toilets. Worst of all, there will be no water for our desert cooler.

When Osane arrives home, I tell him about our water situation. He walks out the door into the hallway, and finds Abdu already there. Abdu feels that the problem is the size of our pipes, and the fact that we are the last homes on the water line.

He tells Osane, "I believe that our water supply in the winter is sufficient, because the larger families up-line use far less of it. This means that there is sufficient water to flow through our small pipes and build up in our hazan. Now in the summer heat, with homes using more water, our tank is getting some water but only trickles. There's not nearly enough."

Osane and Abdu decide to pound on the landlord's door. As they both suspect, his villa is getting plenty of water. Feeling responsible, the landlord hooks up a hose to his hazan. Osane and Abdu unroll this hose into our hazan and our pit is soon full.

This system tides us over for a few days but soon even the larger villas are becoming low on water, while we have *no* water. Trying to solve the problem, Osane hails a cab to the market and buys a large plastic water container. Every morning before work, he walks to the landlord's to fill up the container. Then he carries my water allowance for the day home to me.

To survive, our lifestyle changes radically. We use as few dishes as possible, flush the toilet only once a day, and are very careful with what we wear. The desert cooler is left off, except for two of the hottest hours of the day. We also start sleeping on the roof.

At first, the idea of sleeping on the roof seems very romantic. I picture a prolonged campout. Anticipating another great adventure, we join the generations of Saudis before us and trudge up the stairs with our bedding.

First, we lay out a plastic tablecloth. On that we arrange our mattresses, pillows, and sheets. Falling asleep under the brilliant stars with a breeze to dry our sweat, is all that I dreamed it would be. This pleasure however, is not enough to compensate for the 5:00 am sunrise when the natural world comes alive. The birds are as loud as any rooster. The explosion of the insect community, which rallies every morning in full force, is unbearable. Flies find every open area of flesh, and mosquitoes dive-bomb relentlessly. The last straw is the call to prayer from the mosque loudspeaker no more than twenty feet away.

With the lack of water destroying our lifestyle, Rema and I spend our days visiting the hazan, listening for the refreshing sound of dripping water to come cascading out of the pipes. For relief from the heat, I wet down Nazar's clothes and twice a day I give him a bath out of a small bowl. I can't allow myself such luxury. It is during these long, unbearably hot days that I learn to take a full shower out of a teacup of water.

Then, early one morning, our vigilance over the hazan pays off. We hear water flowing through our pipes! Empowered by joy, we pull aside the iron slabs and watch a stream of refreshing, cool liquid plunge into the depths of our empty pit. The children dance around us in excitement, and we sit there for an hour absorbing the sound of falling water into our weary souls. When it reaches a certain level, we gather buckets and ropes. Rema dips first.

Unfortunately, this is only a small reprieve. The next week passes without one further drop. Meanwhile Osane complains to every official he can think of, but makes no headway. Our hands are tied, until one Friday afternoon in early August. Out of nowhere, a large water tanker pulls down our street. Hearing the commotion, I pull back our curtain and watch the truck wash down our dirt road with precious water.

Osane is also drawn to the noise, and within a few seconds is at Abdu's door. They both dash out to the water truck and begin begging for water. The workers argue that it is city water, meant for the road. Abdu and Osane claim that their families are more important, and have been suffering long enough. The truck driver replies that this is low-grade, unprocessed water. Osane shrugs his shoulders and pulls out his wallet.

That evening our tank is full. Rema and I, knowing the value of water, use every drop carefully. The full tank and resourceful water usage is enough to keep us even with the daily water supply, which seems to be increasing as temperatures cool slightly.

The main water crisis seems to be over, but the cost we paid is too high. The summer and its problems have worn away our reserves. Each new day leaves us barely coping.

One evening, a darker cloud than usual settles over our home. I tuck Nazar into bed and come back into the family room to watch TV. After our programs, I arrange our bedding and we both lie down. I can tell by Osane's body language that sleep, for him, never seemed so far away. Unable to be silent one more second, I ask him for the hundredth time, "Osane, what's wrong?"

At first, my question is met with his customary silence. When he finally begins to reply, I center myself so I can stand in his darkness. He says, "My job, our life, our house, the water shortage, our lack of money, car, or hope are destroying me. I readily admit I have failed you and our son, and I can't stand seeing my family living the way we are. I have spent endless hours trying to figure a way out of this maze, but I can't find the door. It will be much better for us if we can simply leave this nightmare behind, but we haven't enough money for one plane ticket, let alone three.

"The only solution I can find is divorce. I can borrow enough money from family and friends to get you both back safely to the States. There you can create a new life. You'll be much better off without me and my culture, for our Saudi life so far has been a disaster."

As he finishes his soliloquy, my heart stops. Although life has been difficult, never once have I blamed Osane. I know he is trying, and he's giving when he has nothing left to give.

Looking into his eyes I say, "Osane, I have never blamed you for what has happened. You have never failed us. Our family is meant to stay together! Through our united strength we'll pull out of this present life of despair. You'll see."

We spend the rest of the night talking. It takes hours to convince Osane that I want to stay, that I don't want to give up. Finally, after a thousand words and a river of tears, Osane gives in. We will stay together and we will go on. United we will find the door to our steel cage.

With everything said, Osane falls into a sleep of exhaustion, while I stare at the ceiling wide-awake. Somewhere in the deep heat of the summer, reality has eaten away my youthful idealism and actuality has become my bedmate. Now I have to face the cold hard fact that I have just burned my bridge.

Full of unselfish love, Osane has offered me the easy path, the only route that is truly sensible. Out of my belief in our family unit, I have chosen to stand firm. As I watch the dawn of a new day, I know that the States are much further away now than they had been last night.

Chapter 31

Finding Our Way Out of the Maze

"Nothing and everything cannot coexist. To believe in one is to deny the other. Fear is really nothing and love is everything. Whenever light enters darkness, the darkness is abolished."
Dr. Helen Schucman

Knowing we have hit rock bottom, Osane is determined to begin our upward climb. Thinking out of the box, he devises a plan. In the evenings he begins rewriting the traffic rules in Riyadh, using American laws as his model. His goal is to educate ministry officials on traffic control. This will also enable him to broadcast his name in higher circles of government.

Osane works very hard on these traffic rules. When he is finished, they are thorough and complete. He makes an appointment at the Interior Ministry, and personally hands them to Prince Mohsen.

Next, Osane increases his efforts to circulate among important officials in the Ministries. As he broadens his circle of friends, he is finally introduced to the Assistant Deputy Minister of the Interior Ministry, Dr. Ramzi. It seems that Dr. Ramzi has also been educated in the United States. With their American experiences as common ground, they develop a quick friendship.

Osane begins to spend an increasing amount of time in Dr. Ramzi's office. Each day he is exposed to influential contacts. As time passes, a flame of hope grows within Osane. He is beginning to identify Dr. Ramzi as the door out of his steel trap.

Then, at the end of August, Osane receives a phone call from Imad (the man we met at Jane and Naji's apartment sale). Imad, in an excited voice, tells Osane that his Scottish wife and child have arrived. During the phone conversation, Osane invites the family over for dinner the following Friday.

As I ready the house, I remain rather cynical. It is good to have a potential friend in town again, but I picture a dull, heavyset girl with pale skin and plain features. Osane thinks I am wrong. He claims that Imad would only marry a fine wife. With mischief in our eyes, we place bets. As the doorbell rings, we are excited to see who wins.

The second Briannah walks into our home, it is obvious that Osane has won the bet. Her delicate, fair skin contrasts with her deep blue eyes and long black hair. She is tall, thin, attractive, and very stylishly dressed. What pleases me most however, is her lively personality and humor.

Mina, Briannah's beautiful daughter, is also very bright. She is six months older than Nazar and our two children spend the evening sizing each other up. By the end of the visit, they, too, have bonded. Hugging our new friends goodnight, I feel the dread of the lonely summer falling off me like a long-awaited rain in the middle of a terrible drought. With relief in my heart, I know that I also have found a door out of my maze.

The next Friday, our two families share a cab to a foreign compound on the other side of Riyadh. Imad tells us that the employees of a Greek Water Company live here, but they are overseas for the summer. This leaves the facilities open for outside use.

As we drive up to the unmarked gate, I doubt that anything special can exist in such a common neighborhood. However, the minute we walk through the gate, we enter another world. The pool area is not extravagant, but it more than suits our needs. Palm trees shade the picnic tables and lounge chairs, and there are changing rooms and showers.

As we jump into the water, months of stress wash off us. The whole experience is surreal. We are actually floating in this beautiful water, in total privacy. A small tear of relief runs off my cheek and into the cool pool water.

Screams of joy fill the air when Mina and Nazar begin splashing each other. They are both wearing blow-up arm bands, for neither of them knows how to swim. When these two friends grow tired of the water, they chase the monkey, cats, and dogs that roam freely around the grounds. Meanwhile, we sit in deserted lawn chairs, chatting and enjoying the breezes of our own private oasis.

Mercifully, the weather finally begins to cool. The foreigners start returning from abroad, as do the Saudis who come back from the cooler parts of the Kingdom in Taif and Southern Arabia. With the diminishing strength of the fall sun, the occupants of Riyadh settle into their dynamic winter lifestyles.

Productivity is exactly what Osane has in mind for me. It seems our continuing dilemma is Osane's small paycheck. Because the government sent him overseas on a scholarship, he still owes the ministries five more years of service. That means that the higher paying private-sector jobs are out of reach. Working overtime or moonlighting is also against government regulations. Therefore, it is decided that I should apply for a teaching position at the Riyadh International School, to boost our family income.

My heart is not into the prospect of working. The norm of the 70s is that females stay at home, care for the house, support their husbands, and raise the children. Nazar is just two years old, and my whole being wants to remain with him.

Knowing I have no choice, I put on the dress Zora had sewn for me and slip on my abaya. Osane and I walk out the door to a waiting taxi and drive to an interview with Mrs. Mills, the principal of the International School. The driver lets us out at a small, unmarked door. We open this portal, and are magically transported from the East into the West.

When we enter, Ms. Slatter, the school secretary, glances up from her work. After dropping her pencil in surprise, she gives me a cold stare. Her look of rejection unnerves me, and I slip into a corner chair and sit down. Thankfully, my wait isn't long and I am soon in Ms. Mills's office.

The school principal is a very attractive, older American woman who radiates rank and efficiency. She is wearing a navy blue skirt, a crisp white blouse, and a colorful scarf. A trim pageboy hairstyle frames her intelligent face, and her hazel eyes stare at me over bifocals. She sits patiently as I hand her my degree, a copy of my college courses, grades, and some references. Oddly, she seems more interested in my story than in my paperwork. Studying my Saudi dress, she asks me how long I have been in the country, where I lived, and under what conditions.

Sensing the oral section of this strange interview has turned into the history of my life, I finish my last sentence and wait. Somehow, I know Ms. Mills is going to be straightforward with me. She finally looks up from my papers and states, "Christina, I feel that you'll fit more naturally into the Riyadh School."

As surprise registers on my face, she assures me that there are other foreign teachers at this private Arabic School. To assist me, she calls the headmistress and personally makes an appointment for me the next day. Feeling shell-shocked and confused, I thank her for her time and walk out the door to find Osane and my waiting abaya.

The next day finds me in the same dress, but on the way to the Riyadh School for the interview Ms. Mills has arranged. This school is much farther away, but I enjoy crossing town in a new way. The taxi driver lets me off in front of a large gate. As I walk through the gate, nobody stares at my abaya, only at my fair skin and blue eyes.

I make my way through clean, spacious grounds and into the office. Here, one of the girls takes my abaya. After serving tea, she tells me in perfect English that the headmistress will see me shortly.

Once again, I have a short wait before the headmistress comes out, shakes my hand and leads me into her office. She is much colder and more formal than Ms. Mills. As I fill out a long application, she looks over my credentials. When I finish, she states that my application will go before the board and that I will be notified. I leave the office, feeling like nothing has clicked.

Safely back in my own home with Nazar at my side, I silently celebrate two dead-ends. Life slips back to normal, until three days later when Ms. Mills calls Osane. A position has opened up in the English department. The contracted teacher has decided not to return to Saudi Arabia. If I am interested, the teaching position is open to me.

When Osane relays this news, I outwardly remain calm while deafening screams of doubt and fear reverberate within. First, I could never spell or diagram a sentence! Secondly, I have nothing to wear and how am I going to get to school everyday? Most importantly, who is going to take care of Nazar?

Feeling my hesitation, Osane pulls me toward him. "Don't worry, Christy. Just take the job. Together we'll work out all the obstacles."

I know there are no options; the next day finds me once again sitting in Ms. Mills's office, accepting the teaching position. Now that I am officially on staff, Ms. Mills shares the history of the school with me.

"Christie," Ms. Mills begins, "I think you'll find this story very interesting. The Riyadh International School was started several years ago by an American teacher, who was concerned about the education of her children. As the foreign population in Saudi grew, so did the school. Everything was progressing very nicely, until the school televised a skit on a children's TV program. This short song and dance caught the eye of government officials. The little girls' pumpkin costumes were too scant, and the mixing of boys and girls beyond the level of second grade was considered sinful. The government closed down the school and wouldn't allow it to open until it met universal Kingdom regulations.

"Not to be stopped, the International School purchased the villa next door and turned it into the Boys' School. This meant that kindergarten, first and second grades remained mixed. These classes remained at the Girls' School. When the children reached third grade, the girls stayed at the Girls' School while the boys attended the Boys' School.

"Initially the plan seemed promising, but the negotiations came to an abrupt halt when the Saudi government insisted that female teachers wear long dresses and abayas. The Western teachers blatantly refused, and the school stayed closed three extra months while the two parties debated. Finally convinced that there was no give on the issue of apparel, the Ministry officials permitted both schools to open. The teachers were allowed to remain uncovered and could teach in miniskirts. The concession for this compromise was that the schools would now be subject to surprise government inspection.

"It is for this reason Christie, that if you teach here you're never to wear an abaya or a long skirt. Miniskirts are the only acceptable attire. If the visiting government officials spot one teacher in native dress, they might close the school until the rest of the teachers also conform."

I reassure Ms. Mills that I fully comprehend the dress code and the reasons behind it, and she places a stack of books and workbooks in my arms. As I walk out of the office balancing my load, I finally understand Ms. Slatter's initial cold stares.

With only three days before I report to school, the care of Nazar becomes my first priority. After dinner, I knock on Rema's door. I am aware that she has a girlfriend living with her who needs work. If I can hire Fatma, Rema will also be involved. Then both apartments will be open to Nazar, and somehow I feel secure with this.

The next dilemma is solved when Osane hires a cab to drive me to and from work each day. With the major obstacles crossed off my list, I now have enough peace of mind to attempt to grasp my teaching materials.

On my first day of work, I wake up extra early. I put on my one miniskirt, apply makeup, and grab a bite to eat. With an encouraging kiss from Osane, I walk out the door uncovered and step into the waiting taxicab.

As I enter the East/West portal into the school's office, Ms. Slatter glances up and smiles at me. Her expression is one of approval, and an inward sigh of relief that I haven't shown up in a long skirt and abaya. Encouraged by this, I walk through the rest of the day with growing confidence.

Soon a new rhythm develops in our household. Unfortunately, I come home every day exhausted. I throw my books in the corner and play with a demanding Nazar, as I cook our dinner. If I'd been a natural teacher the students would have energized me, but instead they depleted me. Resolved to my fate, I begin living for the weekends (Thursday and Friday) and for the monthly paycheck of 2,000 Saudi raels per month.

As our life broadens, so does our exposure. Not only are we becoming known to an increasing number of Saudis, Americans, and mixed-marriage couples, but we are also circulating among teachers from the International School.

Osane's exposure into the upper levels of the ministries also makes us much more visible. This increased notability also comes with an undercurrent of danger, for unfortunately we live in a police state.

Osane and I are fully aware that we will never be allowed the luxury of truthfulness. It is imperative that opinions on anything to do with the Kingdom's policy or the government are kept safely within. We are both tight-tongued with the foreigners we meet. Ears are everywhere, and beliefs are swallowed before they are uttered. While neither of us wants to become paranoid, an underlying prevalence of caution dots every conversation.

Chapter 32

Daily Patterns

"Buddha means awake, being awake, completely awake; that seems to be his message to us. Buddha saw the world as it is and that was his enlightenment."

Chogyam Trungpa

As the weeks slip by, subtle changes keep appearing within the Kingdom, like spring flowers piercing the damp soil in early spring. For generations, Arabia, surrounded by desert and closed borders, had remained in a biblical lifestyle. Only an occasional roaming romantic would wander into this peninsula of sand. Many of these early settlers were English teachers, who blended into village life. They wore traditional dress, ate native foods, and became quite fluent in Arabic. They lived within the country, and were here for altruistic reasons and not for money.

The winds of change are currently blowing a new breed of teachers onto the desert. These transient educators are hired on two-year teaching contracts and are attracted to Arabia for financial reasons. Without enough time to assimilate into the Arabian culture, they remain culturally detached.

While these changes are interesting, they have little impact on our daily lives. What does concern me is that Ella and her family haven't returned from England. In between homeroom and first period, I often slip into the teacher's lounge of the Boys' School and study Ella's house for signs of life.

Finally, one fine day I'm not disappointed. The curtains are pulled back, the windows are open, the wash is hanging from the second floor balcony and the house is once again full and alive. After school I run out the school's gate, around the corner, and up Ella's stairs. We talk far into the evening, for there's so much to share. It feels so good to have Ella back again, and I begin visiting her regularly on my lunch hour.

As the days pass, the weather becomes quite cold. The Saudi men once again slip into their dark-colored wool thobes and long underwear. The rest of us layer to keep warm.

Motivated by the change in weather, Osane and I decide to redecorate. Using some of the money from my teaching job, Osane taxies to the market and buys a kerosene heater to keep us warm. He then goes to the public auction, where he purchases a set of German, rust-colored chairs and a large couch. Imad and Briannah come over one Friday and help Osane build living room tables. Using Aunt Sarah's rug as a base, we scatter our new chairs and tables around the walls and presto, we finally have a living room. It doesn't matter that the legs are falling off the chairs and couches, and that our only artwork are nailed-up prayer rugs. What's important is that our home is finally furnished!

As the days become shorter, the tempered sun feels incredibly healing in the fall's cool breezes. Our Friday mornings are especially relaxing, for Fatma leaves early for her day off and Osane and I sleep in. Nazar usually sits on a chair by the window, watching the men and boys park their cars outside our house, and then walk to the corner Mosque.

One Friday, right after services, Nazar calls out to me in an excited voice. "Mom, come to the window." I sit down at the window next to Nazar, and watch two pickup trucks park in front of the house directly opposite us. One truck is full of large pots, obviously containing cooked sheep. The other truck is loaded to the brim with rice. The driver is standing on the tail of the truck, shoveling rice onto small trays.

All of a sudden, the guests begin to arrive. The men (dressed in their clean Friday thobes) walk in through the large center gates, while the women and children dressed in their finery enter through the small side gate. In fascination, Nazar and I watch the scene unfold. This unique tradition of elaborate preparations for a feast is decades old, and can only be found in Saudi Arabia.

Only a few weeks remain before Thanksgiving, and the school days pass quickly. During the vacation, Ella offers to introduce me to the markets of Riyadh. She knows the shopping areas well, for her husband Tahar often drives his family to the many suqs.

While sitting in the taxi on our promised shopping trip, Ella explains, "Christie, there are three main markets. We'll start on Wazeir Street where the expensive, Western stores are located."

As we walk down Wazier Street we see many foreigners, and I am impressed by its cleanliness and order. This seems to be an "anywhere in the world" street. Although the prices are way out of my range, I am simply glad it is there.

We then make our way into the two public markets. These suqs resemble the stores in Taif, but on a much grander scale. We wander through stalls of incense, gold, material, and food. Here the prices are right, but they lack the expensive products from France, England, or Italy.

We are barely into the first lane of stalls when I begin to feel nervous and strained. It had never been comfortable to shop with the relatives in Taif, but surrounded by their presence I was at least shown respect. Even though the men and boys stared, they remained at a polite distance.

However, walking through the Riyadh public markets with another foreign woman shifts me into a different realm. Although we are both properly dressed in long pants and long sleeved blouses, our faces are *uncovered*. As we make our way through the masses of males, the confusion and dirt, we have to constantly be on our guard to ward off pinches on our bottoms and grabs at our bosoms. Children follow and heckle us, men stare at us with lustful eyes, and crowds gather anytime Ella and I spend too long at a stall shopping. Overall, it is not a pleasant experience. This marketplace is meant for men, boys, and a few groups of covered Saudi women.

I am contemplating these thoughts, when Ella grabs me and pushes me into a side lane of stores. Sinking into the shadows, she motions for me to be quiet. I look back over my shoulder just in time to see a group of soldiers led by a Matawa. They are walking down the aisle Ella and I have just been on. As I stand there trying to make myself invisible, I recall the many stories I have heard about these religious men, whose duty it is to make sure citizens obey the cultural and religious rules.

These elderly males wear long gray beards and brown cloaks, carry six-foot sticks, and are accompanied by two or three soldiers. It is the Matawas and their soldiers who pound on store fronts with sticks yelling "Prayer, Prayer," ordering owners to quickly lock up their shops and pray five times a day. It is the Matawas who make sure the Saudi men have short haircuts. It is the Matawas who heckle the foreign population into acceptable cultural behavior. If the bell-bottoms jeans are too extreme, the Matawas will simply cut off the flare, leaving the owner to stare at a ruined pair of pants.

The Matawas will also challenge any woman in the market place who is uncovered. They will stand with full authority, and demand compliance with the dress code. Finally, they will badger and follow foreign women who are wearing miniskirts. There was even an incident in Dhahran where women, wearing miniskirts, were taken to the main square. In front of a large group of men, the Matawas painted their legs black.

I return to school after vacation, with my suq adventure still ringing through my soul. Caught up in grading papers, I find that the days pass quickly, and suddenly we are approaching our second Christmas in the Kingdom. Everyone at school is in a holiday mood, for the winter exodus from Riyadh is about to begin. Briannah and Imad are going to Jeddah, and Ella and her family are traveling to Bhahran. Mary and Anwar have already left for Iran and almost everyone else we know is on their way somewhere else. Again, we are left behind.

After a day of feeling sorry for myself, I jump into Christmas preparations. Knowing that only a handful of remaining Christians are celebrating the birth of Christ, my enthusiasm isn't dampened. Nazar and I paste a large crepe paper tree onto our Arab room wall. We wrap up little presents to put underneath it and sing Christmas carols around the clock. We also draw pictures of Santa Claus, reindeers, snow, or anything else Christmas. I cook two stuffed chickens (pretending they are turkeys) and overall, our second Christmas in Saudi Arabia fully surpasses the first one.

Having some time to myself over the vacation, I am finally able to do some pleasure reading. One article I find in our censored edition of Newsweek sticks in my mind. This article is on the amount of change an individual can endure and remain sane. It offers a checklist and a point system exam. Curious, I work my way through the test. Before I add up my score, I reflect on the unbelievable amount of changes I have endured in the last year and a half. Hesitatingly, I add up my points. According to the results of the test, I should be a basket case! Intuitively I realize my score isn't far off the mark. As I throw the magazine aside, I wonder how one goes about siphoning the stress out of one's environment.

The following weekend, our friends return from their vacations. With the cool winter breezes and warm sun distracting me, Ella somehow talks me into going with her to the market again. This time our destination is the women's suq, located in the middle of the public markets. Mary had once told me about this open-air square. It is separated from the main market by a small door, through which only women can enter.

As Ella and I make our way through that small door, I am looking forward to doing some shopping away from the intensity of male eyes and the wandering Matawas. Little do I realize I am entering an unfriendly zone of ill will.

My previous experiences with Saudi women had been full of love and warmth, but I once again enter their turf in a different category. I am no longer in one of their homes, as one of them. I am now a foreigner accompanied by another Westerner. The open anger directed at us shocks and hurts me. As we walk by seated women selling jewelry, their stares are hostile and their voices taunting. Ella doesn't seem to notice, for she is only interested in looking through piles of chunky, Bedouin jewelry.

I separate from her and wander over to the familiar material booths, hoping these Saudi women will be friendlier. I am wrong. I am universally perceived as a Christian, an intruder who dresses and acts sinfully. My uncovered face tempts their men, which is seen as a threat and a danger. As these realizations flicker through my mind, all I want to do is return home and close the door on my world.

That evening, my thoughts haunt me. I envy Ella and my foreign friends, for they don't seem to be affected the way I am. They keep their distance from the East, and therefore maintain their sanity. This lifestyle of being a covered Saudi one day and a mini-skirted American the next day is ripping my peace of mind apart. Somehow, in between as I am, my core identity is beginning to teeter. Gradually my facial muscles tense, my jaw becomes set and my laughter echoes artificially. My friends start to notice the change and try to humor me. Osane also notices and it scares him into silence, but for me there is no way out. I simply live each day at a time, counting the weeks and the months until summer and the end of school.

Meanwhile, Fatma is becoming more and more moody. A dark expression seems permanently painted on her face, and each morning we wake up to her stony attitude. We try everything we can to make her happy, and I eventually ask Rema for advice. She tells me not to worry about Nazar, for he spends most of his time with her children and takes long morning naps. As for Fatma, she was simply born with a "heavy streak."

I try to remain calm, but my anxiety continues to build. One day, a few weeks later, I come home to our redecorated bedroom. Nazar has drawn larger-than -ife stick figures all over the walls. The sun, fish, dogs and giraffes are drawn in every color of the rainbow. Obviously, this project has taken Nazar the entire morning. I wonder aloud to Osane, "Where was Fatma?"

The last straw comes early one morning, when Osane asks Fatma to walk to the corner market for some tomatoes. She looks up with her sulky eyes and says, *"no."* Osane points to the door and says, *"out."* Within three hours she is packed, paid, and once again living with Rema.

We are now in a predicament. Not only is Rema's door closed to us, but we also have no one to care for Nazar. The next day I call in sick. That evening Osane brings home a houseboy called Bagosh. As I train Bagosh, some of my anxiety dissipates. He isn't too bright, but he seems honest. In addition, after Fatma's sulky moods I am relieved to find that Bagosh possesses a sunny disposition. We are once again organized, and within two days I am back at work.

There are many good days at school, and I know I have a rapport with the students. By now, I have also made several friends on the faculty. If I had been left alone to just teach, I could have coped. Instead, I find myself caught in the working mother's syndrome plus all the additional cultural demands.

Each day, already tired from school, I open our apartment door to find an extra demanding Nazar. With all of his young energy, he has been forced to stay inside the whole day with Bagosh. While trying to entertain Nazar, I am also expected to cook (from scratch) Saudi style. Dinner usually includes our family, Bagosh, plus a barrage of relatives and male friends. After dinner and dishes, I grade papers, read Nazar stories, and fall into bed.

The next morning I am up with the sun. While I dress in my one skirt, I grab breakfast, pack a lunch, and wake up Bagosh. I say a quick prayer that he'll work well with Nazar, as I run out to a taxicab Bagosh has fetched from the main street.

Often, on the way out the door, I will walk over bodies of sleeping male visitors. One night the floor is so crowded that a relative has to sleep under the dining room table. I tell this to faculty friends and they just laugh, wondering how I cope.

The regular cab driver Osane originally hired has long ago quit. Therefore, I open the door of the taxicab every morning to a new driver and a unique adventure. Forced to wear a miniskirt to school, I learn to fortify myself against the initial stare, the piercing gaze and the brown eyes that slowly look me up and down. I purposely slide to the far right side of the back seat, knowing the driver will readjust his rear view mirror so he can spend the drive to school staring at my uncovered face. If I sit in the corner however, it is much more of a challenge to zoom in. Some taxicab drivers try to touch my legs. Some turn left when I tell them to turn right and I picture myself being whizzed out into the desert. Others try to mutter endearments to me, while others simply tolerate being in the presence of an infidel. Often they refuse to take money from my unwashed hand. All told, each trip to the school is a question mark. Most of the drivers are very polite, but there are enough harrowing rides in between to persuade me to throw a kitchen knife into my purse as a precaution.

Chapter 33

A Turning Point

" Heroes are made by the paths they choose, not the powers they are graced with."
    Brodi Ashton

As much as I attempt to live in denial, conflicting thoughts constantly pelt my peace of mind. This causes my emotional balance to remain in a continuous spin. My attempt to juggle too many roles also takes a physical toll. Therefore, it is inevitable that I catch a bad case of influenza and land in bed for two weeks. When my sick leave is up, I prematurely return to work. Unfortunately, this depletes any molecule of remaining reserves.

With my body weakened and my life overburdened by responsibilities, my mind, nerves, body, and spirits finally collapse. I spend Monday morning in my classroom trying to control my thoughts, but they slither here and slide there. It is as if I am driving downhill on solid ice, and my tires are spinning out of control, back and forth, with no hope of hitting solid ground.

By noon, I begin to have panic attacks. Afraid of losing control at school, I scribble a quick note to Ms. Mills, hail a taxi, and head for home. When the door closes safely behind me, the rest of my mind snaps, and I tumble down into the abyss. My eyes cloud over with wild fear and my inner world become dark, full of echoing voices and sinful thoughts straight out of the dark caves of the ego.

I am more petrified than I have ever been in my life. I lock myself in the bedroom and begin pacing back and forth, trying to walk away from my body. None of my tried and true stress management methods works. The walls of my pit from hell seem glass smooth. There are no crevasses to hold onto; my thoughts just bounce back and forth in a chaotic freefall.

The only recourse is to slink down onto the floor of my bedroom and hug my knees, as the world around me spins out of control. I know I am doomed. There are no psychiatric facilities in the Kingdom, which means no counseling or medication. My fate is obvious. I am lost with no hope of being rescued!

Osane finds me in this insane state. I look up at him with crazed eyes, and fall into his arms sobbing. I attempt to describe my unhinged mental war zone, but in the end all I can do is sink back to the floor and cover my eyes with my hands. Not knowing how to respond, Osane holds me until I fall asleep.

In my closed bedroom, I battle madness for three endless days. Fortunately Osane is always on the perimeters of my suffering, radiating love and support into my mindless stupor. In the end, exhausted, I wash up on the shores of sanity. My belief in God, the knowledge that Osane and Nazar need me, and my youth plus determination combine to give me the strength to grope my way out of my depths of despair.

On the third day, Ella comes to visit me. She listens with empathy, for during her first year in Jordan her mind had also snapped. I share with her for hours. Finally, she softly offers advice only one who has walked my path can give.

For two weeks, my family and friends strive to create a loving environment around me. In this tranquil space, I begin my upward climb toward recovery. Each day, I am able to control more of my thoughts. Finally, I decide that it is time to go back to work. I know the only way I can truly heal is to chip away at the main stone that has tilted the scales.

After giving myself one further week as a buffer, I once again take an early morning taxi to school. My colleagues are happy to see me. I tell them I have been suffering from complications of influenza. Little do they suspect that my inner war has turned me into a completely different person. Physically I am thinner, all remnants of girlhood have been shed, and my Pollyanna naiveté and romanticism have been shattered. My eyes now see the world with a caustic realism. I finally realize that the ancient Saudi culture is not going to be minutely altered by one twenty-four-year-old reformer. Indifference to everything becomes my mantra as I fight my ghost of insanity. I am painfully aware that it will be several years before I can securely stuff the ramifications of my madness into the closet of the past.

The following week, around sunrise, our household is awakened by a large commotion in the street. Nazar shoots to the window full of curiosity and runs back excitedly shouting, "bulldozer, bulldozer!" We pull ourselves wearily out of bed, and look out the front window to find a road crew busily preparing our dirt street for pavement. As nothing in Saudi Arabia happens quickly, I know we are not facing one morning of noise but months of scraping, tarring, and commotion. As I predicted, through the weeks ahead the dust level from the road construction submerges us into a constant sandstorm. The workers also choose to lean up against "our walls" and eat lunch under "our windows." Luckily, it is not summer, so we can live comfortably with the front windows closed and shuttered.

During the next school holiday, my friend Joan invites me to a coffee. I have often visited her, for she lives within easy walking distance. Her home also brings me joy, for it is full of plants and has a comfortable, down-to-earth feel. Since I know most of the women at the coffee, I fall into easy conversation and the time passes quickly. Soon it is time to leave. I need to get back to Nazar, and it is also time to start cooking the two o'clock meal.

Since I have walked, I have naturally worn my abaya and black scarf. I am standing in the middle of the room saying goodbye to everyone, when, without thinking, I drape the abaya over my shoulders. Unfortunately, I am not prepared for Olivia's ensuing attack. "How can you, an American woman, degrade yourself by covering your identity with black?" she loudly demands.

Silence penetrates the room. As I look from face to face, I realize that the rest of the Western women side with Olivia. The explanation that my husband is Saudi falls on deaf ears. Their anger against a culture that inhibits them at every turn is now directed towards me. Pulling my abaya even tighter around me, I thank Joan. Coldly I say goodbye and walk into Arabia.

Gawking Saudi men soon invade my feeling of relief at escaping my friends' hostility. When I turn down our street, the stares by the workers paving our street become embarrassingly intense. Work stops as I walk by, and I become the only focal point. Pulling within, I keep my eyes glued to our door and the safe zone that will soon shelter me.

With relief I ring the doorbell, but there is no answer. As I stand there facing the gate, my spine tingles with the realization that all eyes are still on me. I count to twenty and ring the doorbell again. Still there still is no answer! "Where is Bagosh?" I silently scream.

As I stand there, my back to the world, I suddenly slip into a cold sweat and tears of frustration run down my cheeks. I refuse to retrace my steps to the hostility of Joan's house. I have no money and no place to go. In desperation, I pick up a rock and pound on the gate. Miraculously, it opens, revealing a smiling Bagosh and Nazar. Without a second to spare, I disappear into the safety of my own space.

With Nazar running around me, I walk into the living room and turn on the light. When the room remains in semi-darkness, I immediately comprehend the reason I was stranded on the street. There is no electricity and therefore, no way to hear a ringing bell. Throwing my abaya into the corner, I sink down into a chair and wonder why I ever leave my home. It seems my house is the only place within the Kingdom I feel secure enough to create some sort of peace of mind.

The following Friday, Osane borrows a friend's car and the three of us drive into the desert for an afternoon picnic. The weather is perfect. The temperate air is a gift from nature, before the sun's relentless rays bake the desert. Because it has just rained, the pebbled sand is full of small, exquisitely detailed flowers. As Nazar piles up stones, Osane and I sip our tea. Taking a deep breath, I watch the fresh breezes blowing through Osane's hair.

Finally relaxed enough to share, we cautiously begin to open up. Hesitatingly at first, we speak of our feelings. Encouraged by the safety of the vast desert, we expose ideas and emotions that can never be broached in rooms that might be full of bugs or curious ears. To speak freely, we had to go out into the desert or turn the music up very loud.

Finally, with soft voices we dare whisper words that mutually paint our current realities. "We have both given Saudi Arabia our best effort, but we have failed to create a satisfying stride in the middle of this ancient, isolated land that time has forgotten."

Our joint decision is quite bold. We will leave as soon as the school year is over. The world is large, we are young, and we have managed to save up enough money to make a modest start in the West.

With the decision to leave firmly resolved, a thousand-pound weight has been lifted off our shoulders. In relief, the evenings find us wandering through our apartment, pad and pencil in hand. Soon we have a price tag on all of our belongings. Most of our possessions are in good condition, and second-hand furniture is always in great demand. Because of the transient nature of the foreign community and the lack of discount stores, we know our property will sell at a good price.

While we wait for the days to pass, our lives continue. A few Fridays later, we are invited to an ancient palace that has been subdivided into small apartments. I have heard a great deal about this historic dwelling from teachers at school, and I am anxious to see it. It is on the other side of the city, so the taxi drive alone is interesting.

When we arrive at the palace gates, it's like driving through a portal into the past. In my imagination, I can picture camel caravans shuffling along the date palm path that leads to the walled-in desert oasis. The many cars, family noises, and children playing soon neutralize the grandeur of the old and instead reveal multi-family dwelling units.

While Osane is paying the driver, his friend greets us. We follow him up the stairs to his second-floor apartment. His wife opens the door, and we walk into a spacious room with an outside balcony that overlooks a date plantation. Hanging from the middle of the living room is a massive crystal chandelier, and beautiful crown molding circles the ceiling.

Sipping tea on the balcony, we are enjoying a vivid sunset when a stiff wind picks up. Literally out of nowhere, heavy sheets of rain begin pelting the earth. The rain gives way to hail, the kind that dents cars and breaks windows. The noise from the hail is deafening, and it drops from the sky with such force that it bounces several times before losing momentum. After the hail, the driving rain starts again. The rain is so fierce that absorption into the soil is impossible, and we watch in fascination as rivers begin forming where only desert has been seconds before.

It is getting late and time to be on our way home, for we all have work the next day. After the main part of the storm is over, we climb into our host's car and begin what should have been a twenty-minute return trip. It soon becomes evident that this drive will turn into an adventure, for Saudi roads are constructed without sewers. Used to dirt paths where the drainage is natural, they developed paved streets in a likewise manner. The result is that heavy rain turns these roads into rivers.

As we continue our journey, we find stalled-out cars everywhere. Only the practically constructed Volkswagens and pickup trucks are able to wind their way through these flowing streams. Luckily, Osane's friend owns a Bug. Although our progress is painfully slow, we at least keep moving. We arrive home exhausted and insist that our host spend the night with us. Thanking us for our hospitality, he declines our offer, for he is determined to get back to his family and his own home.

The next Tuesday is a half-day for me. I arrive home from school early, and have time to cook a special dinner for Osane. The second he walks through the door from work, I can feel another dilemma brewing. Arming myself with my new protection of apathy, I wait. After dinner over tea, he finally shares. It seems that he's been offered a scholarship to attend a three-month Social Defense conference in Cairo. This news, which would have been so eagerly accepted before, conflicts with our plans to depart for America.

For two days, we struggle with which path to take. Spending hours weighing the pros and cons of east or west, we remain unresolved. Mysteriously, destiny steps in to decide our fate for us, for a week later I become ill.

Right before school lunch, I feel a pain in the lower part of my body. By sixth period I can't sit down, and by seventh period it takes every ounce of strength and determination not to double over in pain. Somehow, I make it through the school day.

Osane arrives home from work to find me in a desperate condition. The discomfort comes in spasms, about fifteen minutes in length. During the pain, all I can do is roll from side-to-side and attempt to stop myself from screaming.

The next morning Osane stays home from the Ministry, and takes me from doctor to doctor. Not one of these professionals can diagnose the problem. Each time pregnancy, kidney and bladder infections, influenza, and a multitude of causes are discussed. Then pills are prescribed. Soon it becomes obvious that these determinations are just guesses. By the end of three days, I have a large plastic bag full of pills in every color, shape and size, but I am still in pain!

Pulling at one last straw, we visit a doctor who has just arrived from Beirut. He speaks English, and he finally pinpoints a large infection around my uterus that is swelling and causing my pain. He gives me pills to reduce the swelling and recommends a prominent obstetrician in Egypt.

As hopes for life in the States dissolve into unrealized mists, Osane and I shift. We now focus on our preparations for an immediate departure to Egypt, better doctors, and an opportunity for Osane to advance his career. Osane contacts the people who have verbally purchased our possessions, and tells them they are no longer for sale. Meanwhile, I make an appointment with Mrs. Mills. I inform her that because of health problems, I will not be able to finish out the school year.

Ms. Mills studies the doctors' reports and when she puts them down, she takes a long look into my eyes. I know what she's thinking. Sitting in front of her is a different person, a shadow of my original self. I know I am excessively thin, that my rounded shoulders testify that life has become too heavy for me, and the firm way I hold my mouth speaks of determination but little laughter. I stand up and give her a hug, thanking her for her compassion and understanding during the last seven months. I then say goodbye to my school friends. As a taxi drives me away, I put that chapter of my life behind and begin thinking about the approaching trip. We aren't traveling to America, but at least we will have three months together, away from our battle with the Saudi culture.

At the end of a busy week, we take a taxi to the airport. Covered by my abaya, I automatically walk behind Osane into the terminal and then enter the dark, women's waiting room. Sitting there with the other Saudi women, I am anxious and sick to my stomach for I don't trust this trip. On many levels, I am convinced that the Kingdom has somehow grabbed me forever and will never let me go. Osane's knock on the closed door of the women's waiting room snaps me out of my negative thoughts. In a daze, I follow him into the aircraft. I cross my fingers as our plane becomes airborne. Soon we are gliding over the desert, through layers of windblown clouds and up into the clear atmosphere. It isn't until we are over the Red Sea and out of Saudi airspace, that I finally allow myself to accept our freedom. I yank off my abaya, stuffing it into our hand luggage as tears of relief drip down my cheeks.

From the instant we land in Cairo, our Egyptian reprieve is perfect. We take a taxi from the airport to a hotel that overlooks the Nile. It is pure luxury. Nazar and I spend hours on the balcony, letting the cool breezes blow through our hair. The abundance of hot and cold running water is blissful, as is the joy of walking around the bathroom without constantly looking for scurrying beetles.

Early in our stay, we visit the recommended obstetrician. He confirms that I suffer from a large infection, encompassing my whole cervix. He says that this infection has been growing for months and can become cancerous. He proposes that I be cauterized. So, the next day finds me back in the doctor's office for my in-house operation. Osane and I also complain of my inability to become pregnant, so another appointment is set. This time the doctor blows out my tubes.

In between doctor visits, Osane rents a three-bedroom flat, and the next week he begins attending his conference. Soon our life flows into a daily rhythm. With afternoons off, our family spends time exploring museums, the Cairo Zoo, the pyramids, nightclubs, and the countryside. We go shopping and sightseeing. It isn't hard to fall in love with the Egyptian people. They are easy-going, always smiling, very warm, and child-oriented. Nazar is welcome everywhere. There are, of course, the balancing negatives, such as the dense crowds, the dirt and disease. In general, however, I feel that Egyptian society represents a workable blend between the East and West.

Toward the end of our stay, we take a train ride to Alexandria. I find the Nile countryside to be wonderfully fascinating. In contrast to the empty desert, our train passes through many villages. The lush green fields are full of water buffalo, camels, donkeys, sheep, goats, and a multitude of dogs and cats.

Upon arriving in Alexandria, we stay two heavenly days at the Palestinian Hotel, located on the grounds of King Farouk's old palace. The precious moments spent on the shores of the

Mediterranean are gifts from God. Seeping through our total relaxation are tiny trickles and then rivers of newborn strength, life, and health.

We return to Cairo for the final weeks of the conference. On our last Friday, we meet some Egyptian friends in a restaurant on the top floor of a major hotel. Under a full moon sparkling off the Nile, we watch belly dancers. All evening we feast on marvelous food, and breathe in the Egyptian culture we have both come to love.

As I sadly pack for our return trip to Saudi Arabia, I remember my ride around the Pyramids on a white Arabian stallion. With the wind blowing through my hair, the cantering hoofbeats told of moments of total abandonment.

While boarding our plane, I wave a grateful goodbye to our slight recess from life. As the plane lifts off Egyptian soil and heads toward the Kingdom, I drift into a dreamless sleep. I wake just in time to reach into my hand luggage and wrap my abaya around me. Strengthened by renewed health, I am refreshed and ready for our next chapter.

Chapter 34

Summer Fun and a Second Son

"Life is not measured by the breaths we
take but by the moments that take our breath away."
Hilary Cooper

The heat of the mid-July air suffocates us the second we step off the plane. Osane hails a cab and as we open the door of our home, I survey the ruins. Dust, dirt, and beetles are everywhere. I take off my abaya and begin cleaning in the kitchen, making my way through the whole house until it is once again livable.

The summer days slip into weeks. Nazar has his third birthday party, and Osane begins writing a petition that will enable him to be loaned from the government into the private business sector. This will mean a triple salary raise and many benefits. Thoroughly invigorated by the prospect of working for a foreign corporation, Osane begins circulating his petition through the ministries.

The sun continues to bake our days as we wait for petition endorsements. Finally, Osane announces that only a few more signatures are needed, but these officials have moved to Taif for the summer with the rest of the government. We then decide that a trip to Taif will do us all good. We can spend some time out of the heat, visit the relatives, and complete the petition. Within a few days we are once again on a plane, but this time flying out of the desert and into the cooler mountains.

It's a short flight to Taif. After the plane lands, we collect our luggage and hail a cab to Aunt Sarah's villa. Sarah and her family don't know we are coming. We tell Nazar to sneak into the house and surprise them. Nazar quickly disappears. All of a sudden, loud screams explode throughout the rooms. The children are delighted to see Nazar and they soon surround us with their welcoming, smiling faces. This gaiety sets the tone for the entire visit. Surrounded by happy commotion, we are led into the family room, where tea and coffee are served and Osane shares the many stories of the past months.

The next morning, children's laughter wakes us. After breakfast, Osane leaves for the Ministries to push his petition. While he is gone, I explain to Sarah (using my improving Arabic and gestures), how much I want another child. She keeps reassuring me. "Allah is with you, and you should remain patient." As I look into her seasoned and wise eyes, I pray that she is right.

That evening we sit down to the games Osane used to play in his childhood. There are guessing games, a version of "who's got the button," and a game flipping match cartons instead of dice.

A few days later the joyous atmosphere continues. We load the whole family into one large jeep station wagon and head out of town and into the desert. Sarah's son Mohamed drives quite a ways, before turning off the road. He winds the jeep down a dirt track toward a large outcrop of rocks. We park the car at the bottom of the rocks and race to the top. At the highest point, the landscape spreads out into a sweeping panorama. The view is breathtaking, a marvelous spot for a picnic.

While sipping tea and enjoying the cool, gentle breezes, I begin following two clouds of dust in the far distance. As the dust clouds draw closer, they turn into vehicles. The first car is a large, black limousine full of men and boys riding in comfort. The second vehicle is an open pickup truck. Its cargo is bouncing, wind-blown girls and women.

I watch this mirage pass before of my eyes. My initial reaction is disbelief, then frustration, and then intense anger. Quickly I lasso my emotions, for my breakdown has taught me to give no energy to loaded negative thoughts. If I am to survive in this culture, I must not become an angry person, but an accepting, non-judgmental one. With this in mind, I dismiss the event, and casually ask for another cup of tea.

Our time in Taif quickly draws to a close. Osane has acquired the needed signatures and it is now time to return to Riyadh. On the way to the airport, Sarah lovingly sticks 200 raels in my purse and tells me the money is for a new sewing machine. Feeling that she has a large family of her own to support, I thank her and return the gift. We spend the rest of the ride pushing the money back and forth. In the end, persistent Sarah wins. As we warmly kiss goodbye, I marvel at her ability to sense what is most needed in my life.

As time passes, I begin feeling queasy in the mornings. Noticing I have missed a period, I cross my fingers and make an appointment with Dr. Abdula for a pregnancy test. When the test comes back positive, I am beside myself with joy! For several days, I walk around in a blissful daze. Osane and Nazar can only look on. The last thing Nazar wants in his life is a rival, and Osane doesn't see our financial setup conducive for bringing a new life into the world. However, I know the timing is perfect. Intuitively, I sense that Osane is on his way up the ladder of success.

My look into the future proves correct. The following week Osane comes home from work all excited. It seems he has just met Ibrahim, a top Ministry official. After discussing their education in the West, Ibrahim shares that he also is married to an American. With so much in common, they quickly become friends. Osane invites him to our home the following Friday, and he graciously accepts.

When Ibrahim knocks on our door, all is ready. The house is freshly cleaned and picked up. That morning I bake a moist, buttery crumb pound cake with a delightfully sweet lemon glaze. I dress Nazar in his best outfit, and I choose one of Zara's fashionable but modest dresses for myself.

As soon as Ibrahim enters our home, I feel at ease with him. His charming presence is down-to-earth and at the same time commanding. As he sips his tea, Ibrahim shares, "My wife Catherine and our three children are summering in Spain. They'll return at the end of the month. I'm excited for Christie to meet her, for they've had many similar experiences."

The conversation then turns to Nazar. Ibrahim advises us to enroll Nazar in Riyadh School, the same school his children are attending. I politely reply that we are intending to send our son to Riyadh International School, where I had been a teacher. Ibrahim puts down his cup and takes a deep breath. Softly he explains that Nazar has a Muslim father, and can only attend an Arabic school. While I am digesting this information, he continues. "Since it is important for Nazar to learn to speak Arabic at an early age, I strongly suggest you enroll him this fall."

The rest of the visit goes very well. When Ibrahim leaves, I find my heart is in a quandary. The beginning of school is only a few weeks away, and my mind insists that three-year-old Nazar is too young to attend school. Wrestling with the pros and cons of making the right decision, my thoughts counter with the fact that Nazar will only be attending for half a day. I also understand the necessity of learning Arabic at a young age and the benefit of playing with other children. I remained undecided as the harsh sun gradually acquires a tint of pale yellow. Finally, at the end of the last week, I whisper a small prayer and ready Nazar for his first day at school.

I wake early the next morning, dress my first-born in his new blue-and-white checkered uniform, and pack his lunch. We both put on a brave face and Nazar plays a big man, until he sees the school van turn the corner. At that instant, he breaks into tears and refuses to enter the bus. It takes all of my coaxing to get him seated and as I watch him ride away, I am plagued with doubts. I spend the morning worried and nervous, but am overjoyed when Nazar returns home at one o'clock with a smile. The next morning at seven, Nazar boards the van, this time on his own.

A few weeks after the beginning of school, Ibrahim invites us to his home. He wants to introduce us to Catherine and the children, who have recently returned from Spain. On the drive to their house, we enter a newer area of Riyadh. It's full of grand, newly constructed villas. The extra-large lots are beautifully planted with a variety of trees, and flowering vines cascade down the walls. As we drive down these streets, I begin to feel twinges of insecurity. None of this affluence belongs to our world, and I know we're out of our depth. When the taxi pulls up to Ibrahim's large gate, I glance over the wall and am awed by the size of their villa.

Osane knocks, and one of the many servants opens the gate. We are led through the main courtyard, and are directed to a side lawn where Catherine is pushing the children on swings. On the far side of this velvety green area, I notice a pen with two gazelles. These graceful creatures are munching on alfalfa. To the right of the pen is a fenced-in swimming pool and an outbuilding containing an additional kitchen, changing rooms plus showers, a large concrete sitting area, and a pool table.

As Catherine approaches us, I notice a tall, confident woman who radiates poise and charm. Her brown hair is cut in a pageboy. She is modestly dressed in long camel-colored pants and a light blue blouse with long sleeves. Their two sons are wearing white thobes and their young daughter is clothed in a sundress. Taking one look at the gazelles and the swing set, Nazar's face lights up and he runs off into his own idea of perfection.

Leaving the children in the side garden, Catherine and Ibrahim lead us into their house. Each room is lavishly decorated and when I ask about the furniture, Catherine says that most of the decor has been shipped from Europe.

The tour begins in the two dining rooms, equally grand. In between is a formal living room filled with Italian furniture and plush Persian rugs. Glancing into the kitchen, I see two cooks and a driver sitting in the corner. We continued the trek upstairs. The beds in each of the children's rooms are custom made. The boys sleep in racecar beds, while an exotic, garden trellis surrounds their daughter's bed.

My senses are reeling. Catherine leads us back into the living room. As we carry on a light conversation, I keep glancing around the room at the crystal vases filled with fresh cut flowers from the gardens, the exquisitely made furniture and the intricately carved tables. I am accustomed to the temporary glitz of the foreign population on two-year contracts. I have never been exposed to the established wealth of the Saudi upper class, and I feel like a peasant visiting the Royal Court.

Even though Catherine and Ibrahim are hospitable and warm, I don't possess the emotional maturity or confidence to feel at ease in the midst of such lavish abundance. Unfortunately, I experience nothing but relief when our taxi turns into our newly-paved lane, and we enter the familiar servants' quarters we call home.

The next morning I decide to rearrange the Arab room. After working unusually hard, I bend down to pick up our trunk. The instant I straighten up, I realize I should never have attempted to lift anything that heavy while in pregnancy. My deepest fear is realized when a few minutes later, I feel a slight trickle of blood run down my leg. I immediately lie down, making sure my feet are raised a few inches above my head. Barely breathing, I wait for Osane to return from work so that he can take me to the doctor's office.

Pale and scared, I wait for my turn with Doctor Abdula. Finally, Osane helps me into his office. After examining me, the doctor states that I almost miscarried. Even though I still have the baby, he warns that I have to be extra careful. He sends for his nurse, who turns me over on my side and sticks me with a three-inch needle.

As we drive home I am sensitive to each rough spot in the road, for I am determined to keep my baby. Even with extra care, a few evenings later I start into labor. Once again, I immediately lie down and frantically scream for Osane. He takes one look at my face and knows what's happening. Drained of color, he looks lost and helpless. Meanwhile I gasp, "Go fetch Ella!"

I try to calm my emotions and center my mind. I know there is a war going on deep inside my body. The baby wants out, but the shot the nurse gave me is holding the fetus in. Having no way of knowing which side will win, the only thing I can do is focus on God and wait.

Thirty minutes later Ella comes running through the house and into the back bedroom. Seeing that I still have the baby, she pulls herself together and quietly approaches me. Ella gently lifts my legs, putting pillows under them. She talks reassuringly to me the whole evening, and stays holding my hand long into the night.

It seems my prayers and Ella's reassuring presence has won the first battle. However, a careful trip to the doctor's office the next morning clarifies I have yet to win the war. Dr. Abdula informs me, "If you want this child, you'll have to remain flat on your back for eight weeks or more. As the baby grows and you became firmer, you might be able to get up."

The nurse comes in to give me another jab with the needle, and then we wind our way home. There is no question in my mind that I will sacrifice eight weeks or more of my life for this baby. Realizing this, Osane begins to sort out the practicalities.

He concludes that we need a full-time cook and housekeeper. So, the next evening he brings Medina into our lives. She is a large, elderly, black Ethiopian complete with tribal scars and a domineering smile. She is jolly but controlling, determined to run the household the way *she* sees fit.

The next morning I wake early. With helpless frustration, I watch Medina prepare Nazar for school. As the hours of the first day tick by, the awareness that I have to lie on my back the entire day and several weeks to come almost spins me into a panic attack. Focusing on the baby, I somehow calm my nerves.

As the days creep by, sedentary confinement becomes easier. Soon our family, plus Medina, settles into a routine. My morning and afternoon naps are separated by lunch, reading, knitting, playing with Nazar, and nighttime TV. Many evenings, Osane visits his friends, leaving us alone. While I read, I often feel Medina's eyes penetrating my book in wonderment. It is beyond her that a female can decipher any meaning from the written word.

One evening I hear noises from our Arab room. I suspect that the neighborhood children are once again climbing the bars over our windows. Their game is to peek into the foreigner's house. This has happened many times before, and pulling the curtains usually stops the activity.

This evening Medina is in no mood for rude and curious children. She makes her feelings quite clear as she yanks the curtains shut. The children, challenged by Medina, disappear to find recruits. A mob is soon outside both windows, yelling insults. Completely furious now, Medina grabs a broomstick. With fire in her eyes, she opens the front iron gate and pounces into the street to break up the troops.

Her anger only excites the children further, and she is forced to retreat into the house. I lie on the couch watching Medina pace back and forth, her cheeks flushed, her eyes enraged and her mouth full of Ethiopian curses. The infantile troops, now in full revolt, begin stoning our house. Resigned, Medina stomps into the back bedroom and slams the door. With no resistance, the children finally lose interest and slowly return home.

As the baby grows and I become firmer, Dr. Abdula tells me I can start minimal exercise. Relieved, I begin morning strolls through our neighborhood. While smelling the outside air, I have to harden myself against stares from male pedestrians, construction workers, yells from passing cars, and heckling from hostile children plus an occasional taxi that follows me home.

Meanwhile Osane's petition finally completes the red-tape circuit, and he is loaned to the private sector. After a few interviews, he becomes Personnel Manager at Diotec, a Greek company that is responsible for Riyadh's electricity. His salary triples and the company gives him a car. Then, as a surprise, his family in Southern Arabia sends us enough money to put down the first and last month's rent on a new villa.

With good fortune shinning down on us, another totally unrelated incident blesses our lives. The Saudi Government passes a Royal Decree, expelling a large Finnish corporation and its employees from the country. They have one week to leave the Kingdom, and the home rental market is suddenly full of vacancies.

After searching the vacated Finnish villas, Osane finds the perfect home for us. On Friday, Osane drives us to the proposed house, and I am in agreement with him. It is more than ideal! Two weeks later, we move in.

After we settle into our new home, I am finally healthy enough to give Medina notice. I am anxious to nest without a cantankerous Ethiopian telling me what to do. I am also sick of the way she plunders our kitchen.

Every Friday morning (her day off), she walks out the gate looking several pounds heavier. She is indeed plumper, for under her dress are eggs, powdered milk, flour, sugar and anything else she can waddle away with.

Snuggled into our new home, our family thrives. We all love the new garden villa, and we glide through the rooms feeling majestic. The Finns have landscaped the outside area into expansive yards and gardens. A sidewalk circles the home, and delineates the space into two front gardens and one side garden. Boxed hedges run along the outside of each sidewalk, reinforcing the front and side garden patterns. The twelve-foot high wall encircling the villa is covered with ivy, and flowers are everywhere.

Although the house itself is small, it is more than adequate for our family. The entryway leads into a marble foyer. To the left is the living room, and on the right is the family room. Further down the hallway is the dining room, which leads into the kitchen. In the back of the house are two bedrooms, a Western bathroom, and a stairway to the roof. In front of the kitchen window the Finns have planted a forest of sunflowers, and the glow of yellow reflects everywhere. This villa is, indeed, our dream come true.

To furnish our new home, Osane attends a last-minute furniture sale several Finnish families are hosting. With a new baby in mind, he purchases a large black rocking chair. He also brings home some couches and teak tables.

The next evening, Osane drives out to the Haji camp to buy rugs. After I settle Nazar down for the night, I keep an ear out for Osane. Concerned that he's been gone too long, I am relieved when I hear commotion in the garden. I open our villa door to find Osane pulling three rugs through the gate. He looks up at me with a large grin and says, "Well, Christie, here are our rugs. They only cost the equivalent of $300 apiece, and should last us a lifetime."

After he places the rugs safely in the hall, he takes my hand. "Christie, you have to hear this story," he says, pulling me down on the couch next to him. "You already know that this is the month of the Pilgrimage to Mecca and families are traveling to this Holy City from all over the world. What you don't realize is that these pilgrims, known as the Hajis pass through Riyadh driving large, colorful buses, which congregate in government camps every afternoon. In order to pay for this required trip of a lifetime, families spend several years making their one rug, which they sell along the way to cover their travel expenses. So as the women set up camp, the men take their rugs into the open marketplaces where they meet Saudis and the few foreigners who are searching for rugs. As soon as a potential buyer appears, the haggling begins. The singsong resembles the chants of an American auctioneer. After many prices are passed back and forth, sales are finally made."

Now that our new home is furnished, I begin sewing clothes for our baby. I am in the middle of cutting out an infant jumpsuit, when Nazar arrives home from school and hands me a handwritten note. Full of curiosity, I open the envelope, and find an invitation, written in English, to a school open house.

Knowing Nazar will be disappointed if I don't attend, on the appointed day Osane drives us across the city to Nazar's school. Nazar proudly leads me through the gardens to his classroom, and then leaves to play with the rest of his classmates. His teacher, Abla-Faf, knows only a little English. However, I gather that Nazar is doing quite well. After our conference, Abla-Faf leads me into the teacher's lounge where refreshments are being served.

Many of the other mothers and teachers are already there. The moment I enter, I realize I have made a major fashion error. In my mind, I anticipated attending the equivalent of a PTA meeting and teacher conference, which requires casual wear. I therefore am wearing a hand-sewn maternity dress, a cream-colored cardigan, and everyday sandals.

In blatant contrast, the Arab women are meticulously attired in silk designer dresses, spike heels, gold, and expensive perfume. Since they are only permitted to go to school functions, doctors or dentist's offices, and other women's coffees or teas, they consider this is a formal outing and they are dressed accordingly.

I quickly fill my plate with refreshments, and slip quietly into a corner. As I glance around the room, I notice that most of these females are from the upper echelon of Riyadh's society. They are the wives of Ministers, Ambassadors, and Princes. Many of them are amazingly beautiful. Their long jet-black hair accentuates their olive skin. Their ebony eyes are circled by raven black eyelashes and their beauty is mesmerizing. Their features are classical, their posture is perfect and their body movements paint a picture of grace and poise. A few of them politely glance my way and smile, but mostly I am left alone to observe this excessively guarded slice of Arabian life.

The days in our garden villa slip peacefully by. Homesickness, like surf to the ocean, has been my constant companion for months. One morning I wake and notice that this emotion has mysteriously been replaced by a sense of contentment. Somehow, I now have everything I desire. Osane has a new job, we have a beautiful home and a car, Nazar is in the best Saudi school in Riyadh, we have many wonderful foreign friends plus relatives, and within a matter of weeks I will hold my second child. As an additional surprise, Osane rehires Bagosh to help with household chores. I spend my spare time organizing Nazar's bedroom to include a crib, shelves for diapers, new baby outfits, and all the things needed for a new infant.

As my due date approaches, Dr. Abdella leaves for a six-week home stay in Pakistan. The Egyptian doctor who is supposed to take over his practice lasts only two weeks before he returns to his homeland. This leaves me without a doctor. Our friends advise us to leave the country and travel to Lebanon to give birth. Many of them have delivered at the American University of Beirut's medical facilities, and they compliment the Lebanese doctors.

After seriously discussing the option, Osane and I agree that we simply can't afford it. The tickets, plus the rental of an apartment for a few months, and finally the foreign hospital fees, are too much for our budget.

Realizing that I will have a Saudi birth, Osane and I begin to research our options. The first place we visit is the large, Saudi government hospital that is free. We find this hospital to be dirty and crowded; in some cases there are two women to one bed. Our next option is the Obate Hospital, a private facility that has just opened up. We visit a newly-arrived Syrian doctor who has trained in Canada, and decide to entrust him with the delivery. It seems we've made our decision just in time, for the following week I go into labor.

Osane rushes me to the Obate Hospital. Just as I am being admitted to my room, Ella arrives. She keeps me walking until the labor pains force me to lie down. An hour later, I am wheeled into the delivery room. The labor is not long, but abnormally strenuous and very painful. The doctor, for some deranged reason isn't administrating anesthesia, and I am being forced into a natural childbirth.

With no drugs to dull the pain, I concentrate on the pre-natal exercises I had learned stateside. Toward the end of the birth, the nurses keep shouting "*push*" in Arabic. The baby seems to be caught in my birth canal. No matter how hard I try, I can't dislodge it. I give one last frantic thrust (not wanting to suffocate my little one), and deliver a ten-pound boy.

With the baby out, the doctor has problems birthing my placenta. Unfortunately, with no medication to help me deliver my large baby, I am absolutely spent. The doctor makes an executive decision and stiches me up, leaving the afterbirth inside.

The nurses wheel me back to my room, where Osane and Ella greet me. They are full of congratulations and love. When I tell them it is a boy, Osane dubs the child "Sammy." A nurse knocks on my door. She walks up to Osane and enthusiastically states, "You are the father of a *fair* son. As soon as the infant is cleaned up, I'll bring him to you."

Thinking I am about to hold a blond infant, I am surprised when a light-skinned, decidedly Arab-looking baby with dark brown hair is placed in my arms. The price for being caught in my birth canal is a flat nose, flat forehead and flat chin, but everything else about him is perfect, especially his lungs.

My excitement over the arrival of Sammy is dampened when I soak the bed in blood three times that night. The next morning, the nurses bring Sammy to me. As I attempt to feed him, they coo to him in Arabic.

Throughout the first day, nurses from Jordan, Syria, Pakistan, Egypt, and elsewhere wander through the room. These visits are cumbersome, for only one nurse from India speaks any English. If it isn't the nurses, it is anybody else in the hospital (sick or well) wanting to see the first foreign baby born in the new hospital. I use my limited Arabic to disperse the line waiting to hold my baby.

Sammy himself is my other problem. He is so big. Not only is he constantly hungry, he is also having digestion problems. I soon give up breast-feeding and revert to bottles. His constant hunger plus colic turn him into a constant crier.

My time in the hospital passes quickly. Soon Osane is bringing Sammy and me home. A jealous older brother greets us. With a sly grin on his face, Nazar proudly shows me his new bedroom decorations. Covering all four walls is a life-sized mural of Tanzania's Serengeti, with hyenas, lions, cheetahs, antelopes and gazelles. This is clearly Nazar's artistic protest on the birth of a competitor.

A few weeks later, Sammy's face straightens out and he turns into a beautiful baby. Unfortunately, he suffers from *severe* colic. Instead of peacefully gazing on an angelic infant, our existence is bombarded by a continually crying baby. Sammy's fussing causes stress during the day and lack of sleep at night.

I plod through each day, praying to gain back my strength. Then four weeks after Sammy's birth, I begin hemorrhaging. Osane rushes me back to Obate Hospital. The Syrian doctor finally stops the bleeding. After a few days in a hospital bed, plus blood transfusions, he releases me. As we leave the hospital he tells Osane to feed me thick, red meat. I give him a funny look and recall what I have suspected for some time. His medical knowledge amounts to nothing. I wonder whom he bribed to acquire his license.

For the next month, I struggle to make it through each day. I am consumed with exhaustion. No matter how much I rest in between chores, my condition continues to deteriorate. Just before I give up completely, I develop horrible side pains.

This time Osane takes me to Dr. Abdella, who has finally returned from Pakistan. After a quick examination, he realizes that I am in serious trouble. He immediately admits me into the National Hospital, where I am pumped with penicillin and blood transfusions. Dr. Abdella also posts English-speaking nurses, to check on me around-the-clock. He daily monitors me, and brings consulting specialists to my bedside.

The diagnosis is that my undelivered placenta, which has been rotting in my body for eight weeks, has me knocking on death's door. I can barely open my eyes and when I do I can't focus. I hang on the cusp of life for a few days before the penicillin takes effect. Then Dr. Abdella performs a D&C.

Osane is shaken to his core by my brush with death, for his mother had died in his childbirth. Therefore, as soon as I return home from the hospital he hands me tickets for a four-week stay in Beirut. He is determined to have me undergo a complete medical check-up by Lebanese doctors, no matter what the cost!

Chapter 35

Communal Living

"One can acquire everything in solitude except their character."
　　Stendhal

The flight to Beirut is uneventful and pleasantly short. Our family hails a taxi to the hotel we stayed in on our way from America. As a surprise, Osane rents our original suite. It is on this bed that I spent my first night in the Arab world and out of these windows I first glimpsed Arab culture. Sammy's cries break my trance. With no hesitation I call the porter, and, in Arabic, I ask for a crib.

The next day we visit a well-known Lebanese obstetrician. He confirms that my insides carry the scars of a primitive delivery, but with my D&C he predicts that I will quickly gain my strength. Our next challenge is to find comfortable but reasonable living quarters. Osane locates a one-bedroom apartment across from the American University of Beirut, which suits our needs.

We spend the next three weeks enjoying this complex city, tucked between the mountains and the sea. We leisurely stroll the urban streets, browse the main shopping districts, sip tea at outside cafes, and one afternoon we take a long drive into the mountains. With the ocean not far away, we spend time at the public beaches enjoying the salt breezes and the bright hues shining through the Mediterranean sun.

In contrast to Egypt however, this is not a child-friendly city. There are few parks, and most of the children spend time either in school or in their high-rise apartments. Living with a crying newborn and an overactive child in a one- room apartment, soon becomes a nightmare. I begin to yearn for our garden villa with its large walled-in yards, washing machine, and Bagosh to help with the chores. When I share my feelings with Osane, I find that he also is ready to go back home. We therefore decide to cut our vacation short and return to Riyadh one week early.

Anxious to settle our family into a solid routine, I begin counting the hours until we are tucked back into our Saudi home. Finally, it's time to pack our things. On the way to the airport I say a prayer of thanks, for as the Lebanese doctor had predicted, my strength has returned. As our plane gains altitude I say goodbye to Beirut, "The Jewel of the Mediterranean."

Within a few hours, we are once again on Saudi soil. We quickly make our way through customs and board a taxi to take us home. As we turn into our street, I experience an exuberance that radiates from my inner core. Our family has been through such turmoil in the last few months. It's past time to construct a stable nest!

Our taxi pulls up in front of our villa and Osane pounds on our gate. He is expecting Bagosh to open the door. Instead, he stares in disbelief as Uncle Hamid's son welcomes us. I am stunned. Numb, I walk through the garden. My heart is in my stomach. In the house, six other family members, ranging from two to sixty, greet me. Inwardly I am seething, but years in the Arab world have trained me to hide my emotions.

As I glance around *my home*, I find that the relatives have totally rearranged it. They have taken mattresses off the beds and placed them on the floor, changed the rooms around, and stocked the refrigerator with Arab food.

Mentally searching for some explanation, I remember that Uncle Hamid has been working in Riyadh while his family remains in Southern Arabia. Thinking that we will be gone the rest of the month, he must have moved his family in. This is perfectly acceptable by Saudi standards, but incredibly difficult for me to accept. Knowing I can no longer conceal my indignation, I mouth a quick goodnight to everyone with the excuse of putting the children to bed.

Since our master bedroom is already taken, the four of us have to sleep on mattresses on the living room floor. As Osane hands me the bedding, I furiously begin making up the beds.

"Christie," Osane warns, "You'd better pull yourself together and not hurt my uncle's feelings. You know he hasn't done anything to intentionally annoy you, and you better not offend him!"

Still throwing sheets around, I begin crying. Seeing my tears, Osane shifts. Sensing how unacceptable this unannounced move-in is to an American, he wraps his arms around me. Brushing the tears off my face he whispers, "Christie, the only thing we can do is make Hamid's visit as pleasant as possible. As for how long the family is planning to stay, no one will know, for it is unacceptable to hint for a departure date. With all likelihood, they will be with us for the rest of the summer."

The next morning I wake, resolved to release my personal space to the relatives. Our lifestyle suddenly shifts from west to east. We begin sleeping, eating and ironing on the floor. Our meals become traditionally Arabic, and we pass every afternoon in the garden drinking tea and listening to Saudi music. The men rent an old projector and often bring in Arabic films, which they show on the roof in the cool evenings. We also have Saudi families over for dinner, the women sitting on one side of the house, the men on the other.

Throughout the visit, as the woman of the house I retain a slight dominance. This allows me the luxury of subtle rebellions. Every time I serve tea, instead of beginning with the oldest male I begin with the oldest female. This action results in shy giggling, as the women glance at the men. Also when there are visitors, instead of sitting in the family room with the rest of the women, I often walk into the living room and pass the time with the males.

One Friday morning, the female relatives attend a wedding. This leaves the male relatives and me free for a drive. Osane borrows a large jeep, and our party begins a road trip to an agricultural area outside of Riyadh. With Arabic music blaring, the miles speed by.

After a few hours, during the heat of mid-day, Osane pulls off the main road and into the desert. The relatives open their doors and line up. I watch as they kneel and begin washing with sand. Osane explains that when water is not available for prayer purification, the discipline is to complete the washing ritual with sand.

After prayers, Uncle Hamid opens the trunk and pulls out a watermelon wrapped in a blanket. With no plates or utensils available, he shatters the melon on a rock. We pick up pieces, enjoying the cool liquid as it quenches our thirst.

After another hour of driving, we see green fields magically appear out of the desert. As we wind through the lushness, our eyes soak in the healing colors of pale sun reflecting off the healthy crops. We stop by an agricultural pump, which is circulating water throughout the fields. Leisurely we sit down under the royal palms. As we listen to the flowing water, we drink tea, eat dates, and watch the sun set.

Nightfall finds us back on the road, homeward bound. Inspired by the cool night breezes and the passing open desert, Uncle Hamid begins shouting a primeval desert chant. The cadence and the rhythm are like nothing I've ever heard. Abruptly he stops, and his son takes up the song. Some of the words are the same, but the rest seem to answer a continuing puzzle. Back and- orth they chant, in the same loud, melodic tune. Soon I have heard enough to produce my own pagan dirge. The relatives erupt in laughter at my version.

Osane tells me over his shoulder, "Do you realize you're mimicking a camel herder's song? The lead Bedu uses this chant to keep the other camel drivers awake and in line when they ride through the night."

Uncle Hamid is now animated and full of enthusiasm. For the rest of the drive he tells me (through his sons and Osane) about the traditional Bedouin life. He defines the nomads as ones who live a life that is solitary and independent. He relates that the Bedouin base their life on the camel. This creature carries heavy loads on padded feet cushioned for desert travel, and is able to go long distances without water. The tribesmen also depend on sheep and goats for milk, meat, leather, wool, and transportation.

Eyes shining, Hamid begins to proudly praise the old ways. He describes a complex brotherhood based on traditions, rituals, and morals that developed into a society of alliances and raids. In such an ancient culture (adapted for survival on the desert), emphasis is placed on patience, courage, stamina, and generosity. Arab hospitality is a result of these principles.

For instance, Hamid explains, "If we were to visit a Bedouin settlement, our party would first send out a spokesperson to declare our peaceful intentions. As this representative approaches, he would shout "Salaam Alaikum"—peace be with you. He would then use his right hand to throw sand up into the wind, signaling peace. With good intentions established, the visitors would now be welcomed, even if they came from an enemy tribe. They would be given food, tea, camel's milk, rest, and care.

When Uncle Hamid finishes his stories, I look over at him and find that he is still entrenched in the past. He slowly turns his head and smiles at me. Pulling up the sleeve of his thobe, he points to a scar on his upper arm. His son shows me a similar scar behind his knee, and I remember the mark on Osane's hairline. I nod my head in understanding, knowing that these marks are made when skin is seared with an iron poker to cure disease. Watching me study the scars, Osane comments, "The Bedu still participate in skin searing and also the drinking or applying of desert plants and roots."

We are each lost in our own thoughts as our car continues to speed through the night. We arrive home, totally refreshed after a day of togetherness.

The summer flies by, and as the days lengthen I notice that the relatives are gathering their things. Patiently I watch, until I gather that they are ready to begin their journey homeward. On their departure morning, Hamid's wife walks up to Sammy's crib. She kisses him and then places some coins under his head for good luck.

After warm goodbyes, the relatives are suddenly gone, and the house is quiet. As I reclaim our space, I realize how close we have all become. I reflect on the blatant misconceptions that exist between the east and west. Hatred, anger, misunderstanding, prejudice, and bigotry can effortlessly dissipate if we simply realize we are all human.

On the cusp of each culture are the dangerous extremes, but everyday man occupies the expansive space in the middle. Because of our summer together, each Saudi relative has a face, a name, and a personality to me. I also am real to them and we are bound together by love, respect, and the hours we have laughed together.

Chapter 36

Contentment

"Pull up a chair. Take a taste. Come join us. Life is so endlessly delicious."
　Ruth Reichl

As the seasons change and the sun loses its fierce heat, the overseas population of Riyadh once again begins flowing back. Nazar starts his second school year and Sammy outgrows his colic. I call him my sunshine, for seldom does his smile leave his beautiful face.

　A few weeks after school starts, I am strolling through our freshly watered garden admiring the Finnish flowers we have inherited, when there is a knock on the gate. Bagosh opens it to find Ali and his suitcases on the stoop. Concealing all surprise, I warmly welcome him. Over tea, Ali tells me that he has received a promotion from his hospital in Southern Arabia, on the condition he undergo a three-month training session in a Riyadh hospital.

So once again, we have a relative for a houseguest. Ali sleeps on a mattress in the living room, where I serve him breakfast every morning. After prayers and his meal, he travels by cab to work, returning with Osane around two o'clock. After dinner, he spends his time on the veranda, smoking one cigarette after the other while staring into space.

One Friday in late fall, Osane drives all of us into the desert for a picnic. Somehow, he happens upon a rough, new road that we decide to explore. After some miles the desert surrounding us turns rugged, with rocky pebbles mixed with packed sand, jagged hills, and hardly any vegetation. Osane pulls to a stop on the side of the lane. We jump out and follow Nazar up a little used trail, which leads into a ravine and up the side of a gradual slope. Here we find a cave Bedouin have used, to hide from the sun while tending their sheep. The cave is big enough for all of us and as Nazar, Sammy, and Ali throw rocks down the side of the hill, I blurt to Osane, "I never want to leave Saudi Arabia. The Americans can have the West."

Surprised by my own words, I stare at the wide-open spaces. My occasional feeling of contentment has grown into a constant state. Somehow, I feel one with the Saudi society we now live in. A delicate balance has developed between Riyadh's small foreign population and the urban Saudis. The present group of Westerners consciously attempts to blend in with Arabian culture. Most of them have been in the country for some time, have learned the language, respect the customs, and within both societies there is an intangible moral code.

Recognizing that Saudi trust and honesty have been passed down from an era where nomads lived in tents with open flaps and no doors, the present foreign community mirrors these ethics. It never occurs to either culture to lock houses or cars. Besides, punishment is harsh so crime is almost non-existent.

Nevertheless, a jab of concern pierces my peacefulness. I am aware that the Stanford Committee is developing a five-year plan for the Saudi government. Change is in the air. More isolated American compounds are being constructed and I worry that all these subtle alterations will upset the delicate balance.

Meanwhile, the boys continue to grow and shine joy into our everyday routines. Nazar keeps us all laughing with his perfect imitation of a herd of sheep. After all, he is growing up in a barnyard atmosphere. Our Bedouin neighbors have animals everywhere. On the roof they keep pigeons, and right under our bedroom window live their sheep and chickens. Also (much to the boys' delight), down the dirt lanes in front of our villa, cows, donkeys and horses freely wander. Every day Bedouin herd their sheep and goats past our gate, and at night packs of wild dogs howl as they hunt.

The weeks pass by with Nazar busy in school, Osane involved with Diotec, and Sammy growing cuter every day. Christmas rushes by, and then the wet season hits. With the rains comes sickness.

Riyadh is a very dirty city, thick with flies and uncollected garbage. The intense summer heat keeps the germs under control. With the cooler rainy season, many of these germs spring to life. Nazar is the first one to become sick, and soon our whole household is down with a two-week influenza. Bagosh remains the only healthy one. With his help, we somehow pull through Sammy's feedings, mealtimes, and dishes.

A month later, after we are finally well, Bagosh gives us notice. He explains that he is moving to Jeddah, but that he has found a houseboy called Mohammed as his replacement. When I stare at him in alarm, he attempts to reassure me by telling Mohammed's story.

It seems that Mohammed left his village in Yemen when he was only nine. Under the guardianship of a man called Uncle, a bus full of boys drove through the desert. They slept at night under their bus, praying they wouldn't be robbed by wandering Bedouin. In Riyadh, the boys were placed in menial jobs. Mohammed was assigned to the Ministry of Interior. He spent three years in this Ministry, working from dawn to dusk. He did manage to attend night school, where he met Bagosh. When Bagosh told him about a job opening in a private home, Mohammed was ready.

The next day Bagosh and Mohammed walk through our door. I notice that Mohammed doesn't look like a Yemeni, for he is much taller and stockier, with a light complexion. The only flaws on his handsome face are small pockmarks, which cover his cheeks. I find him shy and quiet, but he wins me over with his ever-present smile, his intelligence, and his eagerness to experience anything new.

Within the next six months, an increasing number of foreigners begin settling in Riyadh. Many move into our area, and can be seen on the streets and in the shops. The discomfiting reality is that these Westerners are a new breed. Signing two-year contracts with huge salaries, they refuse to bend to a new culture during their temporary stays. I begin noticing them in the markets paying expensive prices instead of bartering, and expecting the shop owners to speak to them in English. Even though the Matawas still heckle them for not covering up properly, their sheer numbers tend to shield them.

With this increasing foreign presence, alternative opportunities begin opening up for Osane. He is hired as guide and interpreter for an American party studying the oryx, the near-extinct, gazelle-like animal of the Arabian Desert. One evening, Osane brings home the curator of the Tucson Zoo, a South African photographer, and the wealthy patron who supports this documentary film.

While Osane is in the desert filming, a bulldozer digs a trench in our dirt street. A few days later, one of the workers knocks on our gate and casually hands me a telephone. I am breathless with excitement, and rush into the living room to carefully arrange our new telephone on the bookcase. My exuberance ebbs as the days pass by in silence, and soon the telephone become one more thing to dust.

Two months later, when I hear a ring, I run into the bedroom to turn off my alarm clock. I am halfway there, when I realize that our dead phone is ringing in a new era in Saudi Arabia. I jump around the room in celebration. Even though I know that each call is censored, the shiny wires on my bright red phone connect our family with the rest of the world.

This becomes clear when the phone rings early one afternoon. Excitedly, I pick it up, to hear the overseas operator asking for an American company. I am speechless! The realization that I can stand in my own living room and talk to the States is bewildering. Somehow I mumble, "I'm sorry, but you have the wrong number."

The operator thanks me and hangs up, but I stand there, stubbornly hanging onto an embryo cord to my culture, refusing to place the phone back on the hook. Instead, all my senses concentrate on the buzz of the overseas connection and the small talk of the New York operators. Listening to their chatter, it strikes me that I am homesick. Therefore, after finally hanging up, I begin filling in details to a plan I have been working on for some time.

Throughout my years in Arabia, I have been receiving letters from my parents. As the seasons pass, the letters become longer. With the birth of our second son, my parents have offered to pay half of our travel expenses to the States. Feeling it is time for the boys to visit their grandparents, Osane and I decide that as soon as Nazar's school year is finished, the boys and I will make our trip westward.

June arrives quickly. As we sit waiting to board our flight, I try to control my emotions. Tears keep splashing the green passports I hold in my hand, drenching the Saudi emblem of the crossed swords and palm trees. My emotions are torn.

For the first time I don't really feel a need to leave Saudi Arabia, and my heart aches anticipating a three-month separation from Osane. Yet the other part of me knows I need to touch home base, after four long years in the Arab world. Still not wanting to go, but knowing I must, I painfully kiss Osane goodbye.

Chapter 37

A Long Awaited Family Gathering

"One wants to be together with one's family.
That's what families are about."
   Aung San Suu Yuki

Our flight to Frankfurt, Germany is long and uneventful. This is the first time I have traveled alone, and the responsibility for two small children weighs heavily upon me. I watch out the window as the plane touches down on German soil. I patiently wait until everyone else exits, before making my way out with my assemblage of baby gear. Typically I follow the rest of the passengers to the baggage area, but by the time I make my way through the gate everyone from my plane has disappeared.

Looking for signs to baggage, I begin scanning my surroundings. I observe a modern airport, built on different levels.

These floors are connected by a series of escalators. With all the signs in German, I randomly pick a direction and start walking.

Unfortunately, I discover that my pram will only fit on the escalator if it is folded. It soon becomes evident that it is impossible to load my boys and all my paraphernalia onto these moving stairs. I am forced to halt at the top of each escalator, while the population of Germany steps in to help. Thanks to kind souls, we make it down four separate escalators and finally into the luggage area. An agent helps us through customs, and we are soon standing on the sidewalks of Frankfurt. I hail a taxi, and we speed down forested avenues to our hotel.

We sleep that night between clean, starchy sheets. Still on Saudi time, we are the first ones to rise the next morning. I leisurely dress the boys and then attempt to westernize the Arabian female I have become. My long hair hasn't been cut in four years, and has lost all hint of style. I'm wearing a long dark blue skirt, and a long sleeved white blouse I had bought at a Cairo bazaar. With a shrug, I turn my back on my appearance, and lead two excited boys out the door into the cool, German woods.

Morning mists caress us with moisture. The dewy air takes on the shape of laundry blowing in the wind. Our desert eyes soak in the lush green, as we inhale the scent of pine into our parched souls. After a quick breakfast, which includes side orders of bacon, we are back at the airport and in the air.

Our trip from Frankfurt to Boston turns into a complete nightmare, for I bounce Sammy on my knees for ten straight hours. It is no wonder that by the time we arrive in Boston, I have a splitting headache.

When our plane finally touches down on American soil, my soul explodes into a multitude of emotions. I have so often dreamt of returning to the States. Now that it is finally happening, I am so excited that I feel numb. In my surreal state,

I feel like I'm watching a movie or reliving a dream, as if I'm projected above my body, watching from above.

The next morning, as the boys sleep, I spend long moments at our hotel window. I marvel at the sound the wind makes as it blows through maple, oak, poplar, and pine trees. The yellow-green colors calm my nerves and I breathe in the odors of lush, thick grass and the different flowers basking in the early morning sun. Adrift in this aimless state, my heartbeat suddenly quickens and I tumble into a flashback. I am peeking out a shuttered window, covered with bars. A large group of Saudi men are gathered in the street, pointing and leering up at me. In fear, I jump away from the window. The next instant the image is gone, replaced by blowing leaves and quiet lawns.

The following afternoon we board our flight to Cleveland and the long-awaited reunion with my family. Once again, we are the last ones off the plane. As we struggle through the crowd looking for familiar faces, I feel someone grab me. Before I realize it, I am in my parents' arms. As we hug one another, tears of happiness and relief roll down my cheeks.

On the way to baggage, Father says, "Christie, Mother and I envisioned you two ways. Either, you'd be overweight from being housebound, or you'd appear skinny and tired from the intense heat."

I laugh nervously in response. I can read in their eyes that they are jarred by my appearance. I fully realize that my whole persona is far removed from the daughter they had last seen. As for the boys, they immediately bond with their grandparents. From the minute Mother sees two-year-old Sammy, she adopts him. Meanwhile, Nazar follows Father around, asking nonstop questions.

Tired from our long travels, we are more than ready to pull into the driveway of the house where I grew up. My sister, Jean, and her husband, Bud, are waiting at the door to give us emotional hugs of welcome. As I settle into my old room, I feel layers of responsibilities drip off me and dissipate into the air. I listen to Mother play with Sammy, while Bud teaches Nazar to play baseball.

During the next few days, there are family reunions and old friends to see. Everyone wants to know about the mysterious Arabia, so I speak continuously about my Saudi adventures.

My sister and I spend a lot of wonderful time together. As we visit, shop, and cook, I begin to feel more connected to the Western world. One afternoon, Jean senses my need to transform. She takes my hand and leads me into the backyard, scissors in hand. Clip-clip, my long hair falls onto the grass. Twenty minutes later, I have a new shag haircut.

The next evening, Nazar dresses in his Saudi clothes. After singing the Arabic songs he's learned at school, he hands out presents. Soon Saudi gun belts, tea sets, sandals, incense holders, jewelry boxes, and Arabic material cover the floor. As I scan the faces of my happy family, I realize how far they have opened their minds to the Arabian culture.

The next weekend Grandma and I pack the car, and Grandpa drives us to our Canadian cottage. As we settle into the North woods, time passes peacefully by. The boys and I spend our time under pine trees, or sitting on beaches watching water ripple on the shore. Surrounded by clean air, the call of loons and Canadian sunsets, the real me begins to finally re-surface.

As idyllic as our days are, subtle incidents occur to reinforce the reality that the boys and I are living a double life. Out of nowhere, Sammy throws a temper tantrum because Grandma is driving a car. When I ask him what is wrong he cries, "Only men drive cars!" Another day our little American-Saudi begins screaming again. Grandma has picked up a shovel and is clearing the yard of rocks. "Men work, women don't work!" yells small Sammy.

I also suffer from reverse cultural shock. Learned fears from Arabia follow me like unwanted ghosts. Little do I realize the damage done to my psyche until I attempt to hold conversations with men (even male family members). When I speak to the opposite sex, I can't look them in the eyes. The whole time I am conversing, I suffer from shallow breathing and perspiration. The real impairment is made painfully clear, when I freeze each time my father hugs me goodnight.

On our frequent trips to town, I also suffer from moments of illogical anxiety. Whenever I walk down the sidewalks and a male is behind me, I grab my purse in preparation for a heavy swing, in case he attempts to pinch or grab at me.

Constantly angry with myself for these insane thoughts, I gradually gain enough trust to relax. I even become confident enough to take my eyes off the sidewalk in front of me. Slowly I start to look up and gaze at the entire scene.

As I continue healing, a new dilemma surfaces. I recall how content I had been just weeks before leaving Saudi Arabia. The more western I become, the more I begin dreading my return. I also begin questioning the land we will be returning to. An article entitled <u>An Ancient Kingdom</u>, confirms these worries:

The article begins, "The Kingdom of Saudi Arabia never entered WWII. There was a lot of diplomatic juggling, but no actual fighting. During these war years, Arabia was very poor, for the turmoil stopped the flow of pilgrims to Mecca (a major source of income) and also broke up trade routes.

"Meanwhile, in the States during 1943, the shortage of oil created the realization that America had become the petrol tank of the allies. A frightening 63% of the entire world's oil consumption was coming from US reserves.

"Roosevelt's Secretary of the Interior, Harold L. Ickes, proposed that to save American oil, the world should burn foreign oil. Oil had already been discovered in a British possession along the Persian Gulf called the Trucial Coast. Americans outmaneuvered the British companies to win exclusive oil rights within the Kingdom. Exxon combined with Mobil to form the Arabian American Oil Company (ARAMCO).

"Therefore, in a short nineteen months, Saudi Arabia moved from being far afield to being vital in the defense of the United States. Roosevelt made the Kingdom eligible for Land Lease Assistance that meant nearly six million dollars in cash, goods, and bullion. Slowly, Saudi opened up its doors to the West and each year more Americans arrive."

The article concluded with the statement, "With hundreds of new changes as a result of oil, the pre-industrial society within the Kingdom is rapidly disappearing."

Putting the paper down, I realize that I have already begun to witness these changes. I feel honored to experience the ancient Arabian culture, as it has been for centuries. I am not sure I will bond with the Saudi Arabia of the future. The large wooden gates of the past are being pushed open more each season, and the established honor-based society is being exposed to the monetary culture of the West.

I place my anxieties on hold, determined to enjoy our stay until it trickles to an end. Way too soon we reload the car, store away our summer memories, and Grandpa heads the car due south.

During our short Cleveland stay, my youngest sister, Lee, drives up from Cincinnati for a visit. It is wonderful to reconnect with her. In the last four years, she has turned into a delightful adult.

During the final days of our stay, I have the boys checked by pediatricians and dentists and I finish shopping. In a final act of rebellion, I make a hair appointment. I tell the beautician to give me a boy cut, and she crops my hair to the scalp.

On our sad day of departure, Mother and Father drive us to the airport. After tearful goodbyes, we make our way onto the airplane. Breaking the connection with my family is even harder this time. The summer has gently blended us into a cloud of blissful co-existence.

As we sit in our plane seats waiting to take off, I glance back into the airport. Out of the corner of my eye, I catch the silhouette of my parents. The large airport window frames a picture of an elderly couple, sitting hand-in-hand on a hard bench. Lines of loneliness are etched through their features, but sparks of united strength flicker through their eyes.

Chapter 38

Changing Times

"Worrying is a form of atheism. I don't understand people who call themselves Christian or Buddhist or Muslim or whatever and worry. Because you cannot believe in a power greater than yourself and worry. It does not compute."
Oprah Winfrey

Somewhere over the Mediterranean Sea, both boys settle into an afternoon nap. Lulled by the droning airplane engines, I begin to prepare myself for our landing in Riyadh. I concentrate on Osane's image, and with his face illuminating my mind, I also slip into sleep. We all wake as our plane flies over the Arabian Desert. I know we are close to home when I start sneezing, for desert dust always activates my allergies.

The boys exit their seats quickly, excited to be home. They don't seem to mind disembarking into the heavy, hot atmosphere of Riyadh. We all search the crowd of mingling men, until we spot Osane. Nazar is the first one in his father's arms, but Sammy and I aren't far behind.

It feels so good to be united again, and we share stories all the way home. Osane pulls up to our gate and the children run into the house, glad to be back in their own territory. After greeting Mohammed, they find new bikes waiting for them in their bedrooms. I am equally surprised. On my pillow is a beautiful gold necklace and in the bathroom is an American washing machine. An hour later, there is a knock on the door. We open it to find Ella, Tahar and the children, full of welcoming hugs.

During the next weeks, Osane spends most evenings visiting friends. After the newness of our wonderful welcome wears off, I begin slipping into depression. Especially during the long evenings after the boys are in bed, I settle into despondency.

Taking a chair into the garden, I spend hours looking up into the clear Arabian sky. Not only am I having trouble adjusting back into the Saudi lifestyle, but Osane and I are also at odds. He is unable to align with my revitalized Western behaviors. He doesn't approve of my new western clothes or my haircut. He keeps calling me his little brother. I soon discover that Arabian males hate short hairstyles, for hair is a symbol of female beauty. The longer and fuller the locks, the more beautiful the woman becomes.

As the days drift into weeks, the spring of disharmony in our relationship keeps twisting tighter. I soon sense that if this pattern continues, we will begin living separate lives. This will not do!

In order to save our marriage, I regress into the role of Saudi wife. I pack away my new western clothes and commence wearing long Saudi dresses. I also begin spreading large meals out for Osane. My hair is another concession. Because of the good stateside cut, it starts to grow out nicely. Enjoying all these subtle changes, Osane once again spends evenings with his family.

Meanwhile, under the hot desert sun, Riyadh is transforming. Villas are being constructed, shops and new schools are going up, and the whole city pulsates to the sounds of construction.

The main construction workers are the Yemenis. They are the ants of Saudi Arabia. I am able to observe them first-hand, as they erect a villa in the lot next door. While standing in my kitchen, sheltered from the sun by thick concrete walls and desert coolers, I marvel at their endurance.

For them, work continues through the hottest part of the day. Their only protections from the sun are cloth skullcaps and centuries of built-up desert tolerance. Often singing while they work, their ancient chants filter into our house, holding us in their trance.

With the building boom in full throttle, both Arab and foreign workers flow through the open gates of the Kingdom. While the Yemenis build, the Jordanians, Palestinians, Syrians, and Lebanese teach in schools, operate shops, and hold down white-collar positions. The Pakistanis serve as tailors and gardeners; they share household work with Ethiopian, Philippinos and Yemenis, while the Saudis work in government positions.

The ever-growing foreign population serves as a catalyst for even more growth and upheaval. From all over the world, the ranks of the new vanguard file in. Americans, Germans, Dutch, French, and Japanese come to teach the Saudis about modern technology, to train Saudi armies, to set up financial systems, to build new and better villas, to clean Saudi streets, to open hospitals and factories. Even though the government insists that these new foreigners be housed in compounds, away from the Saudi population, the government can't harness the influence this new influx of foreigners have on everyday life.

Few if any regulations direct this disorderly building and population explosion, which soon outstrips the utility and maintenance accommodations. The electrical generators are old and outdated and they can't keep up with explosive use. The results are hours, even days of electrical cuts. These cuts are difficult though manageable in the winter but absolutely impossible in the summer, for electricity is needed to operate water-dependent desert coolers. Garbage pickup is also suffering, and traffic jams are becoming a new way of life. Finally, for the first time, crime is becoming a consideration and the profits from bootlegged liquor are way up.

As oil springs open the ancient Kingdom, the feudal monarchy is faced with overwhelming challenges. The key is to open up certain segments of the society while protecting the culture and Saudi lifestyle.

Unfortunately, the life of the average Saudi *is* being affected. For instance, household servants and gardeners were once a mainstay of everyday Saudi life. The growing foreign population however, raises these servants' salaries to a point beyond the means of ordinary Saudis. Spiraling inflation is also spinning every day necessities such as food, shoes, and clothing into burdens for large Saudi families. The result is that the men are forced to work extra hours. This increases the pace of life, cuts down on family time, and puts new social pressures on everyone.

It seems the ride into the twentieth century, as I prophesized, is becoming an extremely bumpy one.

While life around us pulsates, I tutor the Minister of the Interior's daughters. This family had hired an English nanny, but after only a few days she returned to England. While awaiting the arrival of their next nanny, the children come to our house.

The days pass quickly, as I am completely occupied with tutoring and childrearing. Just as our lives acquire a healthy rhythm, the foundation crumbles. Osane comes home from work one day and announces that the landlord has decided to move his family into our villa. The blow is a crushing one. Not only will we lose our home and location within the foreign population, but we will also become victims of inflation.

Trying to digest this forced move, I recall that our first apartment was 3,000 Saudi raels a year. The next year we again paid 3,000 raels, which testified to the stable housing market. When we made the move to our Finnish villa, we paid 6,000 for the first year, and 7,000 for our next year. Even before the landlord had expelled us, he warned that he was raising the rent to 40,000 raels a year. Osane's salary has improved with Diotec, but can't possibly keep up with such rapid inflation.

For a month, Osane searches for houses after work and on the weekends. I stay home, for any time an agent sees an American, the already outrageous rents will double. After days of scanning the rental market, he still has no luck. Anything that is at all livable is *way* above our budget.

Our moving date comes and goes, and we still can't find a place to live. Every time there is a knock on our gate, I jump. I vividly picture either soldiers or the landlord throwing our family onto the street, with our belongings heaped around us.

Finally Osane finds a villa, but it's way across town in the same area as Nazar's school. The closeness of the school makes sense, along with the rent of 30,000 raels a year. Unfortunately for me, this will mean exile into an Arab neighborhood. I will be marooned, miles away from any contact with the foreign population or anything familiar.

The following day Osane drives us across the city to our new home. Every mile away from the familiar foreign section twists my stomach into a tighter knot. Finally we turn off the main road, wind down narrow, dirt streets, and stop in front of a gray wall. Osane swings open the gate, and we enter a neglected garden. The bushes are overgrown, the grass is barely growing, and un-raked leaves from the many trees are everywhere.

Upon entering the house, paint fumes engulf us. I quickly grab Sammy's hand, and warn Nazar to stay out of wet paint. The landlord meets us at the entrance, explaining that there were ten people living here previously, and that he is repairing the villa for us.

Staying in the middle of the floor, we continue our tour. Off the marble entryway is a large hallway leading past the living room on the left and another large room on the right. As we continue down the hallway we turn left into the sleeping area, which consists of two bedrooms and a Western bath. At the end of the hallway are stairs leading to the roof, another room on the back right, and a door into the garden. Looking for the kitchen, I ask the landlord for the "matbuk." To my amazement, he points to one of the two outbuildings in the back garden.

Osane opens the door into the garden. As the boys run around, we follow the landlord across a tiled area covered with grapevines, and into the outhouse that serves as the kitchen. As soon as I peek in, I can't believe my eyes! In shock, I say to Osane, "How did the previous family *possibly* feed ten people out of this primitive space?"

Glancing around the filthy room swarming with flies, I note a single sink and one electrical outlet. Horrified, I turn around and walk quickly towards the door. This is a nightmare and there is no way I will raise my boys in such surroundings.

Osane catches up to me in the side garden. "Christie," he says. "Just wait right here. I know what you're thinking, but give me a few minutes with the landlord. Don't move!"

Pacing back and forth, I impatiently wait for Osane's return. Finally, I see him walking towards me. "OK," he says. "Remember, we are a family without options. The landlord has promised to turn the back bedroom into a kitchen, and the old kitchen into a washing room. He has also agreed to clean up the garden and plant new grass. Most importantly, he is willing to give us a two-year lease as a precaution against inflation."

Knowing I have no choice, I study the mature trees growing in the garden, while Osane hands the landlord two years' rent on our new home. Wondering how I am going to survive 24 months of isolation, I walk out the gate and into our car. Putting Sammie on my lap, I hug him and pray for strength plus a miracle. Only God's might will enable me to create a happy space out of such rubble.

I wake early the next day and begin packing. Three days later, a truck and three Yemenis arrive. As they load their colorful red pickup they chant, which sets into motion quick and rhythmic movements.

These small men fascinate me. Through leverage and mind control, they pick up items two to three times heavier than their body weight. I watch in amazement as one Yemeni straps our washing machine to his back. Meanwhile, another barefoot Yemeni picks up our American-size refrigerator and carries it over rugged stones to the pickup. While they continue their ancient singsong, they place tables on chairs and boxes on beds. Somehow these Yemenis create a chaotic puzzle that magically fits into their colorful truck.

By late afternoon, our former happy home is nothing but a skeleton. As I take one last look, I say goodbye to an era and quickly get into the car, cursing this move. Following the Yemenis' red pickup and all our belongings, we slowly drive out of the foreign sector and into the past.

Chapter 39

Life in the Saudi Sector

"There's a pleasure in being reminded
of the value of ordinary life."
   Karen Thompson Walker

During the first month in our new home, I become obsessed with nesting. The living room is the first area to take shape. Our furniture and Aunt Sara's rug fit nicely into the large open space. Next, the room adjacent to it transforms into a sunny playroom, and the wide hallway converts into our dining room.

    The kitchen however, develops at a frustratingly slow pace. The sink, stove, and refrigerator are installed almost immediately, but for weeks I live without shelves or storage. Finally, Osane brings an Ethiopian cabinetmaker to the house. This incredibly large man builds shelves plus cabinets with his huge fingers, and the back bedroom blossoms into a workable kitchen.

With persistence, our new villa with its airy rooms, old-world charm, and trellised grapevines turns into a livable space. Australian pines, pomegranate, orange, and lemon trees are strategically planted outside each window, creating the illusion of a forest. A variety of birds live in the trees and their singing, plus the sun playing through the iron-grated windows, create a peaceful environment.

Mohammed and I make a swing-set and sandbox in the back garden for the children, and I coax the grass to grow in the front yard. The boys spend most of their time in the new playroom, and Mohammed feels at home in his outside quarters next to the old kitchen.

While I am homesteading, Osane grows tired of his position at Diotec. He has reached a deadend, and boredom fills his days. He begins spreading his job availability through his network of contacts. Within a few weeks, he becomes president of an establishment owned by one of the Princes. This challenge is immense, for the Prince's business is near bankruptcy. Osane is more than ready to tackle the job, and begins working around the clock.

This leaves the boys and me on our own. We have no car, and only a censored telephone to connect us with the outside world. Trapped and isolated, I soon feel the newly painted walls closing in on me. With walking absolutely out of the question, I begin spending a great deal of time on the roof. In this open space, I am able to unleash my spirit into the vastness of the open desert.

When even the roof walls begin to close me in, I pile up the loose stones and balance on top of the rocks. Cautiously, I peer down on the neighborhood below. Mysteriously, I am always spotted, which forces me to jump off the stones. Never easily discouraged, within a few minutes I stubbornly remount my stones to gaze out onto the world.

My eyes catch a cloaked female walking down the dirt road. Her three children surround her. They dart around her like moths around a bright light. The two young brothers race out ahead, but always come running back to touch their home base.

My attention focuses on the mother, who walks with calm grace. Her steps are slow but certain, and she wears a shadow of confidence. She has inherited her position from previous generations. Her function is to be the nucleus of her immediate family, while being surrounded by her extended family. The rules that outline her behavior are typed in bold print, and her role is femininity at its essence, to nurture, love, and support. Her career is to be wife and mother. If she is at peace with this and follows this path of least resistance, she will live a life of security and peace.

Finally stepping off the stones and back onto the roof, I ponder the behavioral differences between the east and the west. Feeling like a leaf floating in the ocean between two shores, I once again ask myself the question that haunts my existence. *If I'm supposed to submerge myself into this ancient Arabian culture, why wasn't I born here?*

Early the next morning, there is a faint knock on our gate. Mohammed opens it to find a small girl standing there. After a short conversation she leaves, and Mohammed tells me that I have been invited to the neighbor's house for tea.

Determined to break my cycle of loneliness, I use this opportunity to join the roaming group of women I have spotted from the roof. After Nazar leaves for school, I carefully dress Sammy and we routinely walk down the street to different houses. After knocking on the gate, we are shown into the villa. We sit on the floor while our host serves us tea and coffee, and the little girls bring us nuts. Sammy will never sit beside me very long. He much prefers playing with children or the goats, chickens, pigeons, or cats that live in the back gardens.

After several weeks of visits, I begin to feel the strain. Even though the neighbors are always warm and hospitable, these mornings are becoming too difficult. My Arabic is not strong enough for lengthy conversations. Even if I were fluent, our common interests and experiences are too far apart. I begin refusing invitations and decide to search for other options to fill my long days.

After much consideration, I decide the solution is to return to the foreign sector. I begin asking Mohammed to walk to the main street and hail a cab. After a wait of fifteen to thirty minutes, a taxi will finally appear outside our gate. Grabbing Sammy's hand, I'll enter the cab and go to to Ella or Mary's house. With my old friends, I can communicate in English about topics that are culturally similar. This brings great joy into my life for a while.

As time passes however, each trip across town becomes more difficult. Because of the steady influx of new people, the traffic is becoming unbearable. Cars will often come to a complete standstill. I find being caught in traffic jams with Saudi taxicab drivers very unnerving. The frustration of the trip soon outweighs the value.

Forced to stay home, I watch the days flow into spring. The weather at this time of year is ideal. Every morning I open our windows and let the temperate air filter throughout the house. The breeze off the desert sways the tree branches, and the sun reflects off the shimmering leaves. In the quiet of the mornings I sit on our veranda and listen to the ancient agricultural pumps pushing water through the date fields. These pumps are pulsating at the pace of nature. As I allow the sound to be absorbed into my body, the tempo slows me down and buffers my restlessness.

While it is still cool, our family goes on several Friday picnics. Our favorite spot is an oasis off the Mecca road. After driving down this straight highway for miles, we feel the road suddenly dip into a large ravine filled with date palms and startling green vegetation. After Osane passes through a small village, he turns left down a small, unused lane. After parking the car, we walk down a winding path through date palms. Our destination is a palm shelter near an ancient well.

Osane spreads our blanket, while I prepare lunch. Meanwhile, the boys dip in the cool refreshing well water. After our noon meal, we all lounge on the blanket and the boys chase the goats and sheep that graze underneath the palms. As the filtered sun creates fascinating shadows on the oasis floor, we all enjoy the cool air, the sound of the agricultural pumps, and the rattle of the palm ferns blowing in the wind.

As summer approaches, the fly population increases. I try to mend our screens, but nothing seems to work. At certain times of the day the windows are black with flies, and everything in the kitchen has to be continuously covered. To solve this problem, the Saudi government bought crop-duster planes, and regularly bombs the city with insecticide. As the clouds of spray encircle our villa I grab the boys and run inside, closing our windows. Angered by the fumes, I conclude that the flies will adapt, while the insecticide will kill off the human population of the city.

Osane's hard work is finally paying off. He has transformed the Prince's establishment into a company with wide possibilities. After weeks of negotiations, he constructs an agreement with a Spanish company to sell their agricultural equipment to Arabia. This contract requires a trip to Spain, and a meeting with the company's top executives.

The price Osane pays for these successes: even longer working hours. My contribution is extended stretches in the kitchen. Since restaurants in the Kingdom are few in number, business entertainment falls to the woman of the house. As Osane begins bringing an increasing number of clients home, I start to look forward to these dinners. The executives are from around the world. Just sitting at a table with them is educational.

One of our regular guests is a Sudanese man named Ramzi. He lives in Barcelona, Spain with his Spanish wife and son. Every visit he tells us stories about Spain, and hours pass as he describes the beautiful, hilly region north of Barcelona. At the end of one visit, he offers to find us a house to rent on the Spanish Costa Brava.

I am skeptical that an overseas summer holiday can ever become our reality. Instead, I focus my attention on the boys' education. As Nazar finishes kindergarten, his Arabic becomes quite good. He is beginning to read and write his father's language, but I am concerned about his English education.

So in the late afternoons I tutor him, using a correspondence course I purchase from Maryland's Cambridge Center. This kit includes enthusiastic letters from mothers in far-off parts of the world who are also homeschooling their children. I keep reading these letters, marveling at the patience of these women. Somewhere, the educational flow between Nazar and me is short-circuiting. The more I try to make the lessons fun, the more of a chore they become. Fortunately, schoolbooks are put away so we can prepare for our summer trip to Spain, which is actually becoming a reality.

Osane is too involved in his growing business to get away for a long period. Therefore, the boys, Mohammed and I will spend the first month of our Spanish holiday alone. Osane will join us later.

Our departure date comes quickly, and Osane drives us to the Riyadh Airport. With new oil money, the Government is in the process of building a beautiful international airport. Meanwhile, passengers leave through a temporary World War II quonset hut.

Opening the hut's door, we walk into a wall of heat that makes it hard for us to breath. I slowly become light-headed and sick to my stomach. Osane tends to our tickets, while I guide the children to a bench against the far wall. With the mid-summer sun beating down on the tin roof, the heat inside continues to build.

Trying to keep my mind off the sweat that's pouring off my body, I watch an old Bedouin sit down beside me. She is completely covered. Feeling invisible, she turns and studies every inch of me. I find myself inwardly chuckling, for such audacity is humorous. After her visual inspection, she begins interrogating me. "Where are you going? How many children do you have? Whom are you married to? What does your husband do?" If I didn't get up, I'm sure her next questions will be about my intimate sex life.

The plane, of course, is late. By the time we finally make it out of the tin shelter, I am weak and suffering from the first stages of heat stroke. Our goodbyes to Osane are short, and soon we are heading out of the desert and toward the *cool* mountains of Spain.

Chapter 40

Spain

"Today, I am blessed to be living a dream.
And yet, if it all went away tommorrow, I
know I would still have peace."
    Tim Howard

As our plane begins its descent, I glance over at Mohammed. His face is radiant and his body is tight with excitement. This is his first time on an airplane, and his first trip overseas. It had been especially difficult for Osane to obtain a passport for Mohammed, for traveling restrictions on Yemenis are very strict. Now that he is landing for the first time on foreign soil, he can hardly wait for his adventure to begin.

Our friend Ramzi meets us at the Barcelona airport. He helps us load our belongings into a cab. After we are settled we drive north, up the coast toward a town called Santa Christina.

Outside the city, the countryside turns into green rolling hills, full of old-world farmhouses. Our destination is a Swiss establishment called the Golf Club. Ramzi tells us that spacious townhouses, apartments, and villas dot the rural landscape of this vacation complex. There are also two golf courses, several swimming pools, a gourmet restaurant, and many tennis courts.

After a two-hour trip, we make a left turn and arrive at our destination. Ramzi asks the driver to stop the car in front of a Spanish-style townhouse. I notice that across the street are a playground, tennis court, swimming pool, and clubhouse. I gaze at the green mountains in the distance, while Ramzi explains that he feels this location is perfect for small children, especially since I won't have a car.

As Mohammed carries our suitcases through the front door, the boys run around our new home. After touring the house, I find it to be more than adequate. It has three bedrooms and two baths upstairs, plus a complete kitchen, dining room, and living room on the main floor.

Since we are all tired from our journey, sleeping in fresh, clean sheets is pure pleasure. Early the next morning, Ramzi knocks on our door, and we drive to the grocery store. After buying a weeks' worth of food we sit in the sun and sip tea, while the children play around us. In this ideal setting, I begin to feel faint. The trip, the heat in the Riyadh terminal, and Saudi life in general, have once again worn me into exhaustion.

After three days of rest, my health rebounds and color begins to creep back into my face. The next weekend, Ramzi brings his wife and son for an introductory visit. They both speak English and we connect immediately. Mohammed takes the children across the street to the playground, while we sit in the back garden breathing in the mountain air.

Every day for the next two weeks, we see Ramzi and his family. We travel to the sea and drive through Spanish towns and into the countryside. The weather is perfect and our spirits soar. Way too soon, Ramzi and his family leave Santa Christina for Barcelona, their vacation over. With our friends' departure, life becomes much heavier. None of our neighbors speaks English. With no television, few toys, and no car, we spend much of our time on walks or swimming.

During this time, Mohammed becomes increasingly frustrated. He is a very good-looking boy of sixteen, and his dark complexion and brown hair make him appear Spanish. He has never been allowed to even glimpse a female in Saudi Arabia or Yemen. Suddenly women of all ages are not only uncovered, but are also wandering around in small bikinis.

One day I notice Mohammed looking out the kitchen window while he is doing the dishes. He is extremely interested in something. I sneak outside to find a beautiful teenage girl dressed in a bikini, chasing a puppy around a tree. The more Mohammed looks, the faster the dishes are done.

The crowning frustration for Mohammed occurs one afternoon at the swimming pool. A very attractive girl approaches him. She is obviously interested in Mohammed and starts speaking to him in Spanish. Mohammed gives her an embarrassed look, and she switches into French. Still making no headway, she attempts English. All Mohammed can say is, "I speak Arabic." Giving him a friendly smile, she leaves, and Mohammed jumps into the pool to drown his frustration.

Abruptly the weather turns very cold. Having no warm clothes for the children, we pack our suitcases and hire a taxi to drive us back to Barcelona. Ramzi reserves two rooms at the Avendido Palace, a very old, high-class hotel. As we walk through the grand lobby and across the highly polished floors, I notice a pronounced absence of children.

The rooms are absolutely beautiful, but it soon becomes evident that the maids don't appreciate the boys bouncing on the beds. Therefore, in between shopping trips, we spend most of our time at Plaza de Catalonia, where the boys can chase pigeons. At the end of three busy days we are well stocked with warm clothes, and another taxi drives us back to the open spaces of the countryside.

As soon as we settle into our townhouse, a fierce storm hits. For two days, rain slashes at our windows, hail pounds on the roof, and wind makes the house creak. At points, I wonder if the house will continue to stand. It is difficult to keep the children occupied, for cabin fever makes them impossible to handle. On the third day, the storm moves on. Although the air is still cool, we bundle up in sweaters and splash through the puddles on the golf course fairways.

Gradually we begin to notice fewer people. With schools about to open, the storm causes many families to cut their vacations short and head back to Germany, France, and Amsterdam.

By the time Osane finally arrives, we have the whole area to ourselves. He brings with him a full spirit and continuous activity. Our Spanish home glows with contentment as the fall breezes blow briskly through our lives.

Meanwhile, in the middle of the countryside, where the Arab culture can't touch us, our relationship blossoms. Every day Osane and I are drawn closer together, and a rosy blush becomes a permanent feature of my complexion. While Mohammed takes the boys to the playground or on walks, Osane and I spend long, leisurely hours bonding in body, mind, and spirit.

With my lover's arms around me, I desperately want time to stand still. I search for any way to extend this bliss. I imagine us living happily ever after in this island of green grass and rolling hills, but the minutes keep sliding by. During the dawn of the last day, I once again pack, while the children play in the front garden.

The ride to Barcelona is charming. The sun sparkles off the fields and quaint farmhouses. Osane sits in the back of the taxi with his arm around me. I enjoy every fleeting moment, for I know public affection will soon be sinful. We board our plane without incident and late that evening we land in Italy.

We are planning to spend a few days in a small town outside Rome, but the customs officials have different ideas. Our American passports are processed quickly, and the officer slowly approves Osane's Saudi passport. When the government agent picks up Mohammed's Yemeni passport, he stubbornly stands his ground. He claims he can't let Mohammed into Italy, when nothing in the passport is written in English or Italian.

As Osane tries to reason with him, he runs into a brick wall. Stuck in customs no man's land, we sit for hours as the passport filters from one supervisor to the next. Osane follows the path of the passport, arguing with each agent. His persistence finally pays off, and the country of Italy is open to us all.

We eat a late spaghetti dinner that night. The next morning, Osane sits in a barber's chair, while the rest of us wander down quaint Roman streets and markets. Time passes quickly and we are soon back in the air. During our flight, I glance at the front page of an English newspaper. I notice an article in the left-hand column about the violence in Barcelona caused by the Basque Separation Movement. In the right-hand column, I read about the renewed bombings of Beirut. Uneasiness settles into my stomach, for our journey is from Barcelona, via Italy, to Beirut.

My unrest only increases when I learn that our plane is one of the last flights scheduled to land at the Lebanese airport, before the government closes it down. The crew is jittery as we begin our final decent. As I look down at the familiar mountains, I am deeply saddened. What a shame to destroy such a beautiful city.

As we land, nervous energy fills the air. We make our way into the airport, for we are required to change planes. There is debris surrounding the terminal, and bullet holes in many of the windows. Silence hangs over us, and even Nazar and Sammy are subdued. There is only one thought in everyone's mind: Get in and out as fast as possible.

The airport personnel in the terminal look strained and armed guards are everywhere. The attendants check passports and check us onto Saudi Air with as little communication as possible. In record time, we board our flight to Arabia, passing flight attendants with radios in their hands.

As we sit down in our assigned seats, I notice that the plane is already full. Somehow, we double up, and more people board. The doors finally close. As the plane ascends, many around us are in tears, and a heavy mood subdues the cabin.

A well-dressed Lebanese woman, with her equally attractive husband, asks for the time. It is obvious she is in shock, so we begin whispering. She says her Lebanese family has been forced to leave the city, and is now living in their summer home in the mountains. She lives in Riyadh with her husband, but they have made the trip to Beirut to check on their relatives. She is distressed about leaving them, for she has seen many terrifying things in the short week they have been here. Suddenly she becomes silent. At the end of the flight, I'm not surprised to see them enter a black limousine, which has driven onto the tarmac to pick them up.

Chapter 41

The Seasons Continue

"If you follow the classical pattern, you
are understanding the routine, the tradition,
the shadow....you are understanding yourself."
 Bruce Lee

The next morning I hear Mohammed singing in the kitchen, while happy noises come from the playroom as the boys re-discover their toys. Spirits in the younger generation are soaring. However, as soon as Osane changes back into his thobe, his walls go up.

Effortlessly, we fall back into our familiar routines. Then late one evening, Osane comes home from work with a darling puppy. The boys have been asking for a dog. They shriek with excitement when they find their new friend, early the next morning. Our pup is half Saluki and half Sheepdog, and could easily be cast in any Walt Disney movie. The Saluki is the only dog acceptable in the Arab world. All other breeds are considered dirty. Nazar names his new dog Trusty, and Sammy won't put him down.

With the beginning of school, the time we have to spend with Osane is becoming more limited. Not only is he traveling, but he is also eating many afternoon dinners with clients. This means that he is also seldom home during the evenings, for business in Saudi Arabia is now pursued during the late hours. Even when he is with us, his mind is preoccupied with work. Fortunately, our lives touch over morning coffee. During this shared time, I often study Osane's tired face and count his new gray hairs. They seem to be growing in bunches now, and I wonder if his hard work is worth it.

As profits continue to flow into the corporation, our lifestyle improves. Our first personal upgrade is a new Pontiac. Sammy calls it "the brown car." With it, a driver named Adam enters our lives. Nazar is overjoyed, for instead of arriving at school on the back of Mohammed's bike, he can now be dropped off in style. More importantly, he can finally ride home in air conditioned comfort, avoiding the blistering mid-day sun.

The car plus driver also lightens the load of my life. I now have the freedom to travel to the foreign section of Riyadh. This opens up my world and within a week, I have a job in an English nursery school. It is volunteer work, but Sammy can also attend. This allows him to make new friends and expand his horizons.

Now that all the children are in school, I am seeing more of Hallid, the eleven-year-old boy next door. At three, he was in an automobile accident that left him mentally challenged. Because there are no facilities in the Kingdom for special-needs children, the boy stays home. Left alone, he wanders around the walls and roofs.

One morning, Sammy starts to argue with him. Hallid begins screaming and yelling in an insane way, and jumps off the wall. Suddenly he begins throwing Pepsi bottles onto our marble veranda. As the glass bombs explode, I quickly pull Sammy inside. That evening, Osane speaks to his father, and our war with Hallid ends.

The day Hallid spots our puppy, he becomes a constant part of our lives. He often runs on top of our joint walls yelling, "Tristin, Tristin." He never jumps off the walls, but few days go by that we don't see Hallid.

One day the boy appears on the wall with a burlap sack containing a cat. He lowers the sack to Trusty's level. When Trusty begins to jump and growl, he pulls the sack up. Alternatively, he will take the cat by the tail and lower it down to Trusty's face. The barking, hissing, and commotion are intense, but I don't want to scream at poor Hallid. Luckily, all I have to do is walk out the door, and he will jump off the walls.

Time flies by, and without realizing it, we find Christmas is upon us. Ironically, the Arabian holiday of Id falls on the same day. So we start the morning opening Christmas packages, and end the day by sacrificing a sheep.

The ceremonial Id lamb is delivered in the early afternoon. With Trusty barking at its heels and the children running crazily around, two men manage to guide it through the side garden and into the washing room. The whole night it bleats, and on Christmas morning, after they open their presents, the boys and Trusty spend hours at the washing room window.

During early afternoon, the sheep is turned towards Mecca. A knife that is sharp enough to split a hair offers the animal to Allah. Many of the city Arabs no longer knows how to kill, skin, and chop the sheep into edible sections. These families wait for hired professionals, but Osane is determined to pass this dying art to his sons.

With traditions and customs regulating each step, Nazar and Sammy watch as the sheep is sacrificed and skinned. They learn that the small intestines, bladder, and the organs are cut out and stored in the stomach. They note the meat being cut into certain sections, and observe as these pieces are further chopped into meat slices in preparation for cooking.

Traditionally, one-third of the animal goes to the poor, one-third to neighbors, and our household will keep the remaining third. Around noon, Adam and Nazar drive one section of the meat to a group of Bedouins who live down the street, while Mohammed takes the other third to neighbors. Sammy watches as boys from neighboring homes deliver bags of meat to us.

A tired but accomplished Osane climbs into bed that evening, feeling rejuvenated from the physical activity. I turn off the lights reflecting off our homemade Christmas decorations, and check the door of our fridge, full of freshly butchered meat. Celebrating a dual holiday has certainly been a unique experience.

After Christmas, the evening and nights become very cold, while the days remain warm and sunny. This flux of temperatures is not healthy, and many people come down with colds and flu. We are also entering the rainy season, where short outbursts of violent weather are not uncommon. Hail the size of pigeon eggs, and sheets of rain can appear with no warning.

During one such cloudburst, water comes plummeting to the earth in record quantities. The pounding sensation on the roof is surreal. Within twenty minutes the storm is over, the sky turns blue, and the sun beats down. I open the door to find the entire garden under water. Trusty wiggles out and begins galloping through the submerged yard, sounding like a horse and leaving a wake. I strip the children down to their underwear and watch as they also plow around the yard. The water is up to their knees and they run, slide, splash, and swim after Trusty. What bizarre fun, in such a strange land. Half an hour later the water is gone; only our memories of fun remain.

Over dinner that afternoon, Osane tells me of his next trip overseas. He will be gone for two weeks, and during that time he'll visit many European countries. Suppressing my apprehensions with a smile, I clear the dishes. Within the next three days, he is packed and gone.

Alone again, one day blends into another, and the weekend is soon upon us. That Friday morning, Adam brings us fresh bread and then stops in to visit Mohammed. Meanwhile Nazar and Sammy are playing in their paddle pool, and I am ironing in the back of the house. Suddenly, piercing screams break the quiet of the morning. Nazar runs to find me, and as he stands there dripping wet he cries, "Mommy, Sammy is bleeding!!"

I rush to Sammy and find him one mass of blood. He has slipped on the wet tile, fallen chin first onto the side of the sandbox and gashed his chin to the bone. I grab a towel, pick him up and scream for Adam. Within seconds, we are off to the hospital. Since Friday morning is the Arabian weekend, the traffic is light. Thankfully, our trip across town to the Obate Hospital is made at top speed. An hour later, Sammy is stitched up. As he sleeps in my lap on our return trip home, I give him an extra hug, thanking God for helping us navigate in a man's world.

The next week passes quietly and Osane returns, revitalized by the success of his trip. It is a good feeling to have the household intact again, but our routine only lasts for a short while. Within a week, Adam gives notice, replacing himself with his brother Abdu.

The first time I see Abdu, I try not to stare. He is an exceptionally large, black man with three tribal scars slashing each cheek. Whereas Adam is reserved, Abdu is outgoing and wears a constant smile.

On our first drive across town, Abdu shares that he has left his wife and four children in Ethiopia. He has traveled to Saudi Arabia to make money to support them. Three years has passed since he has seen his family, and he misses them very much. He is pleased to be working for a family with young children, and over time the boys and Abdu become quite close.

All of a sudden, it is Easter. As I turn the calendar, I think of my parents and their impending trip to Spain. Over morning coffee, Osane mentions that it might be fun for us to join them. As we converse about it, a trip begins to seem possible.

That evening I call the States to discuss a Spanish reunion with Mother and Father. At first they are surprised, but the more we talk about it, the more excited they become. Within two weeks, Nazar, Sammy, and I find ourselves in a lovely apartment, in the middle of Torremolinos. From our sixth-floor balcony we can see the ocean, the city, and the distant mountain ranges.

On one of our first afternoons in Spain, Grandpa takes Nazar to a bullfight. They both return full of exciting stories. Another morning, while Grandma and Grandpa babysit, I shop in the village marketplaces. I walk back to the playground, loaded down with packages. As I show off my new purchases, Sammy disappears. I scream at Nazar, "Where has your brother gone?" When he shrugs his shoulders, I begin to panic.

Sammy has obviously wandered off the playground and into the maze of shops below. The alleys he could have wandered down were endless. Telling Nazar to stay put, Mother, Father and I fan out in three directions.

I race down crowded lanes, asking shop clerks if they have seen a little boy in a blue jean coat. In and out of the shops I run, becoming more frightened each minute. Desperate, I dash back up to the playground to see if my parents have had any luck. I find the family standing around Sammy and a big, black dog. I angrily scurry up to him, but as soon as I pick him up all I can do is hug and kiss him. Tears of relief streaming down my cheeks, I thank God that my small son is safely in my arms.

Sitting on the playground benches, Mother concludes, "Sammy must have followed the dog into the shops, and kept following him until the dog wound its way back onto the playground. As soon as a crying Nazar spotted him next to the swings, he ran over and grabbed him and wouldn't let him go until we all arrived."

With the wandering Sammy drama behind us, we leisurely drive up and down the coast during the remainder of our visit. We stop at local villages and visit ancient castles and grand churches. The highlight of our tours is our trip inland, through the mountains to Granada.

The drive is beautiful and the Moorish ruins of Alhambra are fascinating. The gardens, the harem rooms, the exotic architecture, and the Arab mosaics are breathtaking. We then drive up the Pyrenees Mountains into the snow. Our journey ends at a ski lodge, where the boys spend an afternoon slipping, sliding, and throwing snowballs. On the way down the mountains, Grandpa stops the car and leads his grandsons to an isolated snow bank. Then he teaches the boys how to write their names in yellow snow.

Our active days pass quickly and before we know it, our two weeks are up. It is time to say goodbye to the Aleutian countryside with its rolling hills and whitewashed houses. We have felt at home here, for the Arabian culture has woven itself throughout Southern Spain. Moorish influence can be found in the food, architecture, and the tan skins and thick black hair of the villagers.

Our spirits refreshed, we give Grandma and Grandpa parting kisses and board our plane. Soon we are once again heading back to Osane and our life in Arabia.

Chapter 42

The Cracking Culture

"Certain barriers do require a critical mass of action at the right time to overcome the inertia that is greater than incremental change."
   David Jaber

After we board our flight to Riyadh, I glance around the plane and find the seats full of foreign passengers. Accustomed to half empty aircraft, I am once again reminded that the Arabian Peninsula is in transition.

Our plane soon touches down on Saudi soil. After making our way through customs, it doesn't take long for the boys to spot Osane and they are soon in his arms. On the way home, an animated Nazar tells his father about the bullfight and all his other Spanish adventures.

A few weeks later, Ella calls with the news that Marianne Alireza, the author of *At the Drop of a Veil*, is speaking to a women's group. Shortly after World War II, Marianne married into an influential, established Arabian family. She put her experiences into a well-written, informative, and very entertaining book.

The following morning, Ella and I knock on the gate where the women's group is meeting. A houseboy opens it to reveal beautiful grounds and a grand villa. We enter a large living room full of women chatting. I immediately recognize Marianne Alireza from the picture on her book jacket. She is visiting with a cluster of Saudi women, and as we sit down, the hostess quiets the group and asks Marianne to speak.

She talks of her children who had left Saudi Arabia, only to return. They feel they can contribute more to the Saudi society than they can to America. She speaks of how Saudi life has changed. She remembers evenings when families occupied their time with a variety of activities. In one corner children might be playing, and in another a group may be eating, while others play cards, sew, or chat over tea. These households radiate love and a relaxed atmosphere, empty of pressures and stress.

Marianne shares that she is now noticing a dramatic change. The Arabian families are becoming smaller. The men are marrying one wife and having only two children. In the new Saudi society, men work in the evenings and "adult only" social engagements are introduced. This results in children being left at home, and the breakup of the easy lifestyle of the past.

As I listen to Marianne, I glance around the room. Expressions of concentration lace the mixed crowd of Arab and foreign faces. It is this generation of females who are attempting to stumble into the twentieth century. They are hearing a history and perspective from a pioneer. She has experienced the Kingdom from after WWII to the present. Hopefully,

Marianne's wisdom will assist these women in understanding the dynamics of the Kingdom's shifting sands.

I return home refreshed, little knowing that a new chapter of my own life is about to open. I suspect nothing when an American friend invites me to a coffee the following week. Upon arriving, I settle into the living room. Looking around, I find myself surrounded by newly-arrived American women, whose husbands work for Chase Manhattan Bank.

As I sip my coffee, I listen to the concerns of these women. It seems they are finding their transition into the Kingdom quite difficult. Suddenly, something in my memory clicks. I remember hearing that Chase Manhattan is paying each family for the villa of their choice, and is providing unrestricted funds to furnish these new homes. The company is also paying for a servant, gardener, and driver. Finally, every six months each family is given tickets to any place in the world they want to spend their leave. As the complaints continue, I excuse myself and walk out into the garden to check on Sammy.

Outside and away from all eyes, I give way to the anger pulsating through me. I begin pacing. "How can these women think they have problems?" I say aloud. "Do they have any idea how spoiled they are?"

I walk back and forth, kicking stones until I calm down. As I center, I realize that on whatever level, these women are still crying out for help. I settle into a garden chair until my breathing returns to normal. Finally I am peaceful and under control. Slowly, I rise and return to my seat in the living room.

When there is a break in the conversation, I explain that I have been living in Saudi Arabia for the last six years. As the women look at me with interest, I offer. "If anyone has any questions about the culture or the city of Riyadh, I will be glad to help." For the rest of the visit I become the center of attention, and many questions are asked and answered.

Over the next few months, our Chase Manhattan group meets every Tuesday. I am given the opportunity to watch these women adapt and grow. As in everything, some adjust easier than others and some never do. I continually try to put their situations into perspective by asking them, "How do you think the Saudis feel?"

They listen as I explain that the Arabian males are only allowed to see their mother, sisters, and wives. It is no wonder that they stare at uncovered females. I also speak of how warm and polite the Saudis are. Subtly, I attempt to balance their vantage point by sharing the Arabian point of view.

A month before school ends for the summer, a Chase Manhattan specialist is sent to Riyadh. His job is to place the lifestyle of Chase's employees in Saudi Arabia on a hardship scale. Bonuses and funds for vacations and household expenses will be determined according to his findings. When he is through, he resolves that the hardships in Arabia parallel Vietnam during wartime. After his findings are announced at our Tuesday coffee, the women in the room nod their heads in agreement and then burst out laughing.

The last Tuesday before school ends, I invite the group over to my side of town for coffee. It takes some of the women's drivers a while to find our villa. Once they arrive, they love the old-world feel of our home and the mature vegetation in our garden. This speaks to them of permanence, a quality not found in their two-year contracts.

With the weather warming, many evenings after I put the boys to bed I climb to the roof. Gazing up at the brilliant stars, I settle down in my corner. One evening as I relax, circling emotional shadows begin floating to the surface of my mind. Sick of boxing these invisible fears, I allow them to drift into my present reality. The truth, finally admitted, shocks me.

It seems that subconsciously, I am beginning to doubt a successful future for our family. My main apprehension seems to be that if we remain in Arabia the boys will receive a substandard education. I recall a conversation I had with an American acquaintance who teaches at Riyadh School. She shared that in the Saudi schools, the education is limited but adequate. The main downfall is that the students are never trained to ask, "Why." Deductive reasoning is not meant for a monarchy, where a questioning adult population can cause unrest. Therefore, the children spend their time memorizing school assignments or the Koran.

My second fear is that all of a sudden the yard isn't big enough for seven-year-old Nazar, and he wants out. This is not possible. "Good children never play in the streets but remain inside the gardens." The main threat is kidnapping by homosexuals. Many times while watching the news we see pictures of young boys who have disappeared. Their parents and the police continue to search for them, but few are found. It was incredibly stressful to have to keep the children so confined.

Feeling better because I have finally faced my fears, I begin the next morning to pack for our summer abroad. The boys and I plan to depart first, flying directly to Canada. A few weeks later, Osane will join us. We will all meet in Cleveland and after visiting my family, we will fly back to Saudi Arabia through Paris.

Our flight from Riyadh to London is uneventful. The boys and I spend the night at a hotel near the Heathrow Airport. The next morning we eat a large breakfast, treating ourselves to English pancakes and three orders of bacon.

After breakfast, several African students step onto the hotel elevator with us. Half of the group exits on the first floor. The front students yell back to their companions, and are startled when three-year-old Sammy mimics their language perfectly. They have no way of knowing that during Sammy's short time on this earth, he has been exposed to English, Ethiopian, and many different dialects of Arabic.

A few hours later, we are sitting in the first class section of our Pan Am flight. As I ready the boys for our take-off from Heathrow Airport. I reflect at how smoothly the journey has gone so far. Ironically, the captain's voice suddenly comes over the loudspeaker announcing that our departure will be delayed until the ground crew can replace a defective part. The passengers shuffle in their seats uneasily, for it is always unsettling to add extra time to an already long flight.

After almost an hour's postponement, we are finally airborne and heading for Boston. I hope the delay won't make us late for our connecting flight from Boston to Toronto. As I ponder time changes, Nazar makes friends with the family sitting beside us. We soon begin conversing, and they ask if I know about the Canadian air strike. Shocked, I ask for more information, and find out that the Toronto airport is closed. Leaning back in my seat I can feel myself tense up, and a headache that had begun in London builds momentum.

We land in Boston and clear customs as quickly as possible. We swiftly race to the nearest American Airlines counter, hopeful that the delay in London won't cause us to miss our flight. The American agent informs us that we will be flown to Buffalo, and then be bused to Toronto.

Stepping onto our domestic plane, we find out that first class means you sit in the one row that faces backward, while the rest of the plane sits forward and stares at you. Our flight from Boston finally lands in Buffalo, in the middle of a downpour. All passengers are led to the far end of the airport terminal, where we find our bags. As we claim our luggage, an airport official checks tickets and a porter loads our belongings into the luggage compartment of the bus.

After everyone settles in, our bus forges through the storm. By now it is dark. Horizontal rain pounds our windows, and thunder rumbles all around us. We wind our way onto the freeway. Fifteen minutes later our bus pulls into a gas station, and the driver runs into the office. He re-enters the bus with a grim expression on his face, and quickly turns the bus around. Soon, we are back on the freeway, retracing our route. Apparently, this new driver has been driving toward Pennsylvania, instead of heading into Canada.

Four long hours later, we finally pull into the Toronto airport. I watch out the window as our bus drives into the back section of the terminal. I wake the boys when passengers begin to file off the bus. We follow our fellow travelers through dark underground tunnels, which seem to go on forever. Our progress is slow and we soon fall behind. I am carrying Sammy in one arm, the heavy diaper bag hangs over my other shoulder, and I am pulling a half-asleep Nazar. All the while I am afraid of getting lost, and being forced to wonder through dark mazes forever.

We walk for an eternity, and finally end up in the lighted customs area. By now Sammy is sleeping in my arms. When we finally stop Nazar falls asleep on the floor, with his head on the red wait line. Exhausted, I yearn for a quiet hotel room, a retreat from all this insanity.

Finally it is our turn, and I walk confidently up to the customs agent. The official casually glances through our American passports and automatically asks, "Where are you traveling from?"

I answer, *"Riyadh."* With the mention of that word the officer shakes himself awake, and begins to scrutinize us. His mouth becomes tight, his eyes harden and he begins keying in lines of information on his computer.

Every moment Sammy is becoming heavier, and Nazar is still sound asleep on the red line. I can't imagine what the complication can be. Suddenly, the official coldly hands us three yellow cards, and motions for a police officer to escort us into the adjoining room. Once inside the room, the officer tells us to sit down and wait our turn, while Nazar and Sammy continue to sleep on a new floor.

As I glance around the small occupied space, I realize that we are the only ones in the room who speak English. Furious, I find the supervisor. I explain that we have traveled from Saudi Arabia, have been in the air for countless hours, and demand to know why we are placed in a room full of non-English-speaking aliens.

In a loud, razor-edged voice he informs me that he has been on his feet for twenty hours, and that the air strike isn't his fault. He coldly motions for me to go back into the room. When I protest further he yells at me, "Shut up!"

Defeated, I make my way back into the detention hall. Beside myself, I begin crying. Nazar and Sammy wake up. Startled by my emotions, they also begin bawling. Through my tears, I notice a customs official elbow another agent and say, "Look at that wilting heart in the corner."

Afraid that I am going to crack, they gently lead the boys and me to a side-office. Through tears I ask, "Why are we being held?"

In a kind voice, the agent explains that this is the year of the Montreal Olympics, and millions have been spent on security precautions. The problem is that I live in Riyadh, Saudi Arabia. Therefore, I have been red-flagged as a security risk.

He then asks me my destination. When I tell him the Georgian Bay his eyes brighten, for he has family in that area. As we reminisce, his attitude softens even more. A few moments later, our passports are officially stamped for customs clearage. Picking up Sammy and leading Nazar, our new friend guides us through the customs gates and into Canada.

By now, it is four o'clock in the morning. After calling our hotel, we are met by the Hilton shuttle bus. Within half an hour, I have the boys tucked between clean sheets, and I am asleep before my head hits the pillow.

Chapter 43

A Time for Reflection

"Life is uncharted territory. It reveals its
story one moment at a time."
 Leo Buscaglia

The next morning even the boys linger in bed, for we are all exhausted from the trip and time changes. We leisurely dress and eat breakfast. By noon, my parents are at our hotel. We load the car and during the three-hour drive to our cottage, I tell them about our nightmare trip from Saudi Arabia.

A few days later, life in the Canadian North Woods has returned my health but not my spirits. The activities of our busy days help to suppress my turmoil, but at night, emotions pound to the surface. Worries about the boys' future in Saudi Arabia whirl through the dark. I also fret over the changes within the

Kingdom. And the schizophrenic battle between my American and Saudi selves is becoming a brutal inner war zone.

Depleted from my conflicted nights, I become tense and irritable. Peace eludes me until I finally have an epiphany. I suddenly realize that the choice to leave the Kingdom is not mine. The only way a son of Saudi Arabia can leave the Kingdom is by his own choice. When I surrender control for the direction of our future to Osane, my haunting worries disappear.

Halfway through our vacation, my youngest sister, Lee, drives up from Cincinnati with her baby daughter. Our Canadian cottage is now full. The days pass happily by, with trips to town and picnics on different islands. The children go fishing with their grandparents, and we boat and swim. Every morning we wander up to *Train Rock* with our orange juice to wait for the train to whistle by.

Way too soon, it is time for us to leave the North Woods. The next leg of our vacation takes us to my sister Jean's house. I am excited to visit my sister and the boys can hardly wait to play catch with their Uncle John.

A few days later, we board our flight from Toronto to Cleveland. On the airplane I pick up an article by the Los Angeles Times staff writer, David Lamb. The title, "Overnight Change: Saudi Arabia—a Story of Success," catches my eye. The article begins:

"This is the story of a people transformed by instant wealth and challenged by sudden change, clinging to one of the world's most conservative life styles as though words and prayers would keep the past secure.

"Flying across Saudi Arabia, a kingdom the area of India, one is struck by the emptiness below. This is a land with no rivers and no permanent bodies of water, a forbidding place where scarcely forty years ago tribes warred, camels wandered, and mud towns stood.

"Today, the grandchildren of those warriors go off to the United States and return home with Master's degrees and Doctorates. The camels have given way to Toyota pickup trucks whose drivers careen at maniacal speeds through Riyadh's new unnamed boulevards, paying no heed to signs that carry such messages as: 'Dear drivers: Your life is precious for your family and your country. Protect it.'

"American businessmen sit with their Saudi counterparts in hotel piano bars that serve orange fizzes and pineapple delights—the punishment for consuming alcohol is eighty lashes in public—and put together deals of Rockefeller magnitude.

"Not far from "Chop Square,' where murderers are occasionally beheaded in public after Friday's noon worship session, is the souq (market). There elderly, bearded men known as religious policemen tap on storefronts with their canes, warning the merchants to close for prayers. Five times a day, the government, the banks, the offices and stores shut down while this nation of seven million bends in prayer.

"If nothing else, prayer time gives the Saudis a chance to catch their breath. For what has happened to Saudi Arabia, a medieval society propelled almost overnight into the 20th Century, is astonishing.

"Many ask if the pace of progress does not threaten the religious and traditional pillars of society that are held so dear. Many reply that moderation is the answer. We don't want excesses in either direction. Islam is adaptable. It is capable of serving us as it has served generations before us.

"Saudi authorities, though, have learned that ripping out "offensive" advertisements from Time and Newsweek before placing the magazines on newsstands is not enough to protect the purity of their society. Alien influences have cracked the shell of this austere, xenophobic Kingdom. Fighting that intrusion with the teachings of the Koran is testing the sensibilities of religious scholars who prefer to make the narrowest interpretations of what Mohammed the Prophet would deem acceptable.

"The lifestyles of many Saudis traveling abroad stands in shocking contrast to the righteous attitudes at home. A homemade illicit whiskey labeled Siddiquay (My Friend) is readily available at $35 a bottle for those with strong stomachs. In Jeddah, the most common offense that judges must deal with is the drinking of cologne, which carries the same punishment as other alcohol consumption.

"The Saudis have reacted to the frightening changes around them by retrenching, seeking refuge in the two constants that offer comfort—family and Islam. This results in a society that is probably more conservative today than it was five years ago, one where gender segregation flourishes and entertainment, as known in the West, simply does not exist. Tradition has triumphed over innovation.

"Women, veiled and forbidden by law to drive, are basically sequestered in the home to idle away their hours chatting with each other. Love is a forbidden subject; no poets write of it, no novelists weave plots around it, no singers romanticize it.

"Even a recent cartoon that showed Popeye giving Olive Oyl a smack on the cheek was considered too risqué to pass the Saudi television censors.

"There are no movie theaters in Saudi Arabia, no legitimate theater, no ballet, no opera, no nightclubs. All are viewed as corrupting influences.

"With 15,000 Saudis already studying in the United States and thousands more ready to follow, the Kingdom will find it increasingly difficult to isolate itself in a puritanical and religiously intolerant society that makes apostasy a crime, bans Christian prayer meetings, and, as a matter of policy, does not grant visas to Jews or unescorted women.

"The choice will be for the next generation to decide, for unlike the youth of so many developing nations who go abroad to get an education and often stay there indefinitely, *the Saudis always come home.*"

Putting the article down, I mentally note that it confirms the demons I have been shadowboxing the whole summer. Refusing to ponder further, I organize our belongings for our descent into Cleveland.

After spending the night with Jean and John, we drive back to the airport to welcome Osane to the United States. As we watch Osane's international flight pull into the gate, my stomach churns with excited anticipation. We watch a beaming Osane exit the plane, and we are soon in each other's arms, but this time on my soi). Then the boys jump into their father's arms and Osane gives Jean and John a polite hug.

When we arrive back at my sister's home, Jean shows Osane around their house, while Sammy opens his father's suitcase to find the present he knows will be waiting for him. When the family settles in the living room, Osane gives Jean the Waterford Crystal wine carafe and glasses he has hand-carried off the plane. My sister is a connoisseur of fine things, and immediately realizes its value. At that moment, the ice between Jean and Osane breaks, and soon they are good friends.

A week passes. The entire time we are in top spirits, for Osane's re-entry into our lives brings with it the feeling of a continual party. The next weekend, Mother, Father, Lee, and her baby arrive to visit with Osane before we take off for Paris. It is an intense few days, for there are relationships to be re-explored and developed. The visit goes well, and a firm foundation for further growth is forged.

After the events of the weekend, we take a cab to the Cleveland Airport. Early that evening, we land at the Charles DeGaulle Airport. While the boys watch French TV, I pore over maps of Paris and a collection of tour books.

The next day we become tourists. The goal is to visit the most important sights in the least amount of time. In between our tours we eat delicious French food, and I re-clothe the boys in jackets, boots, pants, and shirts. Our favorite location is the Eiffel Tower for the children love the ride to the top, and Osane enjoys the restaurants in the park surrounding the tower.

Eventually, it becomes necessary to rejoin everyday reality. Packing our things for the last time, we say goodbye to Paris and board our flight back into the Kingdom. Looking out the plane window at the gorgeous cloudbanks, I feel refreshed and ready for another year. Little do I suspect how intensely we will be tested, or how severely the decisions made in the next few months will shape the rest of our lives.

Chapter 44

Success

"The greater the difficulty the more glory in surmounting it. Skillful pilots gain their reputation from storms and tempests."
    Epictetus

As soon as our plane enters Saudi airspace, I find it hard to breathe. The contentment and the jovial, lighthearted attitude I have grown accustomed to in the west begins to shatter like brittle glass. All of the forces I fought so hard to suppress in Canada are once again rising to the surface of my awareness. Heaviness begins to hang over my every thought, like a cloud blocking the sun. In desperation I conclude that after six years of east and west living, I have become a transitional person. I find virtue in both worlds, but contentment in neither.

A few days after our return, I notice a change in Mohammed. Before we left for the States, he had graduated from his sixth grade night school. Over the summer, he had also taken a driving course, another step toward independence.

It soon becomes clear that Mohammed has outgrown us. Each time I ask him to do something, I am met with a negative attitude. As he becomes more difficult to live with, so do I. Therefore, it is not a surprise when Mohammed gives Osane his two-week notice. He claims he is returning to the Yemen to visit his mother and little brother. We are sad at his departure, but console ourselves with the fact that he is finally returning to his village.

With Mohammed's departure, I am forced to run our household alone. I have tried solo housework before, and I know it is backbreaking. Because of desert living and all the unsealed doors plus windows, the entire home has to be dusted once or twice a day. The floors also need constant mopping, washed clothes have to be carted to the roof and hung on lines to dry, dishes need to be hand-washed, and stacks of clothes ironed. Guests keep coming for dinners that are cooked from scratch, milk has to be made from powder and fruits and vegetables have to be cleansed with a special product from England.

All this physical labor has to be completed in the heat of the September sun. As the days progress, I know my strength is ebbing. After attempting to train two houseboys, it becomes necessary to hire a woman. Most of the female servants come from Ethiopia, but there are a few from Egypt, India, Somalia, and the Philippines. Regardless of the nationality, women are more expensive, and demand more comforts.

Therefore, the following Friday, Osane and I begin to upgrade Mohammed's old room. We put in a bed and a television and replace Mohammed's fan with a desert cooler. We also buy furniture, and clean up the Arab bathroom in the adjoining room. Finally prepared, we open our home to our first female employee.

She barely makes it through the day, claiming that her last place of employment was with a *wealthy* American family. Only a little discouraged, we try a few other women, to no avail.

Finally, our driver Abdu tells us of an Ethiopian woman called Fatma, who is quiet, clean, and hardworking. The next day, Abdu brings Fatma and a group of female friends. As I question her, they scrutinize me. Somehow this informal job interview is successful, for the next day Fatma moves in.

A few days later, both boys start school. Nazar by this time is a pro, but my heart goes out to Sammy. At the age of three he is following in his brother's footsteps and attending school five half-days a week. With a feeling of anxiousness, I dig up Nazar's old school uniform and put it on Sammy. I kiss them both goodbye and watch Abdu drive our car around the corner, the whole time worrying about Sammy.

I busy myself throughout the morning, but I can't keep my eyes off the clock. At noon when Sammy finally comes through the gate, I am relieved to find him intact. He doesn't seem too damaged. Over dinner, he shares that he kept asking the teacher to go to the bathroom. Not understanding English, the teacher ignored him. That evening Osane teaches Sammy his first Arabic phrase. If necessary, Sammy will now be able to use the facilities.

With both boys in school, I keep busy with visiting relatives and entertaining a steady stream of Osane's business clientele. I also become involved in Osane's newest venture, an Asian restaurant. In fast growing Riyadh, there are few if any first-class restaurants, and Osane's opportunistic mind becomes determined to fill the void.

As head of the Prince's Establishment, he rents a large villa in the foreign sector. In the center of this two-story villa is a large swimming pool, which he covers to increase the square footage. He then tears down several interior walls and enlarges the entrance.

After many weeks of construction, the restaurant finally begins to take shape. To staff the business he hires an Asian crew, and houses them on the second floor of the villa. These employees bring with them several boxes from Asia. These containers are full of decorations, cooking equipment, serving dishes, and the native dress they wear as uniforms.

Each Friday, Osane drives us to the restaurant to check its progress. We enter through large gates and into a lush replanted garden. A thick red carpet leads up the stairs to the restaurant entrance. In the waiting room we lounge in one of the comfortable couches and watch TV, which is hooked up to a Beta-Max that plays and re-plays an Asian variety film.

While the children watch the video, Osane guides me through the three rooms that lead off the main waiting area. These detached spaces offer the privacy required in the Saudi culture. Elegant contour arches serve as entrances into these rooms. Each dining area is sprinkled with Asian flower arrangements, grass cloth wallpaper, filtered lighting, expensive carpeting, tables, and chairs.

Finally, just before Christmas, the Asian Steak House opens its doors. The head of Osane's company (Prince Ali ibn Saud), plus other dignitaries, attend its grand opening. From the first night, it becomes an instant success. Word spreads throughout the capital that the Steak House is a first-class establishment, and lines start outside the door.

Most of the males patronizing the restaurant are foreigners, but Saudi Ministers, Princes, Embassy Officials and businessmen of all nationalities also begin entertaining at the establishment. Customers enjoy being served by the waitresses. These Asian females are married to members of the staff, and each evening they gracefully flow between tables in their native dress.

Knowing that he is setting a precedent by using female waitresses, Osane has not taken this step lightly. First, he conferred with Prince Ali. Then he obtained legal entry and work documents for each male and each female member of the staff. Only after the Ministry had returned the signed permits, did he put the waitresses on the schedule.

Our life is so full that in no time the holiday season comes and goes, and the winter rains are upon us. One drizzly day, Osane begins talking about a move. He tells me over morning coffee that it no longer makes business sense to bring his contacts across the city to our villa.

When he leaves for work, I begin pondering. I admit to myself that I won't mind returning to the foreign section. However, without realizing it, I have rooted in this house close to the boys' school. Overall, it has been a happy home. The spacious, old-worldly atmosphere and the grapevines and fruit trees have been such comforts. Its location on the edge of open desert, and the happy memories of three-years spent behind its walls are hard to leave behind. On the other hand, Osane's career needs to remain a top priority. So with mixed feelings, Nazar, Sammy, and I step into the car, and Osane drives us to the new home he has found for us.

Several traffic jams delay our drive across town. We finally enter a newer area of the foreign section. Where there used to be bare desert, there are now villas. As we begin to slow down I tense up, for I know this will be our new neighborhood. Finally, we turn a corner and stop at a large gate.

In front of us lies empty desert. Other than this one open acre, the rest of the area is filled with large, modern, and impressive villas. Suddenly, Sammy tugs my hand. He pulls me through the gate, and onto a tiled area that runs around the house.

The inside walls of the villa are lined with oleander bushes in full bloom. In the side garden is a swimming pool, and next to it is the servants' quarters. Re-directing the boys away from the unfenced pool, we walk through the main entrance.

We find ourselves in a living room, three times the size of our present one. Making our way through a door at the end of the living room, we enter the kitchen plus washroom. Between the living room and kitchen is the dining room, and through another hallway we find the women's living room.

As we climb the stairs to the second floor, I wonder why anyone would need more space. At the top of the stairs we enter an expansive family room, a gigantic master bedroom with adjoining bath, and two other bedrooms plus baths. Climbing the stairs again we walk onto the roof, which offers a beautiful panoramic view of the city.

After our tour, I conclude that this villa is absurdly excessive and filthy. It has been unoccupied for months, and flies and insect droppings are everywhere. None of the bathrooms work and neither does the swimming pool. Personally, I have no desire to turn this vast building into a home, but Osane's mind is set. It is therefore decided that within a month we will move in, and a massive rejuvenation begins.

Chapter 45

Strife and Pain

"The gem cannot be polished without friction,
nor can it be perfected without trials."
    Chinese proverb

Two weeks later, I interrupt my packing to share a cup of coffee with Osane before he leaves for work. After I kiss him goodbye, I finish taping the boxes that are already loaded. Around mid-morning, a friend drops in and we are in the middle of tea and cakes when the phone rings. The voice on the other end of the line is Osane's.

Christie," he says. "I won't be home for dinner this afternoon, and I will be out late this evening. Don't worry."

I sense a strange tenseness in his voice. Just when I am going to ask if anything is wrong, he continues. "Christie, I've got to hang up. Just know that I love you and the boys."

All of a sudden the line goes dead. I stand there for a few minutes, unable to put the phone down. My intuition tells me that something is *very* wrong, but my friend's voice breaks my trance. I push the incident out of my mind and the rest of the morning passes quickly, full of light conversation and fun.

Around twilight, there is a knock on the gate. I open it to find Ramzi, a Lebanese man Osane has recently hired as maitre d'. He stands there looking distracted and ill at ease. Finally, he tells me that Osane has been called away on an emergency business trip. Looking at the ground, he stammers that he will be gone for a few days. He keeps repeating that Osane is fine, and that I am not to worry.

I ask, "Where has Osane gone?"

"Jeddah," Ramzi mutters. Quickly he steps into his truck. As Ramzi pulls away, he looks back over his shoulder and waves. A taught, white face speaks of fear and pity for me, as he drives into the setting sun.

Shaken, I close the gate and sit on the veranda. This whole day has been bizarre, but I am determined not to panic. My mind takes me back to Egypt. I remember sitting at our dining room table submerged in worry, for Osane is four hours late. I am convinced that he is in trouble. I am just about to panic, when Osane drives up in a cab.

"Osane," I yell. "I was so worried about you! Where have you been?"

I can still see Osane's angry face when he coldly states, "Christie, you should never allow fear to overcome you. I am just fine. Only after I have been missing four days, are you to take action!"

With his words ringing in my ears, I tuck the children calmly into bed. When I wake the next morning I push away a growing dread, and continue the activities of the day. That afternoon the relatives come to visit. When they ask where Osane is, I tell them he is in Jeddah on a short business trip.

That evening as I lie in bed, suppressed emotions force me to toss and turn most of the night. The next morning after the children leave for school, I call Osane's office and ask for Ramzi. I am sure I hear his voice in the background, but the male secretary claims that he isn't in the office.

I ask the clerk which hotel Osane is staying in. Again, I sense confusion. Leaving my question unanswered, he simply tells me not to worry and that Osane is coming home tomorrow. Angered by obvious lies, with a strong voice I ask again for Osane's hotel. He mumbles the Sheraton. I thank him and hang up, silently cursing everyone in the office and the whole situation.

That afternoon, I call the Sheraton in Jeddah and ask for Osane's room number. The hotel receptionist answers that Osane is not listed. Quickly I dial a few other hotels, with the same result. Suppressing panic, I begin pacing. Only one reality is brutally clear. As a female, I will never be able to unbury the truth. I need help, and that assistance will have to come from Uncle Hamid.

As I am determining my course of action, the boys arrive home from school. Not wanting to worry them about their father, I quietly feed them and hail a taxi to Uncle Hamid's apartment. As the boys and I climb the stairs to the relatives' third-floor flat, I wrap my arms around myself. My breathing is rapid and I am very aware that my control is hanging by a thin thread.

I knock on the door, praying someone will answer. I am greatly relieved when Aunt Sarah's son opens the door. Pulling myself together and remembering the proper protocol, I calmly ask for Uncle Hamid. I am told that he is on a picnic with the visiting Aunt Sarah. While the children play, I am forced to sit and wait for their return.

Finally Uncle Hamid, Aunt Sarah, and several children arrive, exhausted from the fresh air of the desert. Mustering all my restraint, I wait until Hamid has washed. As he sits down and drinks his cup of tea, I ask him if I might speak to him. He gives me a nod, but first he must pray. Therefore, I am compelled to wait again, while my stomach ties in ever-tighter knots. When he eventually returns, I am ready to explode.

Attempting cool-headed composure, I start telling Uncle Hamid about Osane. As my tongue stumbles around Arabic words, frustration explodes within me and I break into uncontrollable sobs. Startled, Uncle Hamid stares at me, and then goes into action.

He chases the children out of the room, brings in Aunt Sarah and his wife, and sits his oldest son beside me to translate. Once assembled, the relatives wait patiently while I gain control. I tell them about Osane's strange phone call, Ramzi's weird visit, and my inability to locate Osane in any of Jeddah's hotels. Looking slowly around the family circle, I confess that I am worried and don't know what to do.

After a short pause to digest the situation, Hamid and his oldest son Hayder rise. After gentle words, they walk out the door to find their missing family member. As I watch them leave, I feel a huge burden lift off my shoulders. Aunt Sarah holds my hand the rest of the afternoon. The boys and I are only allowed to leave for home late that evening, well fed, loved, and reassured.

Early the next morning, there is a knock on our gate. I open the door to find a very serious Uncle Hamid and Hayder. Over tea, the relatives finally tell me the truth. *Osane is in prison.*

I sink back into my chair, assimilating what I already know. I have suspected this fate from the beginning, but denial mercifully clouded my reality. Now I am faced with the naked truth.

As I sit in my seat hardly breathing, Hayder goes on to explain that the police raided the restaurant a few nights before. Not finding Osane, they arrested Ramzi. Soldiers then closed the business on the grounds that it is against the law to employ female waitresses, and Ramzi spent the night in prison.

The next morning, Osane finds out about the events of the previous evening. Knowing what must be done, he locates the proper prison and walks through the gates. He tells the authorities to let Ramzi go, for *he* is responsible for hiring the waitresses. Osane is then allowed to make one phone call. With officials listening, he attempts to assure me that he is alive and that he loves us. After the censored call, he is interrogated through the day and into the night. Then the guards take him into his cell, where he is imprisoned *indefinitely.*

After a long silence, Uncle Hamid tells me that this evening Ali is arriving from Southern Arabia and Saeed is flying in from Jeddah. In short, the men of the family are congregating and all proper doors will be knocked upon.

Days pass with little progress. Uncle Hamid takes a leave of absence from his work and every morning he comes to our home to pick up Ali and Saeed. They see one official after the other. They also try to contact the head of Osane's company, Prince Ali, but he is in Europe with his soccer team.

Throughout these various attempts, one unstated fact is always lingering in the background. When dealing with a monarchy based on fear, whose government is protected by secret police, each one of the relatives is walking on touchy ground.

Every evening our group congregates around tea and reviews the events of the day. We call the prison, "*the hotel*," to protect Nazar and Sammy from the truth. Spirits are kept high, thoughts remain positive and a language of hope is constantly spoken.

Finally at the end of two-and-a-half weeks, Uncle Hamid is granted permission to visit Osane. He asks me to gather some clothes. So in a perfumed suitcase I pack Osane's toothbrush, fresh underwear, pajamas, and thobes. In a Koran I place a little note saying, "Your family loves and misses you."

Then Uncle Hamid takes the suitcase, and returns two hours later to share details of his visit. He says that Osane is growing a beard, that his health is good and that his spirits are high.

Hamid shares that he only has one more prince to see. Hopefully Osane's homecoming will occur in the next few days, but that I am to be patient. He then quotes an old Arab proverb: "The gates into prison are wide enough for all, but the gates out of prison are so small it is like threading a needle."

After Uncle Hamid leaves that evening, I say goodnight to Ali and Saeed. I enter my bedroom with a resolve to be extra tolerant a few more days, but dark thoughts keep sleep away. Besides the emotional strain and anger at having Osane in jail, his imprisonment can't have come at a worse time. Our rent is running out on our present villa and down payment is due on our new villa. As a woman, I have no access to our funds.

My worries increase as the days pass and still no Osane. The third morning slowly crawls by. I have spent every moment listening for the doorbell (*anticipating Osane's footsteps*), and feeling his arms surround me. By that afternoon, I have worked myself into a traumatic state. For the first time, I refuse to come out of my room. Dinner comes and goes, and I simply stare at the ceiling.

Uncle Hamid arrives for his visit, but my door remains closed. Finally late in the evening, I pull myself together and walk out to a bench in the side garden. As I look up at the stars and the galaxies beyond, I slowly gain strength and hope. Deep in meditation, I pray for courage. I finally resolve that no matter how long it takes, I will remain strong. With God's help, I can outwait the storm.

The next morning, Ali and Saeed are relieved to see me smiling again. I wait for Uncle Hamid so I can reassure him that I am once again patient. I listen the entire morning for him, but he never appears.

Around noon, while I am out back in the washroom, the gate opens and the whole house reverberates with screams. Hearing Osane's voice, I drop my load of clothes. With adrenalin pumping through my veins, I leap into a run. Within seconds I am in his arms, and he is spinning me around in circles. In my joy, I catch the smiling faces of Uncle Hamid, Ali, Saeed, and Hayder—the relatives who created the miracle of Osane's release.

When Osane puts me down, I study him. His jet black hair is now laced with more gray, a full beard covers his face, he has lost weight, and his entire body is shaking.

I am also emotionally shattered. Even with him standing in front of me, I can't trust my eyes. I have waited so intensely for this moment. Now that this instant is finally a reality, I am too numb to feel anything.

Throughout dinner, Osane keeps shaking. Nazar, Sammy, and I sit next to him like glue. When we are alone for our afternoon nap, Osane shares his release story.

It seems Uncle Hamid had been so upset by my emotional condition of the previous day, that he had taken a taxi to Prince Talal Aziz Ibn Saud's Palace. He asked for an audience with one of the highest officials in the Kingdom. Forcefully, without fear, Hamid stated, "Why hasn't Osane been released from prison?"

Prince Talal replied that many high-ranking authorities were upset that a native son had ignored the norms of his society, and had allowed women to work in a public place. Uncle Hamid argued that these women were working with legal work permits. That if they were punishing Osane, they should also punish their brother, Prince Ali, whose corporation sponsored the restaurant.

Taking the risk that he too might be thrown into prison, Uncle Hamid stated without hesitation, "Our son is in prison, while yours walks free in Europe!"

Prince Talal stared at Uncle Hamid for a long moment and then slowly signed his name to the release document. Late the next morning, the prison gates opened just wide enough for Osane to slip through.

After naps, we gather over tea. The room is aglow with peace and contentment. Conversation is limited, for we are just thankful to be together.

Before sleep that evening, Osane shares some of his prison experiences with me. The interrogations of the first day were the worst for him. After the police had completed their questioning, he was handed prison clothes and a mattress, and was assigned to a cell in which no talking was allowed.

As the days passed, Osane began to learn the system. He noted that many of the guards were from the South. Carefully, he began speaking to them in his Southern accent, and gradually the guards began warming to him. During his final days, they slipped him food from the outside, and allowed him minimal speaking privileges.

Osane also shares that during his initial questioning, he discovered that he had been followed for some time. It seems his rise to power has been too quick, and that he has been too outspoken. When he hired female waitresses, he finally went too far. His prison episode is simply a warning. It was now clear that he will be watched, and conformity to the Saudi culture is mandatory.

Talked out and exhausted, Osane slips into sleep, leaving me staring at the ceiling. My husband is finally home and lying beside me. Instead of relief, all the suppressed feelings of the previous weeks become exploding land mines. I have suffered so much, and for what? Realizing that Osane might disappear back into prison at any moment infuriates me and leaves me feeling vulnerable. I pull myself to my feet, and pace the floor far into the night. Exhausted, I finally let sleep engulf me.

The next few days are put aside for rejuvenation. Our family gathers as Osane symbolically shaves off his beard. After a few good meals, he begins to look like himself, though no force can erase the new lines under his eyes.

Ali and Saeed fly back to their families, and we resume our daily routine. A week later, Osane announces that in three days movers will arrive. Within the hour, cardboard boxes begin arriving. Fatma is driven to her new quarters to supervise the cleaning crew Osane has hired. In between cooking, I once again continue packing. Somehow on the third day, my boxes are ready and it's time to say goodbye to our happy home.

I know I don't want to leave, but that I have to. Osane begins his final walk out the door, pulling me reluctantly behind him. With tears in my eyes I break away, and run back into my house. I kiss the walls, and race out the door and into the waiting car.

As we turn the corner, I glance back and see Hallid (the crazy one), balancing on the wall. He is waving goodbye to Trusty. When the house is out of sight I turn forward, realizing that another era in our life has ended.

Chapter 46

The Princess' Villa

"Yes, your home is your castle, but it is also your identity and your possibility to be opened to others."
    David Soul

As we drive across town to our new home, each of us is occupied with our own thoughts. These contemplative moods abruptly dissolve when we walk through the gates, for we find our new villa buzzing with activity. The cleaning crews are hard at work, the movers are unloading our possessions, plumbers are installing four water heaters, and electricians are filling empty holes in the walls with eight new air conditioners.

As twilight falls, all the work crews finally disperse. Relieved to have some privacy, I slowly make my way through our new living space. The furniture that had become too much for our old villa is lost in the vastness of the many large rooms.

I walk up the stairs to our bedroom. Thrown on the bed is the letter I have just received, announcing my sister Jean and her husband John's visit. They are planning to arrive in just six weeks. It is beyond me how we can possibly make this barn livable for our first family visitors.

Life in our new villa quickly assumes a regular cadence. The boys and I wake at 5:30 am. School starts at 7:00, and it takes half an hour to get across town. Osane is the next one up. After our morning coffee, he leaves for his office.

My days are occupied organizing the army of workers who attack our villa each day. With the Asian Restaurant temporarily closed, Ramzi becomes my foreman. I am delighted to discover that he is a natural decorator with a French flair.

The first week, Ramzi hires his Lebanese friend, a fellow refugee from the Beirut war zone. This man is an old-school artist. When he arrives, Ramzi leads him into the women's living room and points at the walls. "This, my old friend, is your new canvas," Ramzi informs him with a warm smile.

After bringing in all his supplies, our in-house artist begins sketching the walls. As the days flow by, he hand-paints the women's living room with mosaics and intricate designs. When he is done with the walls, he hand-sews cushions made from the finest materials and colors. His work is outstanding, and this room blossoms into an exquisite work of art.

While Ramzi's friend is busy creating, we carpet the entire house and paint all the walls. Much of our energy is channeled into the vast living room. Because of the space in this room, we create two conversation areas. They are defined by two sets of elegant Italian furniture plus glass and chrome tables.

We purchase pictures for the walls, and hire another Lebanese tailor to hand-sew our draperies. At the far end of the room, we placed an oak bookcase from Czechoslovakia. On these shelves we arrange all of our books, a set of encyclopedias, and our stereo equipment. Finally, we select a mirror, coat hanger, and picture set for the entryway. With the living room area complete, Ramzi and I start on the dining room.

I decide to keep our teak dining set from Finland, even though the heat has melted the glue. Anytime guests sit down for a meal, I hold my breath, hoping they don't end up on the floor. Ramzi puts a few nails in strategic spots, and that remedies that problem. We then hang a large picture, given to Osane by one of his prison guards, on the accent wall.

Our decoration crew then proceeds to the kitchen, which can never be labeled the focal point of the house. This room contains only the basic culinary equipment, and the floor has a distinct downward tilt. As I gaze around my new kitchen, words like "barely adequate," "primitive," or "needs a total remodel" come to mind. After we hang a few pictures, it at least becomes homier.

When the whole downstairs is complete, the outcome is quite breathtaking. It is now time for our crew to climb the carpeted stairway to the second-floor family room. It is on this level that we live, sleep, and trip over toys hauled out of the boys' bedroom.

A few weeks later, most of the important work has been done on the villa. Over coffee one morning, Osane and I decide to open our refurbished home to our friends. A small party will be a relaxing chance to entertain in our new surroundings.

The following Friday evening, our guests begin to arrive. As soon as they walk through the door and look around, they are thrilled and impressed by our new space. While Osane and I are occupied with entertaining, our landlady the Princess and her two adult daughters decide to pay us a surprise visit.

Fatma leads the covered Princesses into the women's living room, where they ask to see Osane. I continue talking with our friends, wondering why Osane is taking so long. Finally, I hear him say goodbye to the Princesses. With a sheepish grin, he re-enters the room and shares his story with the entire party.

Everyone in the room quiets down as Osane begins. "I have just had a very interesting conversation with our Princess landlady. After tea, she casually offered me one of her daughters, for a wife."

I can feel my backbone bristling. I marvel at the nerve of that woman, even if her actions are culturally acceptable. The rest of the evening, our friends kid me about missing my one and only chance to live in a "royal harem!"

During the first days of May, the weather begins to heat up. For the first time, air conditioners are necessary. Each time I turn on more than three of our eight conditioners, the fuse blows. To solve the problem, Osane brings home an Egyptian electrician. This "professional" stands in front of the fuse-box with a questioning look on his face. I wonder if he will survive the afternoon, as he crosses and re-crosses the wires.

After the Egyptian leaves, we can only turn on two air conditioners. I begin to worry, for with new carpet throughout, our villa is a potential firetrap. With this thought in mind, I keep pressuring Osane to find a reliable electrician.

After a few days, Osane brings home two Americans, who are moonlighting handymen. They take one look at the fuse-box, with unmarked wires running everywhere, and compare it to a 16-sided Rubik's cube. They spend the whole evening tearing out undesignated wires, in an attempt to uncover a pattern.

At the end of the second evening's work they inform Osane that telephone, not electrical wires, have been pulled throughout the house. They comment, "It's a miracle you can get three of your air conditioners working." A week later, our Western electricians have rewired the entire house and have installed two new fuse-boxes. Everything is finally marked, organized, and *safe*.

The next Friday, Fatma answers the gate and finds eight Asian men. She watches as they walk through the side-garden to the swimming pool. Pulling out some cleaning pads they have brought with them, they begin energetically scrubbing down the sides of the pool. When they are finished, they sweep out the debris on the bottom.

Hearing the noise, the boys and I run to the window. Osane joins us and explains, "These men are part of the restaurant staff. This is their way of repaying me for my time in prison."

With the pool scraped and clean, Yemeni workers surround it with a childproof fence and install a new pump. Then water-trucks empty two truckloads of water into our now-functional swimming pool.

The next evening I cook a special dinner to celebrate. After weeks of round-the-clock work, pockets full of money spent, and creative energy flowing in from many sources, our house is *finally* a home. We have only one week left for last-minute touches. Then Jean and John will be on their way.

On the day before my family's visits, the hours barely tick by. I am overly excited! Finally, the hour comes for our trip to the airport. We park the car and make our way into the terminal. I am wearing pants and a long sleeved blouse, but for this special occasion, I have left my head uncovered.

As Osane and I thread our way through the crowds, we become the center of attention. Saudis have conditioned themselves to the masses of foreigners who are now crossing their borders, but mixed couples are still a novelty.

Quickening our pace, we arrive at the appointed gate. I find a chair in the corner, while Osane blends into the crowd. Feeling less obvious now, I watch the passengers from arriving planes. I notice many foreign children coming home from overseas boarding schools, for it is Easter vacation. Western schools within the Kingdom only provide education up to the sixth grade, making it necessary for older children to be educated abroad.

Suddenly I cease my crowd watching, for I spot Osane leading Jean and John. With two leaps, I am in my family's arms. After hugs and kisses, we make our way to the baggage pick-up area. Bags claimed, we walk back to our car and drive homeward.

It has become quite late. Osane shows Jean and John our new home, and we then linger in the living room over tea. An hour later, Osane and I help my sister and John carry their luggage upstairs to their bedroom. After warm hugs, we kiss them goodnight and walk down the hall to our bedroom. I hear them whispering in their room and I know they are too tired to sleep. They are living in the space between cultures. It will take some time before they will be able to adjust to the mass of new stimuli and time zone change.

The next morning, the relatives wake to the boys jumping into their bed. The house explodes with laughter, chatter, and excitement. Nazar and Sammy are ecstatic when their aunt and uncle unpack gifts and stage an unexpected Christmas.

The family party continues for the next two weeks. We walk through markets, visit riding stables that board the Prince's racehorses, and tour the city. One afternoon, we drive out of Riyadh and ride through a desolate desert. Unexpectedly, our car dips into a riverbed, and lush green surrounds us. We follow the wadi to the oasis of Da-harea, the Saud family's home village. Stopping the car, we explore the remains of the ruins. We then wander among date palms, jump irrigation ditches, and walk down the green river bed.

Halfway through their visit, we introduce Jean and John to our Saudi family. On the way over to Uncle Hamid's apartment, I share with John that he will be the first foreign man to see the female relatives unveiled. Knowing this will be a special moment, we are all quiet as we ride the elevator to the third floor.

The moment Hayder opens the door to their apartment, we are surrounded by Arab hospitality. As the relatives of the East and West become acquainted, everyone has a marvelous time. Tea and Arab coffee are served, along with assorted dishes of nuts, popcorn, and sweets. Laughter rings in the room, and stories are shared through Osane, the ever-patient interpreter. Just as the evening ends, Uncle Hamid invites Jean and John to a desert picnic the following day.

Hoping it isn't going to be too hot, Osane borrows the company's station wagon. Right after breakfast, we drive over to Uncle Hamid's apartment. He greets us, standing amidst a pile of provisions. As we pack rice, tea, pots, and pans into both jeeps, Hamid's middle son comes around the building leading a live sheep. Much to my horror and the boys' delight, this, too, is tied into the back of our van. Finally loaded, Osane follows Hamid's car through the city and out into the desert.

We drive for about an hour, before turning off the main road onto a dirt path. As our car bumps and bangs over the ruts, the pots and pans jingle and the sheep bleets. Our caravan finally stops in the middle of sand dunes. Hamid puts a longer rope around the sheep's neck and ties the leash to the roof of the station wagon, while we unload both cars. Meanwhile, the children fly kites and slide down the dunes on cardboard sleds.

After our camp is organized, Jean and I take a hike into the desert, arm in arm. Our magical stroll takes us past beautiful sand formations and tiny desert flowers, whose delicate perfection has sprung up after the last rain. Further into the desert we meet Uncle Hamid and the children in search of firewood. The wood patrol is a difficult task, for fuel is scarce among the rock rubble. Somehow, they manage to find enough wood to keep a fire burning throughout the afternoon and into the night.

When Jean and I return, we find the sheep carcass hanging from the roof bars of Uncle Hamid's station wagon. Osane and Hamid have already skinned it, and are now cutting out the organs. John impresses the male relatives when he joins them as they feast on raw liver.

Meanwhile the women are cooking rice over a gas burner, and Hyder and the older boys are cutting up fresh meat for dinner. Right before the meal, Hamid leaves the group of men and walks over to the fire. He stoops down and picks up a brass mortar and pestle. Gracefully he pours coffee beans into the mortar, and begins chanting the Bedouin song of hospitality. As he grinds up the coffee, he clangs the pestle to keep time with the chant.

I sit down beside him and close my eyes. Slowly, visions of campfires dotting the desert in the early morning sun begin to take shape. Over these fires, I visualize young Bedu boys preparing coffee, while the camp slowly stirs to the clanging of the pestle and the aroma of fresh-brewed coffee. I open my eyes and find Hamid smiling at me.

Osane, drenched in sweat from the butchering of the sheep, joins us at the campfire. As he roasts kabobs, we sample appetizers and watch the women spread our meal on a large Arab rug. We feast on wonderful and exotic food as the sun sets.

Afterwards, we sip tea as we drink in the vastness of the desert, while the children play around us. Finally, the cold and the flying beetles force us to gather up our equipment and head back to the city.

The next morning our household wakes up coughing, for a sandstorm from Sudan is smothering Riyadh. The heavy winds blow dirt into our villa through various cracks. To prevent the air conditioners from clogging up, it becomes necessary to turn them off. Fatma and I spend the day stuffing rags into any gaps we can find, but there is no way we can fight the flying sand. Our only option is to wait out the storm, but it is hot and muggy and breathing is difficult.

The next morning the wind is finally quiet, and the desert is once again at peace. Fatma and I clean the sand dunes out of the house, while Jean lies in bed with a temperature and no voice. The cold dry air of our evening picnic, the sandstorm, and the trip in general have been too much of a strain. I only hope she will be well enough to attend our "Meet the Family" party.

The night of our grand party, John dresses in a thobe, otra, and egal that Osane has presented to him as a gift. Surprisingly enough, with his tanned skin and dark beard, he looks 100% Saudi.

As our guests arrive, I take their wraps and mingle among the different groups. Luckily, Jean is healthy enough to meet our friends, a fascinating lot from all over the world. She spends much of the party visiting with a Sudanese princess, while John circulates through the international smorgasbord.

Guests stay long into the night. As the Asians from Osane's restaurant begin clearing what is left of their outstanding food, Osane attempts to pay them. Through their interpreter they reply, "The party plus the plates the food has been served on, are gifts." With teary eyes, Osane and I give a thankful bow to each one of them.

After the party, the hours slip by. Jean and John finally have one last day to spend with us, before they are off to Egypt and back to their jobs in the States. John wants to stay in Riyadh, for he can see the dollar signs of a two-year tour. Jean blatantly refuses.

Ever since my sister has entered the Kingdom, her health has been affected. In addition, as a female who stands in her own power, she refuses to tread the secondary road Saudi women walk. Finally, she feels that the Arabian culture is "physically separating" her from her husband. Ever since their arrival, they have mysteriously stopped touching. Although she has thoroughly enjoyed her visit, when the plane leaves for home, she will be on it.

Early the next morning, with tears in our eyes, we kiss Jean and John goodbye. As their plane gains altitude, they fly out of our lives. Their short stay however, has planted an invisible seed. This new thought has been silently growing throughout their stay. With unstoppable energy it breaks the soil, even before their plane disappears into the clouds.

Chapter 47

A Decision Is Made

"Waiting hurts. Forgetting hurts. But not knowing which decision to make can sometimes be the most painful."
   Jose N. Harris

On the way back from the airport, instead of turning toward home, Osane heads the car into the desert. We both sense that unspoken words need to be shared, in the open air, away from ears or government bugs.

We drive down a dirt path and find a shaded wadi. Exiting the car in silence, I follow Osane to a clump of thorn trees that line the bank. As we sit down, both of us realize that this is a critical moment. The words that might be spoken have the potential of changing our lives forever. Osane shares first, and then I open up. Our thoughts, concerns and goals mirror the same conclusion. *It is finally time to leave the Kingdom.*

When this thought is actually spoken into the physical dimension, our world pauses. Our future shines before our eyes, as blank as the vast desert. We both linger in this void between present and future. Only the desert wind has substance. Finally, Osane gently picks up my hand and whispers, "My God, Christie. I pray we are making the right decision."

With the words finally said, our footsteps begin treading down a path that veers away from Arabia. As we continue our daily routines, we struggle. Both of us are torn up inside, and wracked with indecision.

We each ponder a multitude of doubts. After years of incredible sacrifice we have finally reached the top, but was the climb too fast? Are we mature enough to handle our present wealth, or wise enough to invest it properly? If we leave for the States, can Osane create a business that will give him the same importance and power he now has? Are the children better off growing up in the suppressed but moralistic Saudi society, or will the free but drug-and-alcohol-ridden American society be more beneficial? Will my conservative principles be able to blend in with the Western feminists and their fight for women's liberation? Can Osane be happy in the West, and is it possible to find such a warm circle of friends and family in fast-paced America?

Exhausted by our inward battles, we once again sit knee-to-knee, this time on the roof. We make a list of pros and cons, and find them equal. It is Osane's weeks in prison that tip the scales, for we both refuse to live in a country where loved ones disappear without a trace.

Life continues through our time of indecision. Used to rising at 5:30 every morning, I begin grabbing moments to memorize my environment. Looking out over the sleeping city, I usually find a few goats getting into the garbage.

Frustratingly, there is now *no* garbage pickup. For years a Yemeni garbage man used to knock on our door every two weeks. He wore an orange coat and pushed a wheelbarrow with cardboard boxes sticking up from the sides. For a short time, Indians and then Koreans replaced these Yemeni garbage men. The heat in the country had been too much for these nationalities. Now the Government is taking bids to bring a modernized disposal system into the Kingdom. Meanwhile the city is filthy, the fly population is immense, and the only thing that keeps disease under control is the intense sun.

As the weeks pass, summer weather arrives. Osane is still traveling, so when he leaves the country, I move into the guest room. I discover that our bedroom is too large for one air conditioner to adequately cool.

I also begin to notice that even with all of our air conditioners working, the cool spots throughout the house are localized behind closed doors. This leaves the heat in the hallways..

To ease the heat, the boys and I jump into the cool water of the pool. Even this enjoyment is conditional, for across the street workers are constructing a two-story villa. This house looks down on our garden, and the view of a foreign woman in her bikini is 100% more interesting than plastering or painting.

Regardless of the heat, every Thursday morning Abdu drives me to the grocery store. Each month the traffic seems to get worse. What normally took twenty-minutes can now turn into an hour's journey. As we sit in these backups, even an air-conditioned car becomes uncomfortable.

In one traffic jam, a bizarre situation unfolds. As we creep by the Ministry of the Interior, a white donkey strolls through the gate, with no trace of a harness or rope. It meanders down the sidewalk, slowly disappearing down the street.

Finally, the jammed cars begin moving. As we speed down the road, we pass the donkey, which is keeping up its methodical pace. Suddenly Abdu slams on the brakes. We are once again baking in the heat of the sun, as the donkey passes by. For another three-quarters of an hour, we play leapfrog with the donkey. At last, we skid into the grocery store parking lot, just in time to see the white donkey clip-clop his way past the front door.

With the days ticking by, Osane and I begin mental preparations for our departure. We decide that our best escape strategy is to leave for our usual summer vacation. This year Osane has rented a villa in the same club we visited previously. The only difference is that this year, *we will never return.* This means that we will ship a few of our most precious items, and the rest will have to remain.

Osane quietly arranges an agreement with an American corporation to buy our things and take over our lease. With this resolved, we place ourselves on automatic pilot. When our determination wavers, we look out our bedroom window. As sure as vibrant flowers in spring, a white truck will be parked across the street. Even during the warm afternoons and late into the night, this surveillance truck is manned.

Needing to release some of our pressures, we invite Ella and Tahar over for dinner. Late that evening, we turn the stereo up and whisper to them about our planned departure. They are sad, but not surprised. They share that they also are thinking of leaving. This doesn't make separation from each other any easier. Ella and I look at each other, tears streaming down our faces. As we hug, we swear that we will always keep in touch.

When school ends, the real heat of the summer becomes an unwanted reality. With the long days and baking sun come the electrical outages. Over the winter too many villas have been built, and the existing generators are old and inadequate.

No electricity means unworkable desert coolers and air conditioners and no water. We try to conserve our energy by unplugging the pump to the pool, and making sure the water storage tank on the roof is full. We also stop living in large sections of our house, and use only three air conditioners at one time.

When the cuts are in the middle of the night, we walk downstairs, open the windows, and sleep on the couches in the living room. This lifestyle is wearing, the heat draining, and it is still weeks until our scheduled departure.

One afternoon in early June, Osane walks through the door and finds the boys and me sitting listlessly in the living room. He instantly makes a decision. Without uttering a word, he walks back out the door.

From his office he calls several travel agents, searching for tickets out of the heat to the cool Spanish countryside. After much persistence, he finds a cancellation and books three tickets to Barcelona. Osane then purchases a July 1st ticket for himself, so he can join us. Finally, he calls his Spanish business contacts and they arrange for us to rent our Spanish villa a month earlier.

That evening he returns home with the tickets. The flight is scheduled to leave in four days. The decision is mine. Either I choose to wait until the beginning of July, or I jam a month's preparation into four days. Looking into the boys' listless eyes, and pushing their sweaty hair off their foreheads. I know I have no choice.

The next three days I sort out our belongings. I wander through our huge two-story villa, passing through full, elegantly decorated rooms. My mind flashes back to our first home. I remember that it took months to furnish our servants' quarters.

Our family has certainly come a long way. Now, my challenge is to walk away from this splendid villa and all our worldly possessions. To participate in this cleansing, we are only allowed to take five hastily packed suitcases.

Soon, I have piles all over the house. I put our most precious objects in the storage room upstairs. This small assemblage includes our Oriental rugs, knickknacks gathered from around the world, teapots, trays, coffee pots, incense holders, and prayer rugs. It will be Osane's job to ship these items to the States, just before he leaves Saudi Arabia.

We also have to make a decision about our dog. It will take $1,000 to fly Trusty to the States, but he is part of the family. So, we have carpenters build a plywood container in preparation for his flight.

Finally I pack my five remaining suitcases, trying not to dwell on what I am leaving behind. I say goodbye to the boys' toys, my china set, beautiful Spanish blankets and bedspreads, most of my clothes and shoes, the beautiful hand-painted Arab room, our Italian living room sets. The list goes on.

Thankfully, packing details occupy my every thought, and our departure date arrives quickly. Switching off my feelings, I ask God to direct our path and lead my family out of our Saudi home without a backward glance.

Chapter 48

The End of an Era

"It's the end of summer. It's the end of it all.
Those days are gone, it's over now,
we're moving on."
    Unknown

No one speaks on the way to the airport. While standing in the customs line, we are surprised by the arrival of Uncle Hamid and his family. Osane walks over to greet them, and I swear under my breath. Breaking away from the Kingdom is hard enough, without any added pressure.

Since we are early and our bags are already checked, Hamid suggests buying a Pepsi for the children. Since I am dressed in long and appropriate western clothes, I am able to join them.

As we make our way to an out-of-the-way cafeteria, I fight for control, for I hate deception. After days of internal struggle, Osane has decided not to tell the relatives about our departure. The idea that we are leaving to live in a new country will be incomprehensible. Saudi students travel abroad, families leave the Kingdom for vacations, and Saudi men travel for business. But Saudis and their families *always return!*

Somehow we make it through our drinks, and wander back to stand in the customs line. The queue is agonizingly slow, but it finally becomes our turn. The official flips through my American passport, stamps it automatically, and then reaches for the boys' Saudi passports.

Suddenly he holds both documents up and speaks to Osane in Arabic. Osane's cold reply is short, and results in an intense argument. Passengers in the boarding lines begin to look our way, and I feel myself becoming faint. Unable to understand what is going on, I feel the fingers of the Kingdom encircling us, attempting to suffocate our flight to freedom.

This assumption is enforced when I see two police officers making their way through the crowd, heading toward Osane. They grab Nazar and Sammy's passports and lead Osane away. I fall back against the wall. Has Osane's name been on an airport blacklist? Are those soldiers taking him away to prison?

As these ideas shoot through my heart, tears well up in my eyes. I look at Hamid for support, but I find no fear in his face. Sensing my turmoil, in simple Arabic he explains the situation. It seems the boy's passports have expired.

Osane tries to barter us through customs, but the official will not be swayed. Therefore, Osane motions to the soldiers to take him to the supervisor. Thirty minutes later, Osane returns. He hands the updated passports to the official, and as he stamps one and then the other, I know that this is it.

Mustering my strength, I casually say goodbye to Hamid and his family. I give Osane a kiss, grab the children and run through customs. I walk to the far side of the women's waiting room and choose a chair. Somehow, even symbolically, I have to place space between my pain and myself.

We are kept in the waiting room a full two hours. A heavy sand storm is beating against the windows. It is hot, close, and eerie in the room. To appease the passengers, flight attendants serve cold drinks. I watch the restless children, study my fellow travelers, and stare at the blowing sand. It is far too dangerous to think or feel. I will have a lifetime to sort out the last seven years. It is best to live in the present, and let the lessons of my desert life filter in, one at a time.

The storm finally settles down, enabling us to board. As our plane speeds down the runway, I look at the faces of my Saudi children. I know we are leaving our Arab halves behind.

Glancing out the window, I wonder if we are making the right decision. Slowly our flight climbs above the turbulent desert. As we enter the clouds, a heavenly calmness centers over me. Hugging the boys and thinking of Osane, I allow the peace of the moment to filter through my being. With a conviction born in my soul, I know that the four of us will grow and flourish. Wherever we go, the years within the Kingdom will become our foundation, and will burn internally, *forever.*

Epilogue

As our plane landed on American soil, our family began another adventure. We put our roots down in familiar soil. Buying a beautiful home in my childhood community (around family and friends), seemed to guarantee a smooth transition. However conservative Ohio during the 1970's, wasn't conducive for mixed marriages.

For two years Osane attempted to integrate. He eventually concluded that he simply couldn't connect with mid-western suburban males. Feeling like oil dripping into water, he finally opened an import/export business and we moved to California.

Finally, our family was able to breathe. We moved into a wonderful community over looking the Pacific. For the next ten years the boys grew and Osane spent half the year in Saudi Arabia developing his export business.

As time marched on, Osane and I grew apart. Gradually our relationship evolved into a friendship. After twenty years of marriage, we lovingly divorced and went our separate ways.

My path took me north, onto a fifteen acre spread in Northern Idaho. My second husband and I designed and built our interpretation of heaven. For the next twenty five plus years, we peacefully watched the seasons change.

Osane's road took him east....back into the Kingdom. He became the proud father of three additional children. He also created another very successful business and now lives in a grand villa in Arabia and also spends time with his daughter in the United States.

Nazar, after a very loving and successful life in California, dies in a car accident at the age of thirty-two. His gift to us was our grandson and his lovely widowed soul mate. Their visits enrich our lives.

Sammie lives in Idaho with his family. His career in higher education has enabled him to help many students find their way.

I hope you enjoyed my story. Please feel free to comment on Amazon or my website: www.annhellewell.com

May God Bless

About the Author

Ann Hellewell presently lives on her 15-acre homestead in the hills of Northern Idaho, with her husband and border collie.
She is also the author of *Anna's Journey*. This novel is written for the seekers of life and follows a young girl's quest to find herself and a "home" or a place of belonging.

Thank you for reading *Seven Years Behind the Veil*. Hopefully you enjoyed the story line and can now perceive the Arab World with a deeper understanding and appreciation.

To purchase copies of <u>*Seven Years Behind the Veil*</u> and <u>*Anna's Journey*</u> please visit the authdor's website at **www.annhellewell.com**.

Ann

Made in the USA
Middletown, DE
25 June 2017